SWORD ART ONLINE phantom bullet

003

ART: KOUTAROU YAMADA
ORIGINAL STORY: REKI KAWAHARA
CHARACTER DESIGN: abec

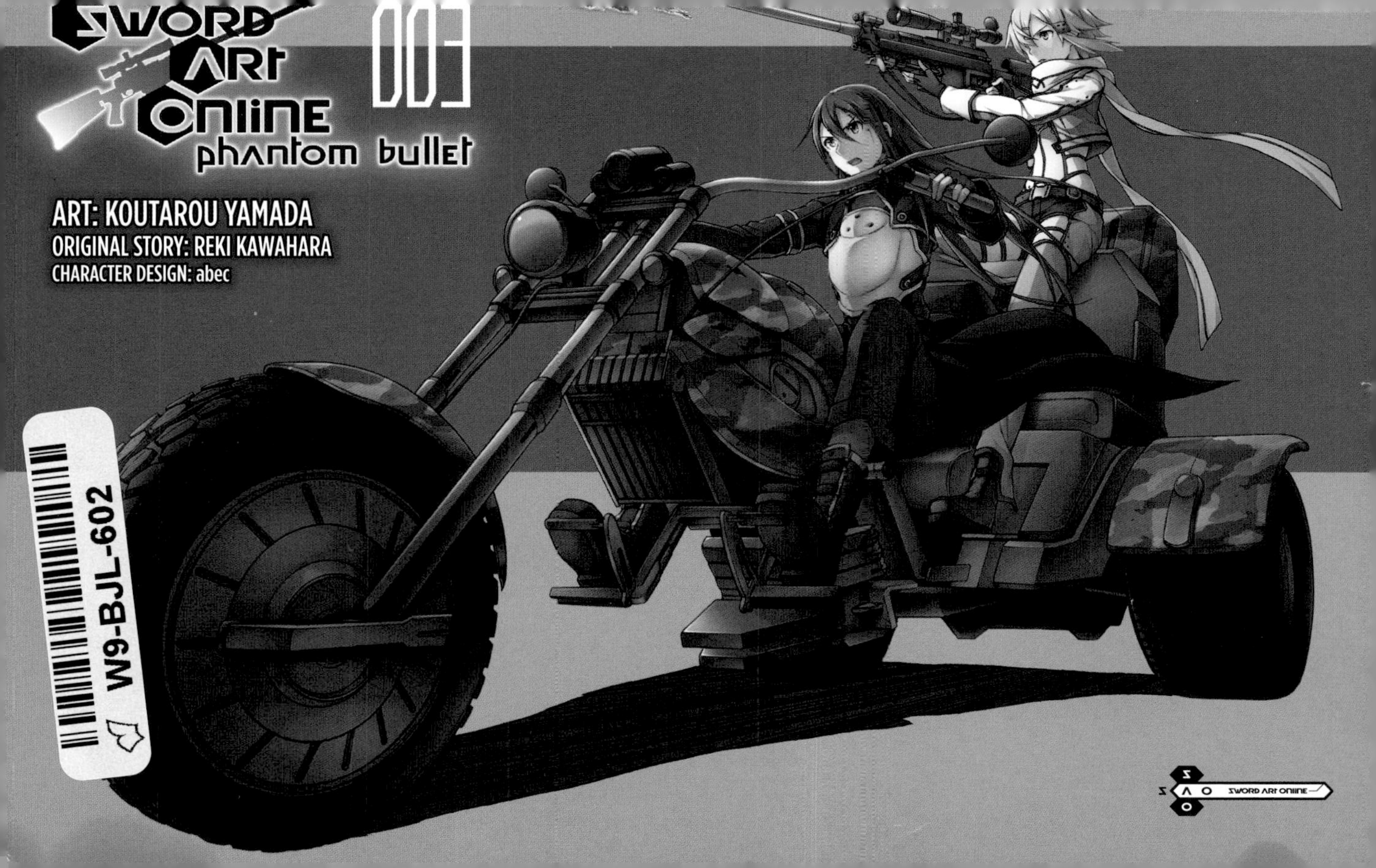
SWORD ART ONLINE

SWORD ART ONLINE

003

SWORD ART ONLINE phantom bullet

ART : KOUTAROU YAMADA
ORIGINAL STORY : REKI KAWAHARA
CHARACTER DESIGN : ABEC

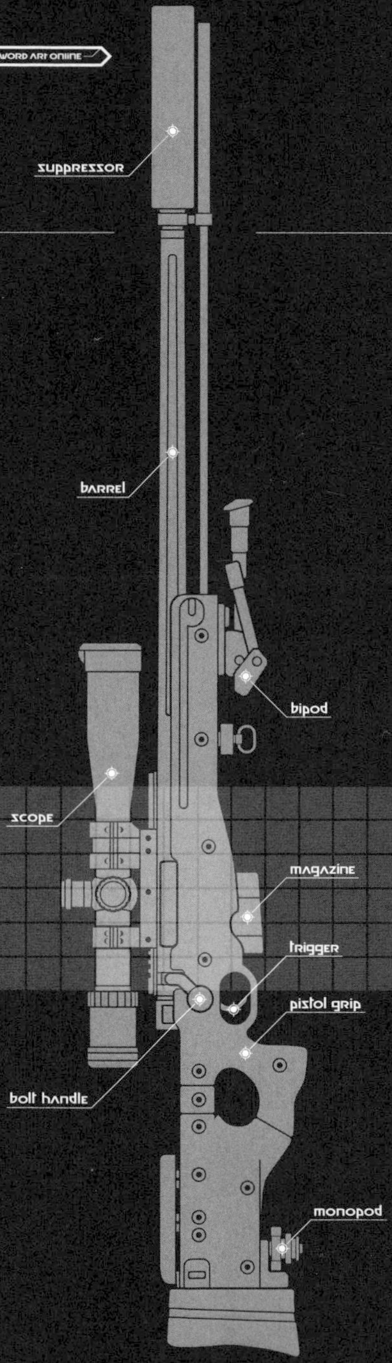

suppressor
barrel
bipod
scope
magazine
trigger
pistol grip
bolt handle
monopod

contents

date : 14 dec 2025 sun

ZASKAR gun gale online

L115A3 silent assassin

cartridge : .338 lapua magnum
5-round detachable box magazine

SWORD ART ONLINE

phantom bullet

003

SWORD ART ONLINE phantom bullet

ART: koutarou yamada
original story: reki kawahara
character design: abec

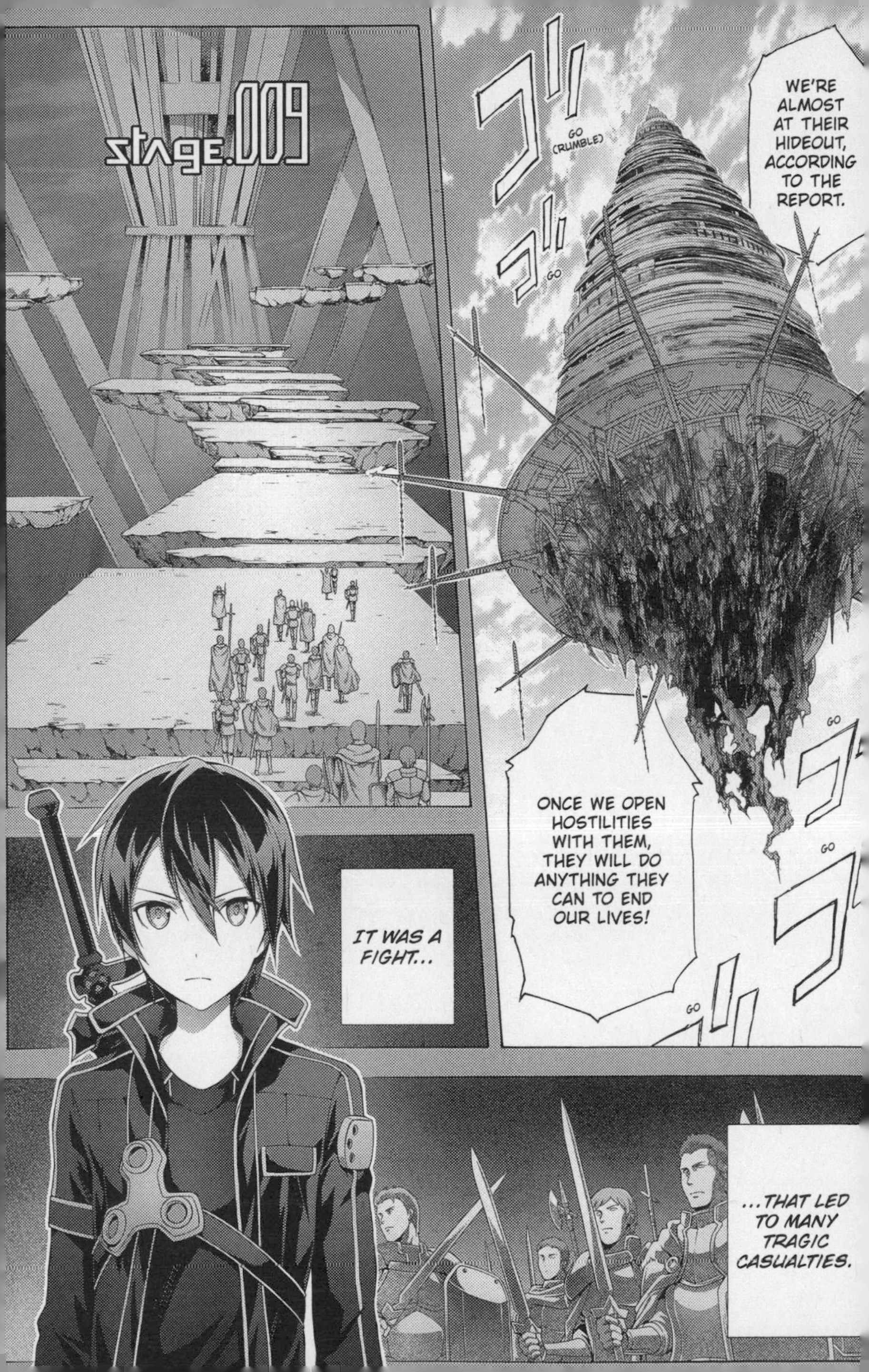
WE'RE ALMOST AT THEIR HIDEOUT, ACCORDING TO THE REPORT.
GO (RUMBLE)
GO
ONCE WE OPEN HOSTILITIES WITH THEM, THEY WILL DO ANYTHING THEY CAN TO END OUR LIVES!
GO
GO
GO
stage.009
IT WAS A FIGHT...
...THAT LED TO MANY TRAGIC CASUALTIES.

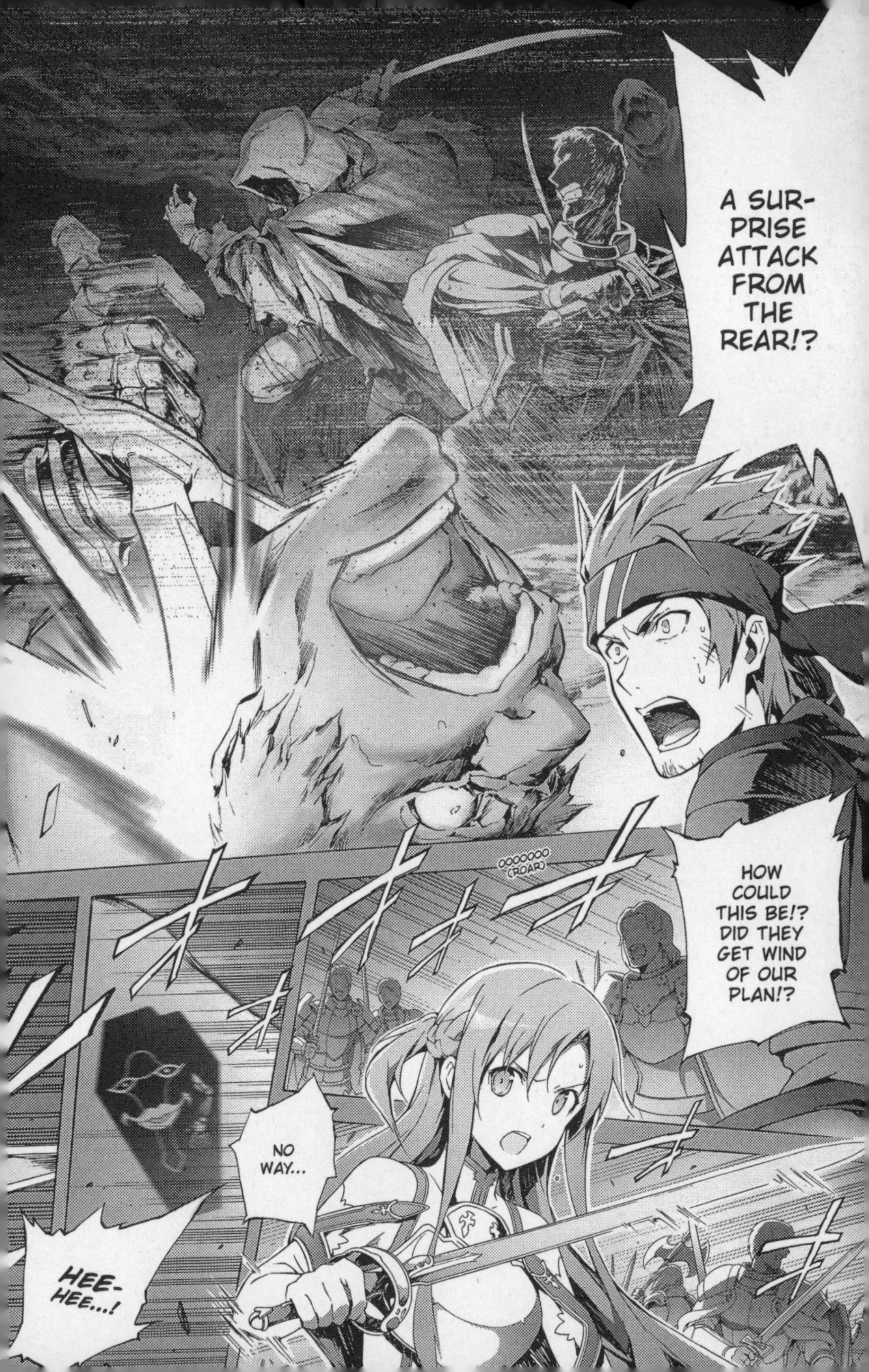
A SUR-PRISE ATTACK FROM THE REAR!?
OOOOOOO (ROAR)
HOW COULD THIS BE!? DID THEY GET WIND OF OUR PLAN!?
NO WAY...
HEE-HEE...!

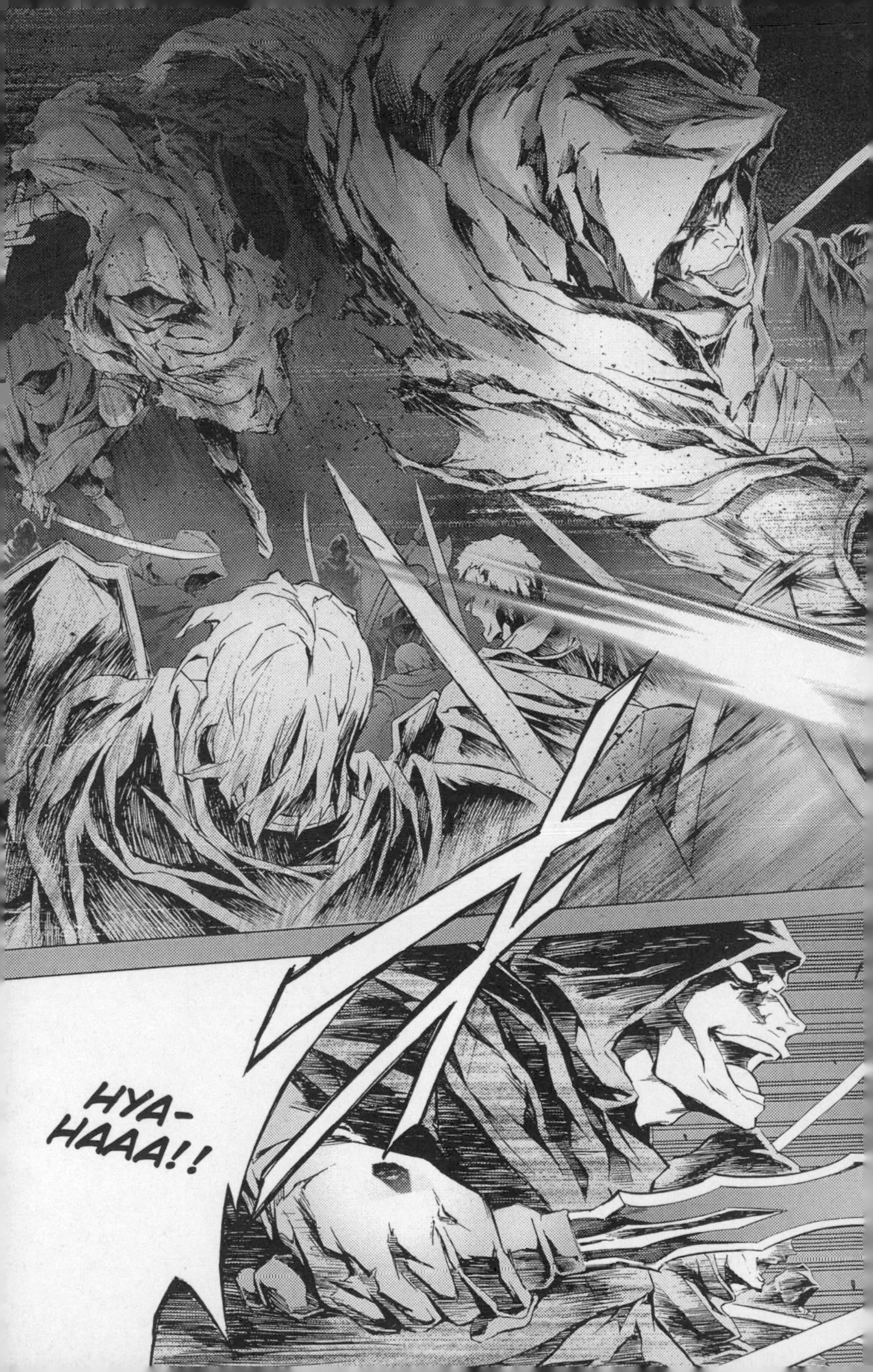
HYA-
HAAA!!

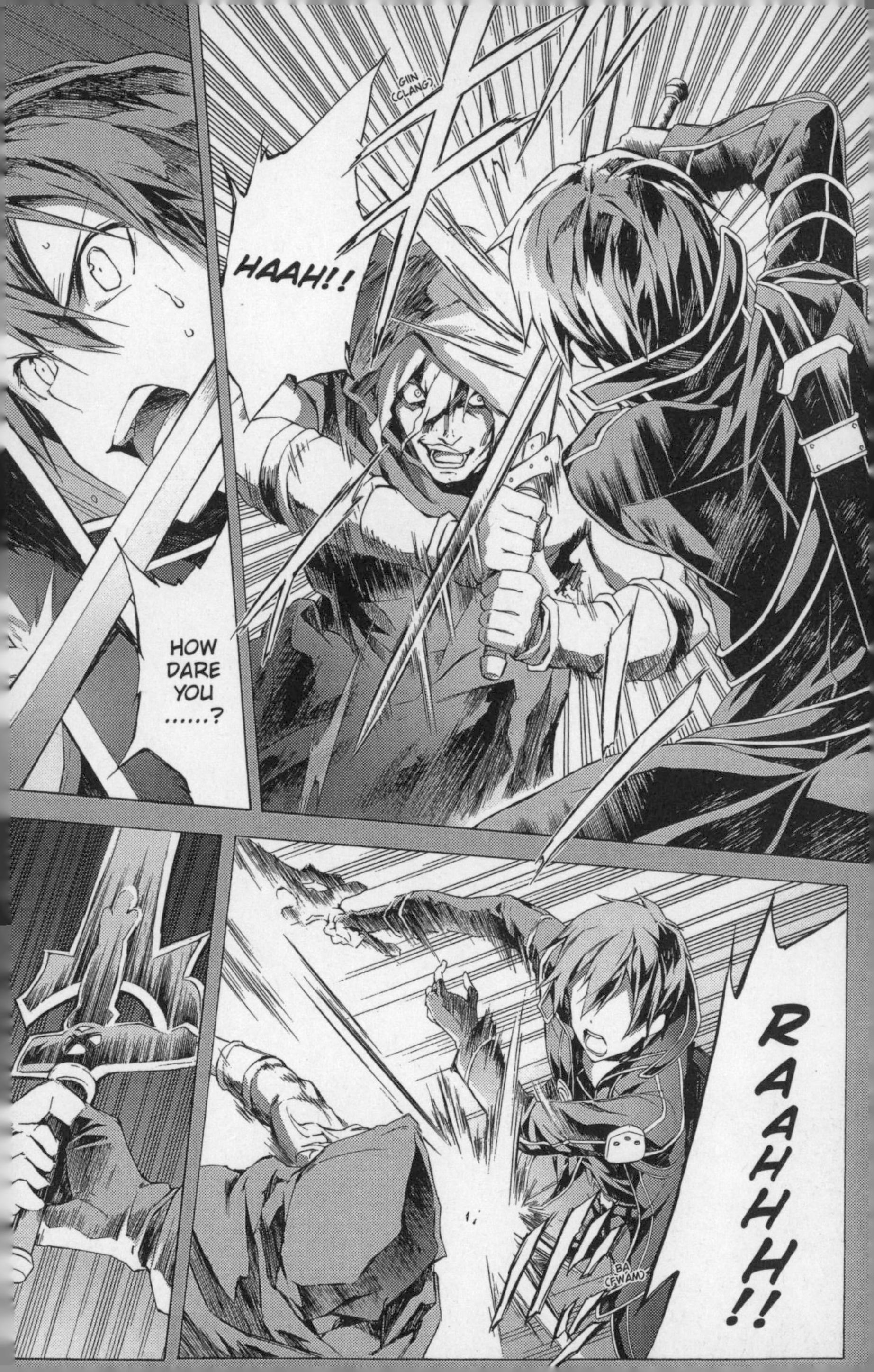
GIIN (CLANG)
HAAH!!
HOW DARE YOU ......?
RAAHHH!!
BA (FWAM)

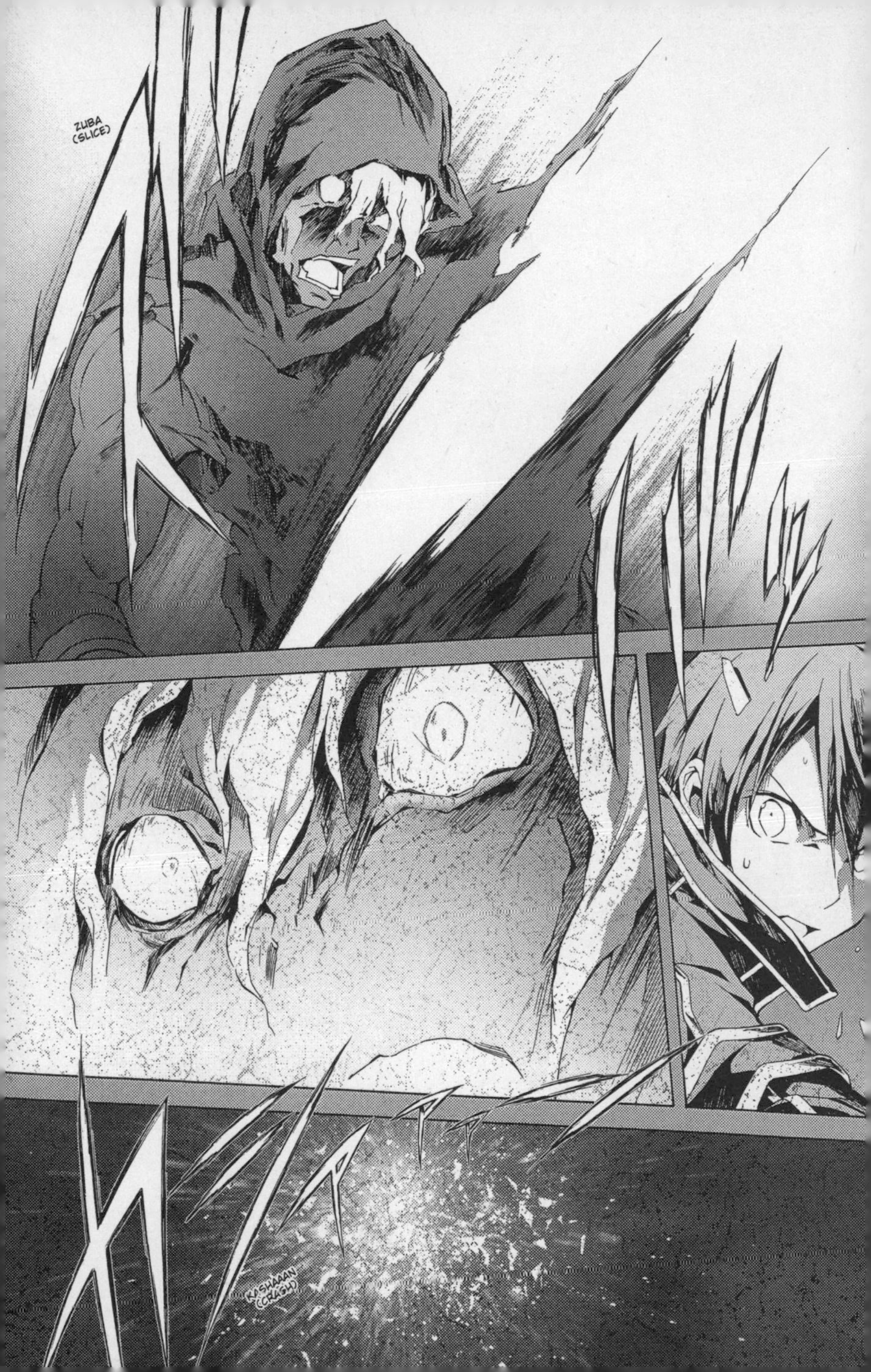
ZUBA
(SLICE)
KASHAAAN
(CRASH)

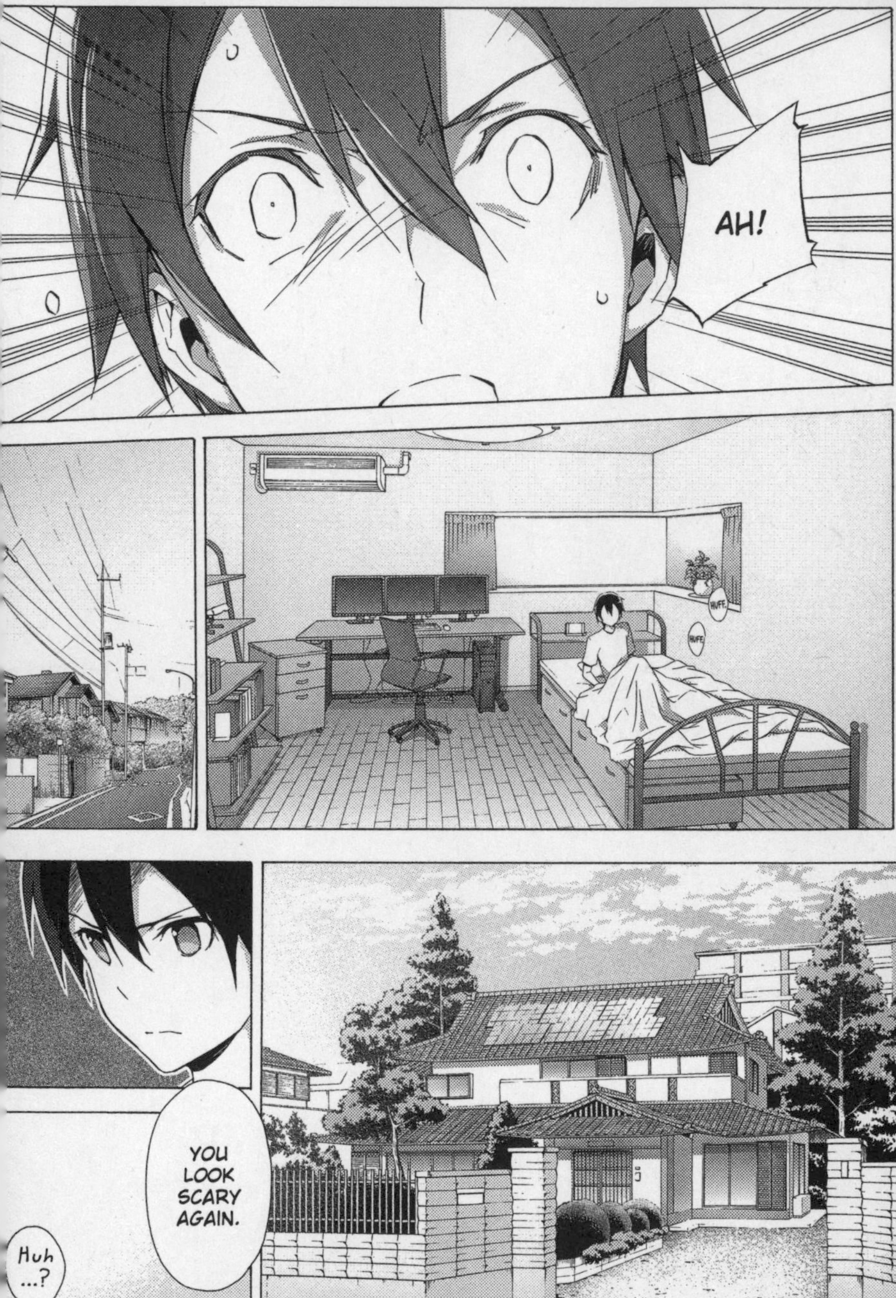
AH!
HUFF.
HUFF.
YOU LOOK SCARY AGAIN.
Huh ...?

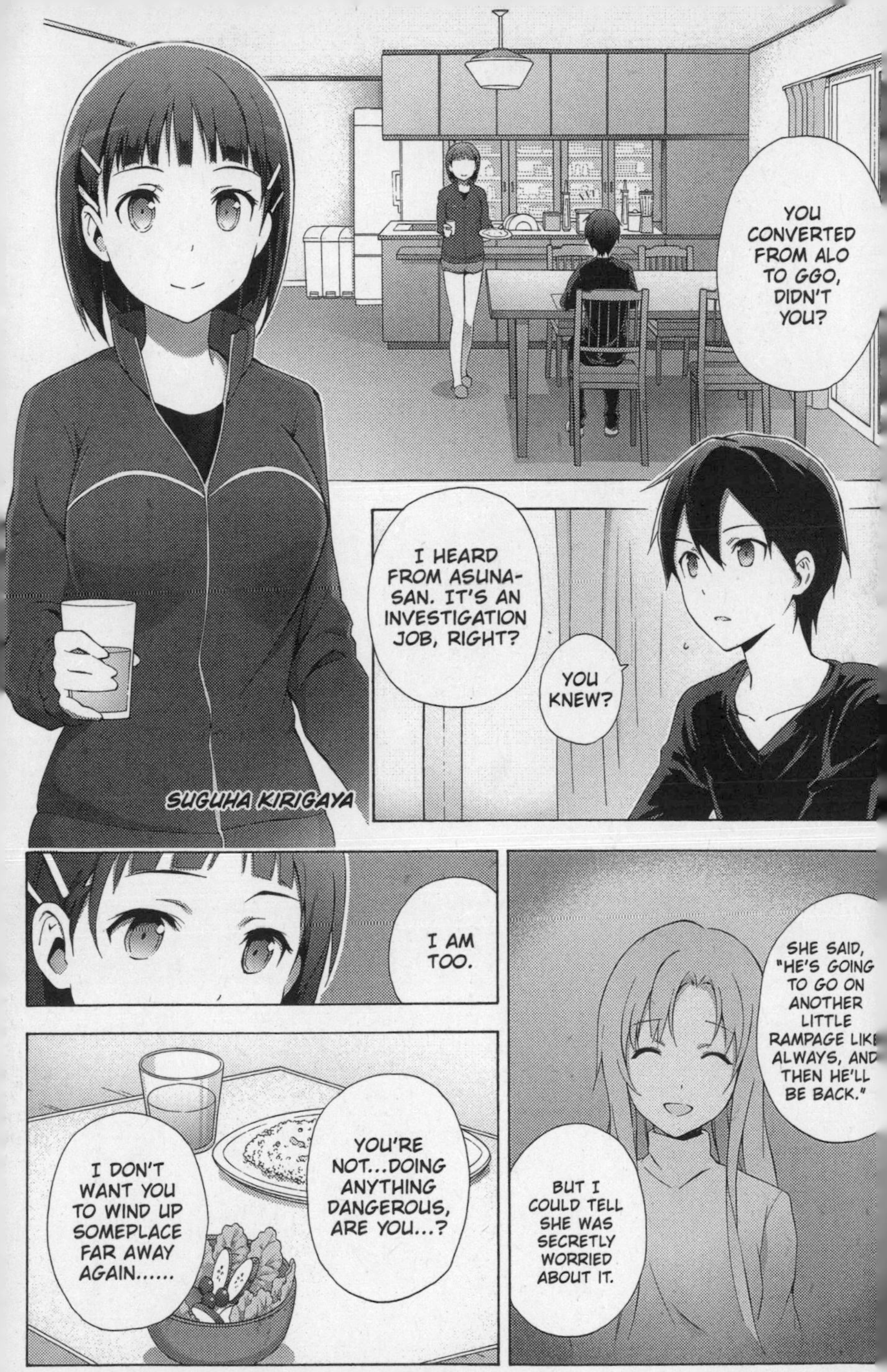
YOU CONVERTED FROM ALO TO GGO, DIDN'T YOU?
YOU KNEW?
I HEARD FROM ASUNA-SAN. IT'S AN INVESTIGATION JOB, RIGHT?
SUGUHA KIRIGAYA
SHE SAID, "HE'S GOING TO GO ON ANOTHER LITTLE RAMPAGE LIKE ALWAYS, AND THEN HE'LL BE BACK."
BUT I COULD TELL SHE WAS SECRETLY WORRIED ABOUT IT.
I AM TOO.
YOU'RE NOT...DOING ANYTHING DANGEROUS, ARE YOU...?
I DON'T WANT YOU TO WIND UP SOMEPLACE FAR AWAY AGAIN......

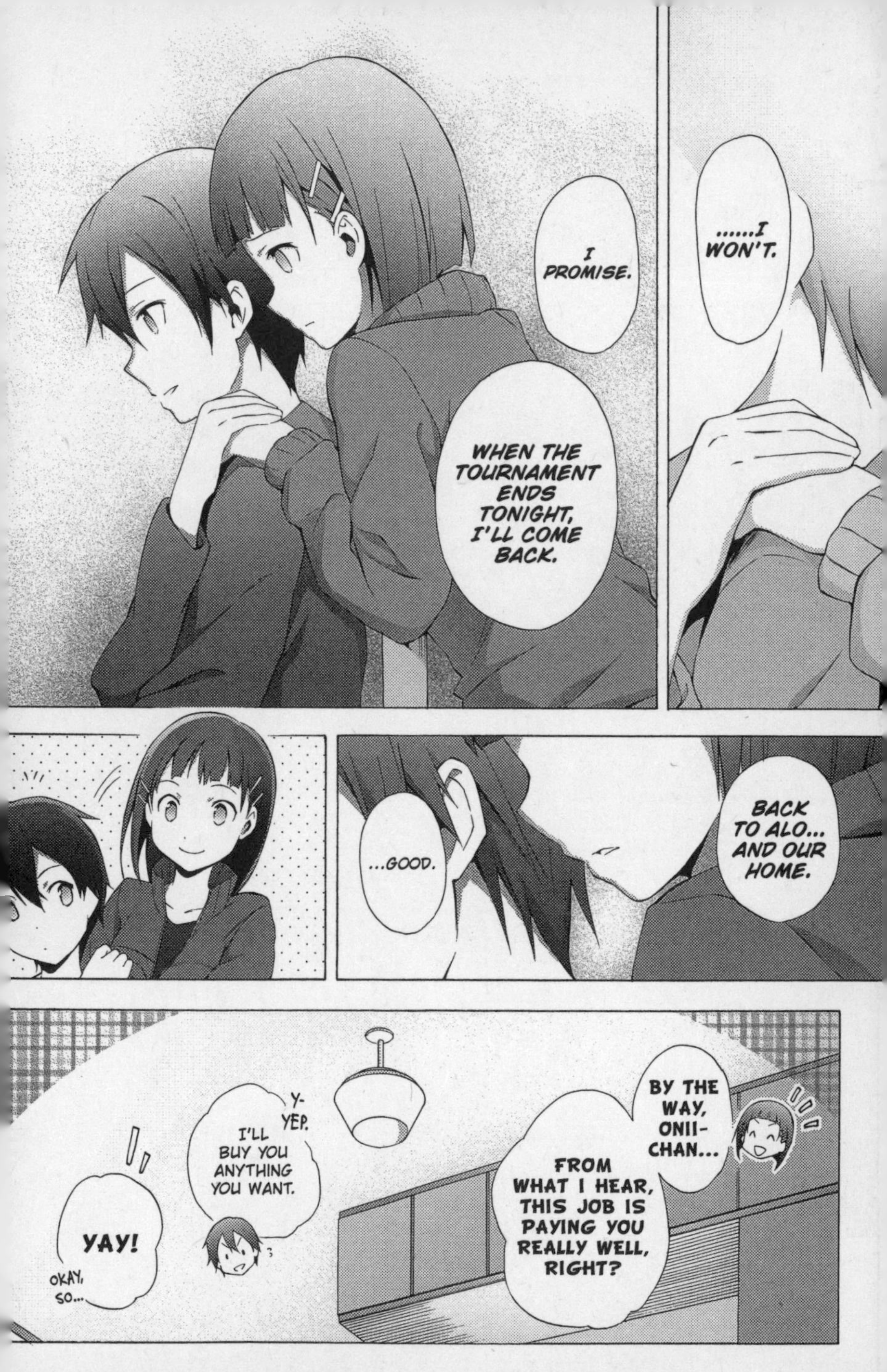
......I WON'T.
I PROMISE.
WHEN THE TOURNAMENT ENDS TONIGHT, I'LL COME BACK.
BACK TO ALO... AND OUR HOME.
...GOOD.
BY THE WAY, ONII-CHAN...
FROM WHAT I HEAR, THIS JOB IS PAYING YOU REALLY WELL, RIGHT?
Y-YEP.
I'LL BUY YOU ANYTHING YOU WANT.
YAY!
OKAY, SO...

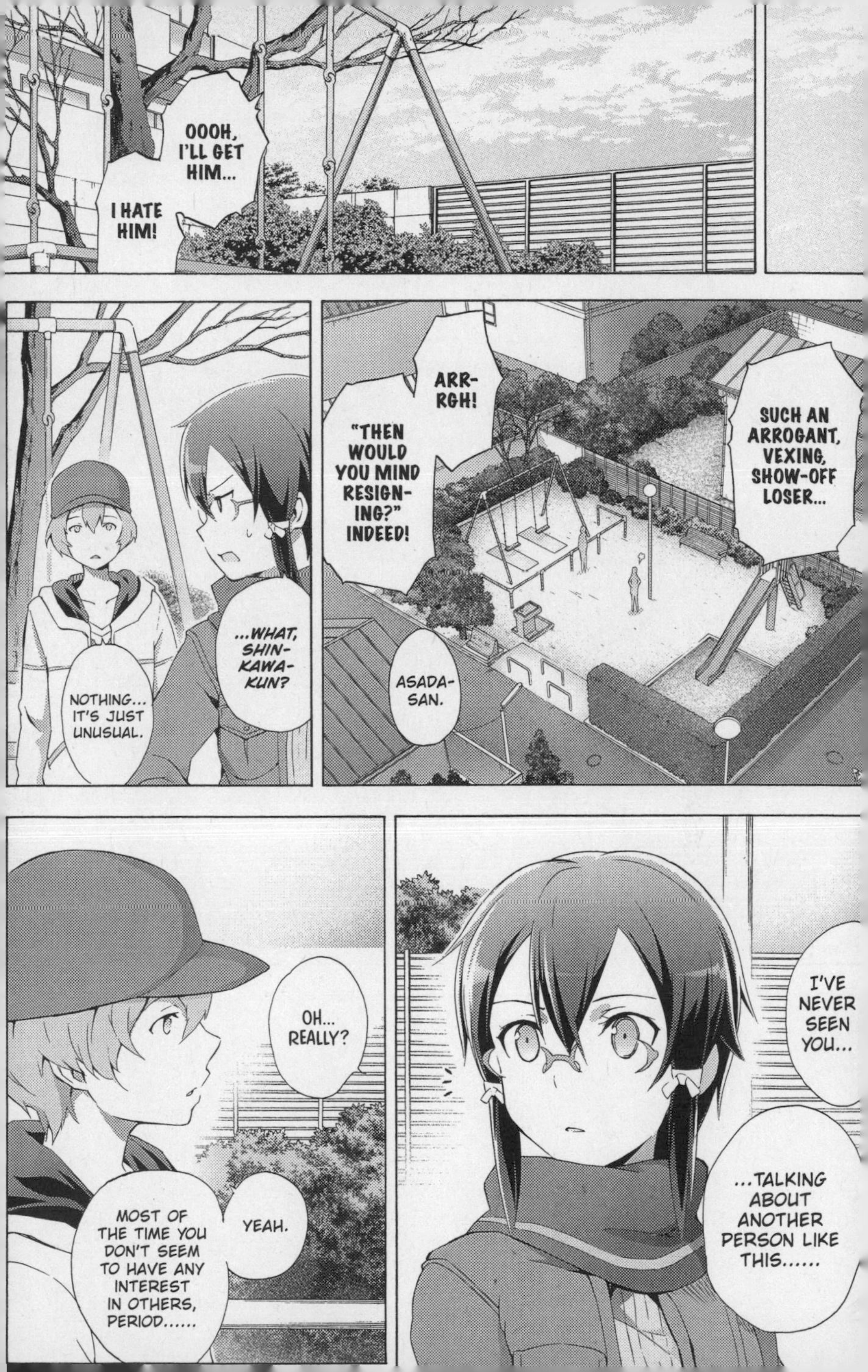
OOOH, I'LL GET HIM...
I HATE HIM!
SUCH AN ARROGANT, VEXING, SHOW-OFF LOSER...
ARR-RGH!
"THEN WOULD YOU MIND RESIGN-ING?" INDEED!
ASADA-SAN.
...WHAT, SHIN-KAWA-KUN?
NOTHING... IT'S JUST UNUSUAL.
I'VE NEVER SEEN YOU...
...TALKING ABOUT ANOTHER PERSON LIKE THIS......
OH... REALLY?
YEAH.
MOST OF THE TIME YOU DON'T SEEM TO HAVE ANY INTEREST IN OTHERS, PERIOD......

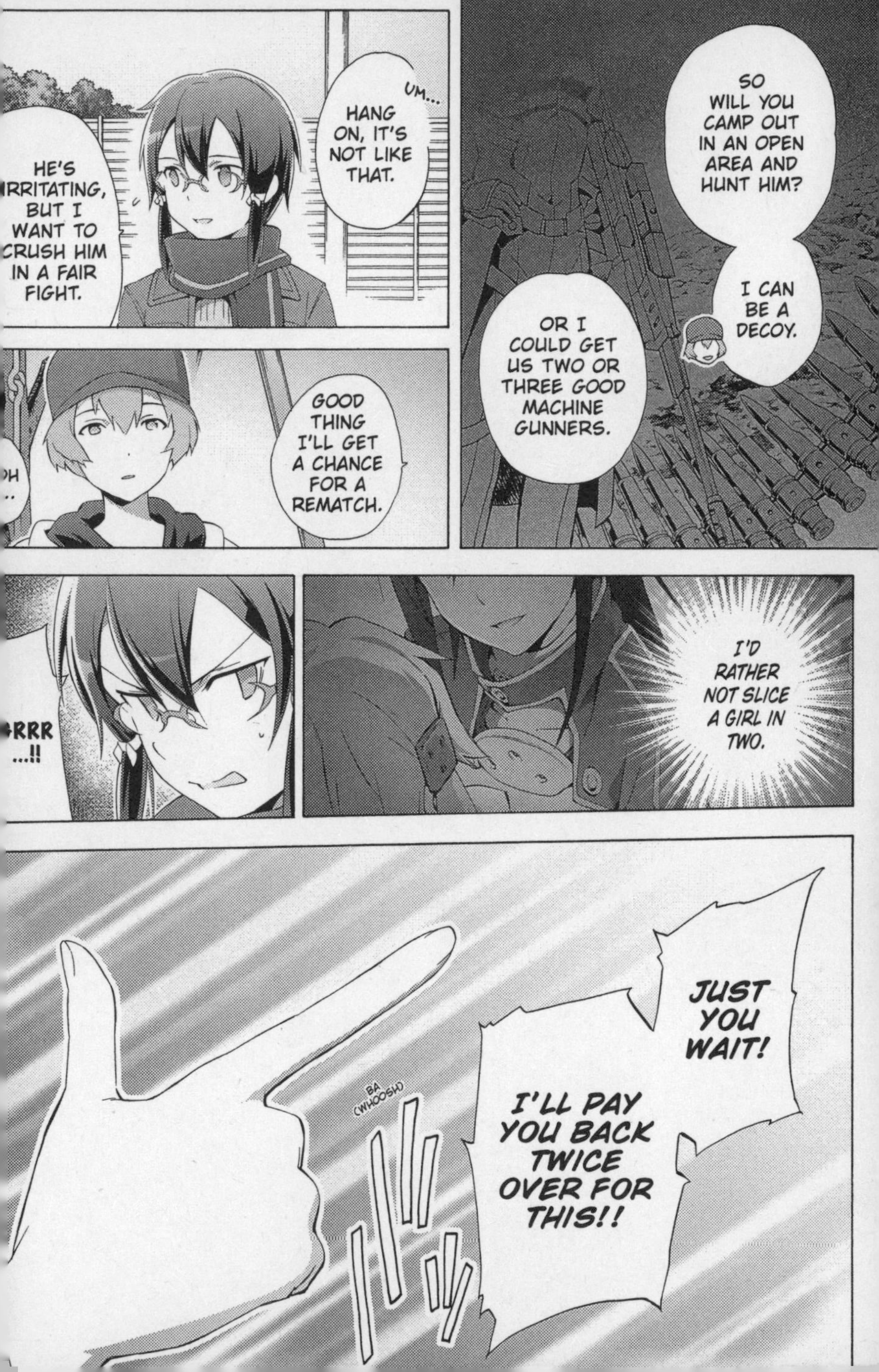
SO WILL YOU CAMP OUT IN AN OPEN AREA AND HUNT HIM?
I CAN BE A DECOY.
OR I COULD GET US TWO OR THREE GOOD MACHINE GUNNERS.
UM...
HANG ON, IT'S NOT LIKE THAT.
HE'S RRITATING, BUT I WANT TO CRUSH HIM IN A FAIR FIGHT.
GOOD THING I'LL GET A CHANCE FOR A REMATCH.
I'D RATHER NOT SLICE A GIRL IN TWO.
RRR ...!!
JUST YOU WAIT!
BA (WHOOSH)
I'LL PAY YOU BACK TWICE OVER FOR THIS!!

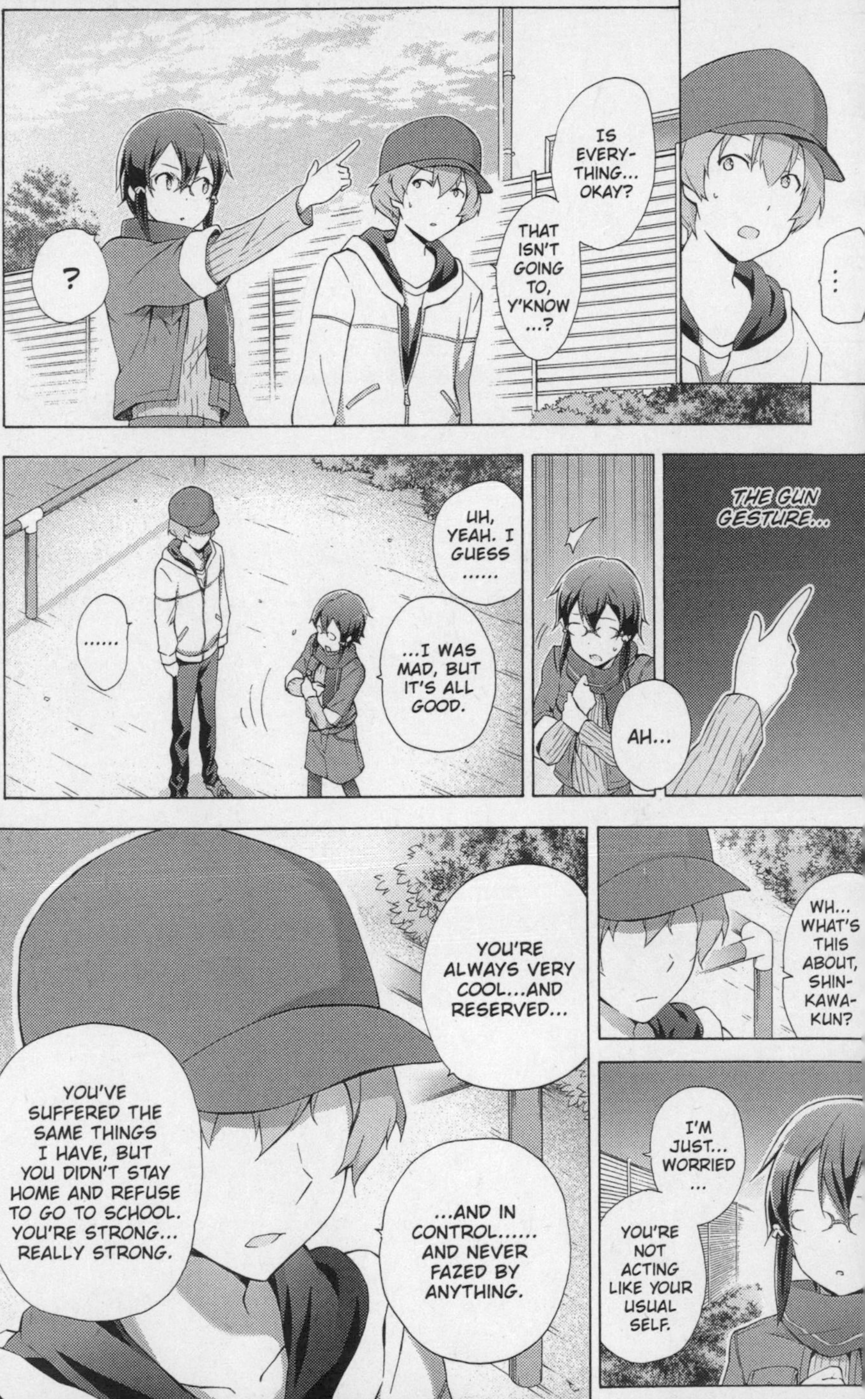
…
IS EVERYTHING… OKAY?
THAT ISN'T GOING TO, Y'KNOW …?
?
THE GUN GESTURE…
AH…
UH, YEAH. I GUESS ……
…I WAS MAD, BUT IT'S ALL GOOD.
……
WH… WHAT'S THIS ABOUT, SHINKAWA-KUN?
I'M JUST… WORRIED …
YOU'RE NOT ACTING LIKE YOUR USUAL SELF.
YOU'RE ALWAYS VERY COOL…AND RESERVED…
…AND IN CONTROL…… AND NEVER FAZED BY ANYTHING.
YOU'VE SUFFERED THE SAME THINGS I HAVE, BUT YOU DIDN'T STAY HOME AND REFUSE TO GO TO SCHOOL. YOU'RE STRONG… REALLY STRONG.

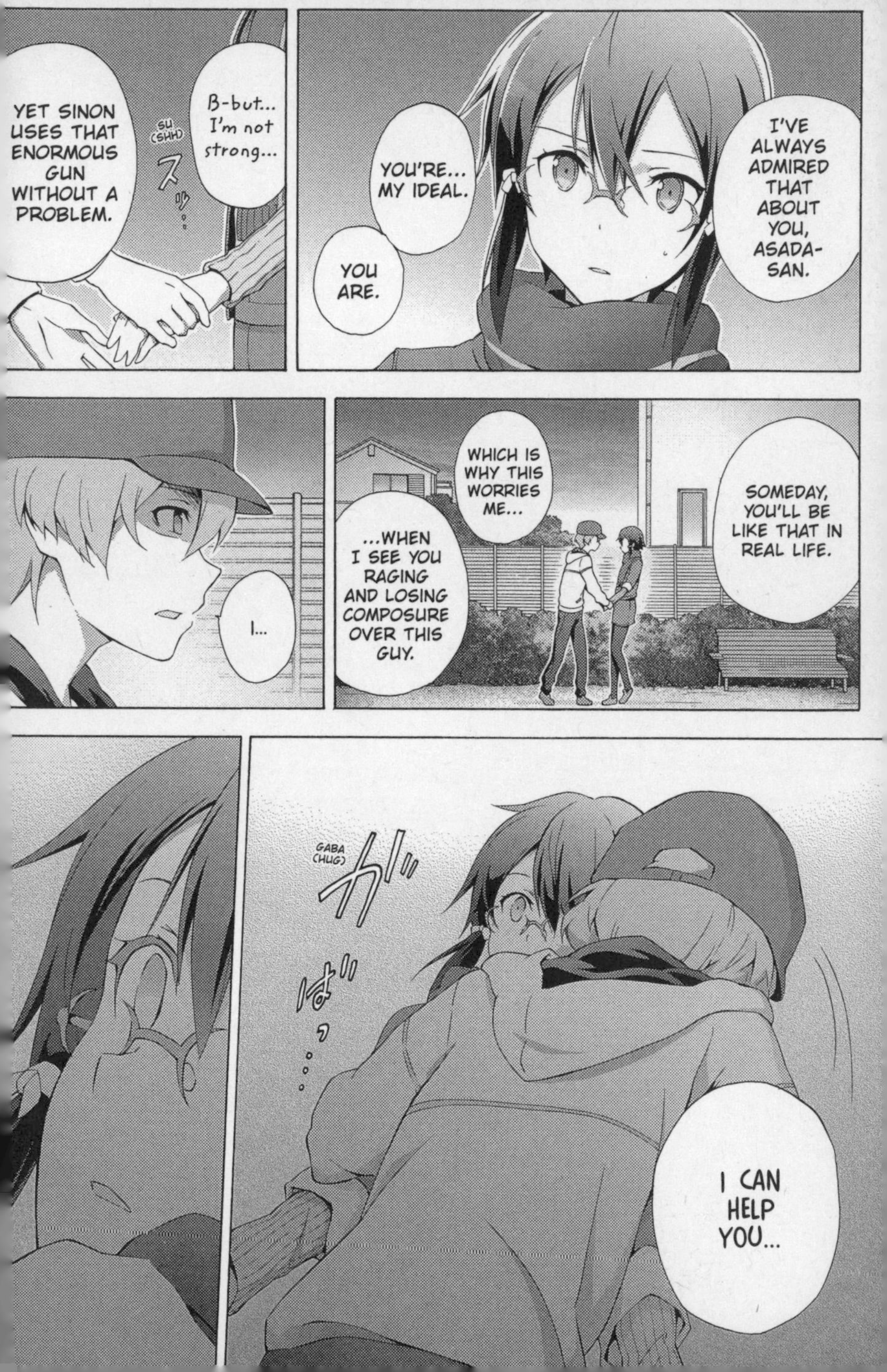
I'VE ALWAYS ADMIRED THAT ABOUT YOU, ASADA-SAN.
YOU'RE... MY IDEAL.
YOU ARE.
B-but... I'm not strong...
SU (SHHH)
YET SINON USES THAT ENORMOUS GUN WITHOUT A PROBLEM.
SOMEDAY, YOU'LL BE LIKE THAT IN REAL LIFE.
WHICH IS WHY THIS WORRIES ME...
...WHEN I SEE YOU RAGING AND LOSING COMPOSURE OVER THIS GUY.
I...
GABA (HUG)
I CAN HELP YOU...

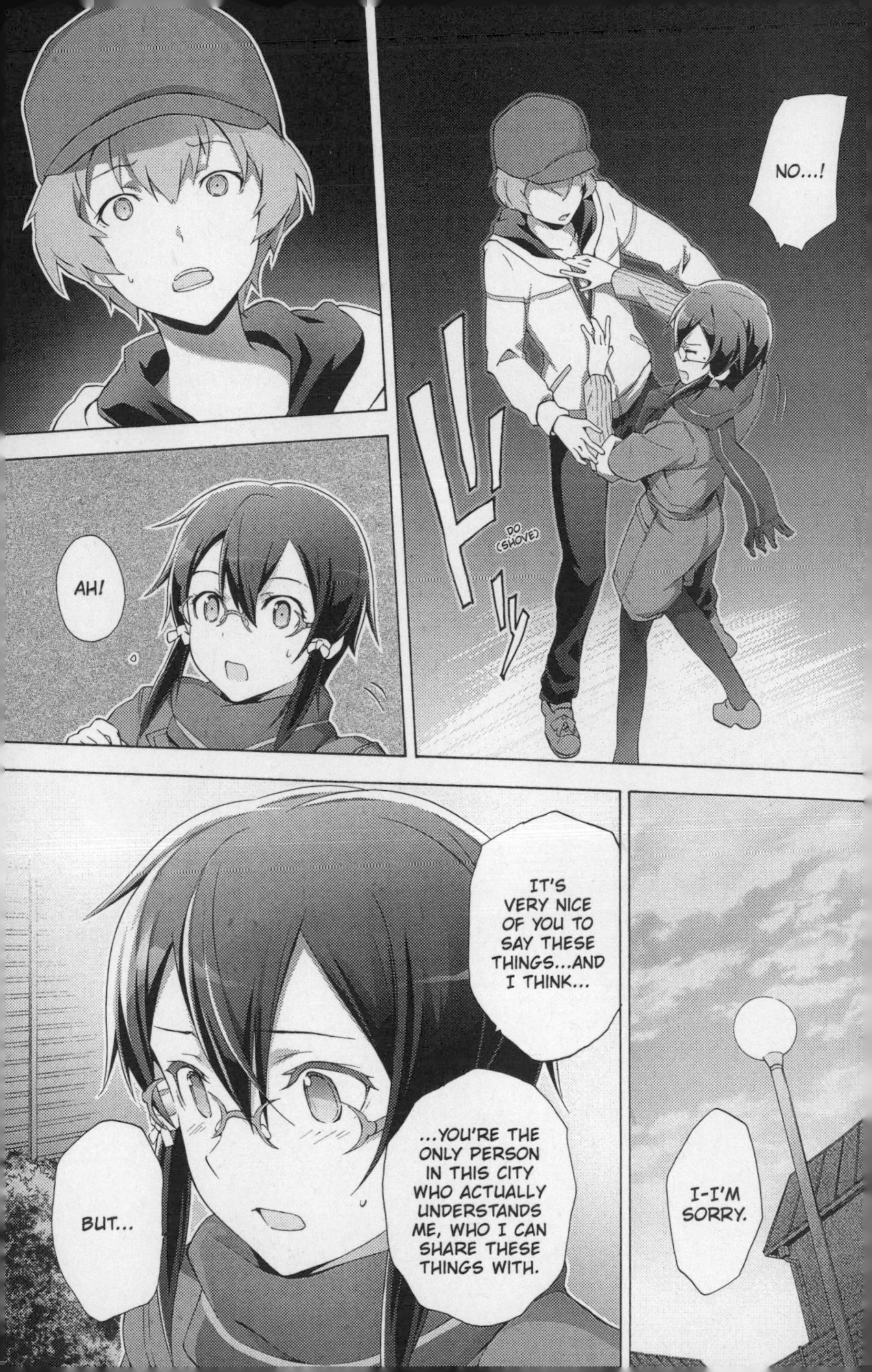
NO...!
DO (SHOVE)
AH!
I-I'M SORRY.
IT'S VERY NICE OF YOU TO SAY THESE THINGS...AND I THINK...
...YOU'RE THE ONLY PERSON IN THIS CITY WHO ACTUALLY UNDERSTANDS ME, WHO I CAN SHARE THESE THINGS WITH.
BUT...

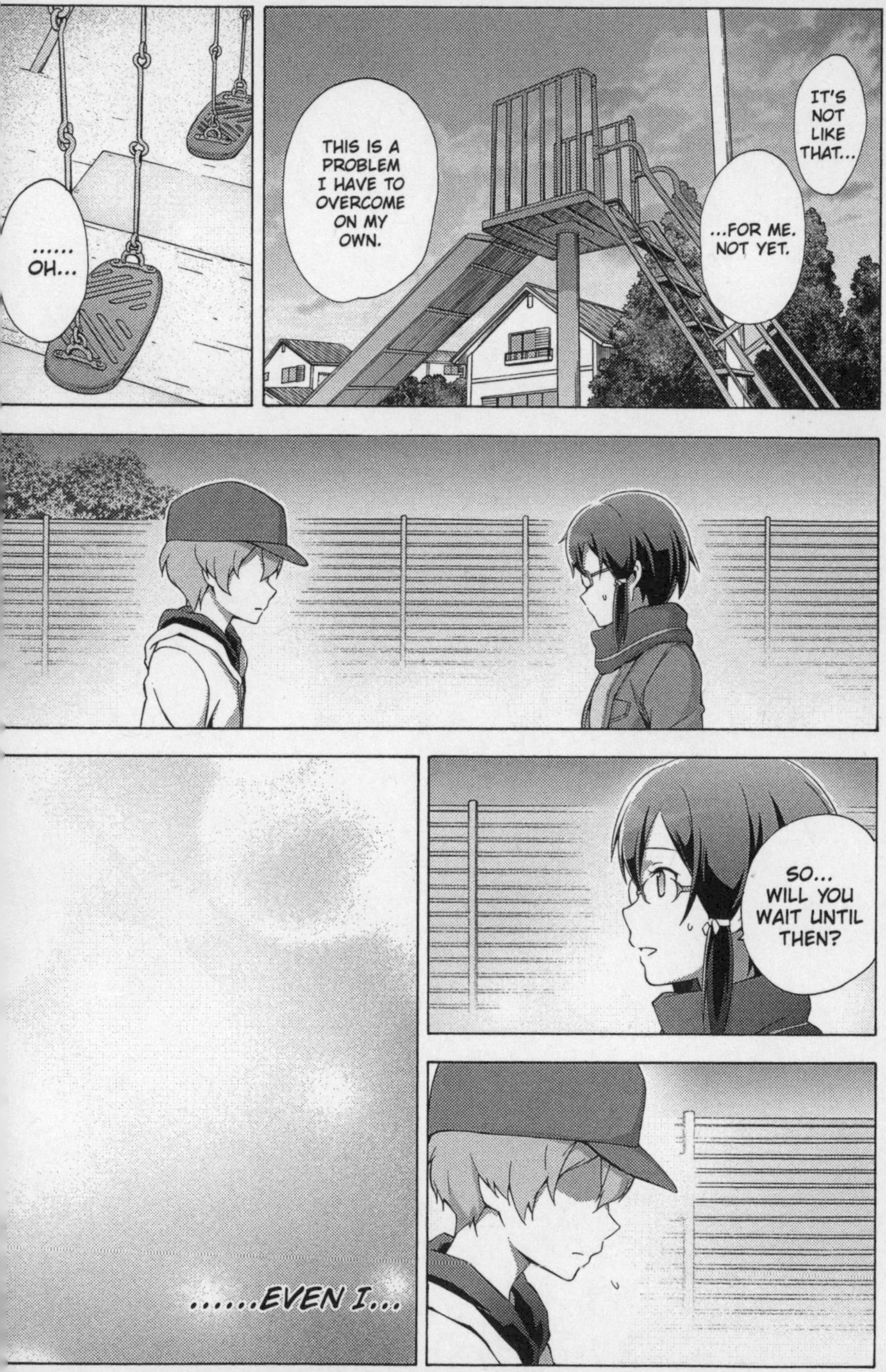
IT'S NOT LIKE THAT...
...FOR ME. NOT YET.
THIS IS A PROBLEM I HAVE TO OVERCOME ON MY OWN.
...... OH...
SO... WILL YOU WAIT UNTIL THEN?
......EVEN I...

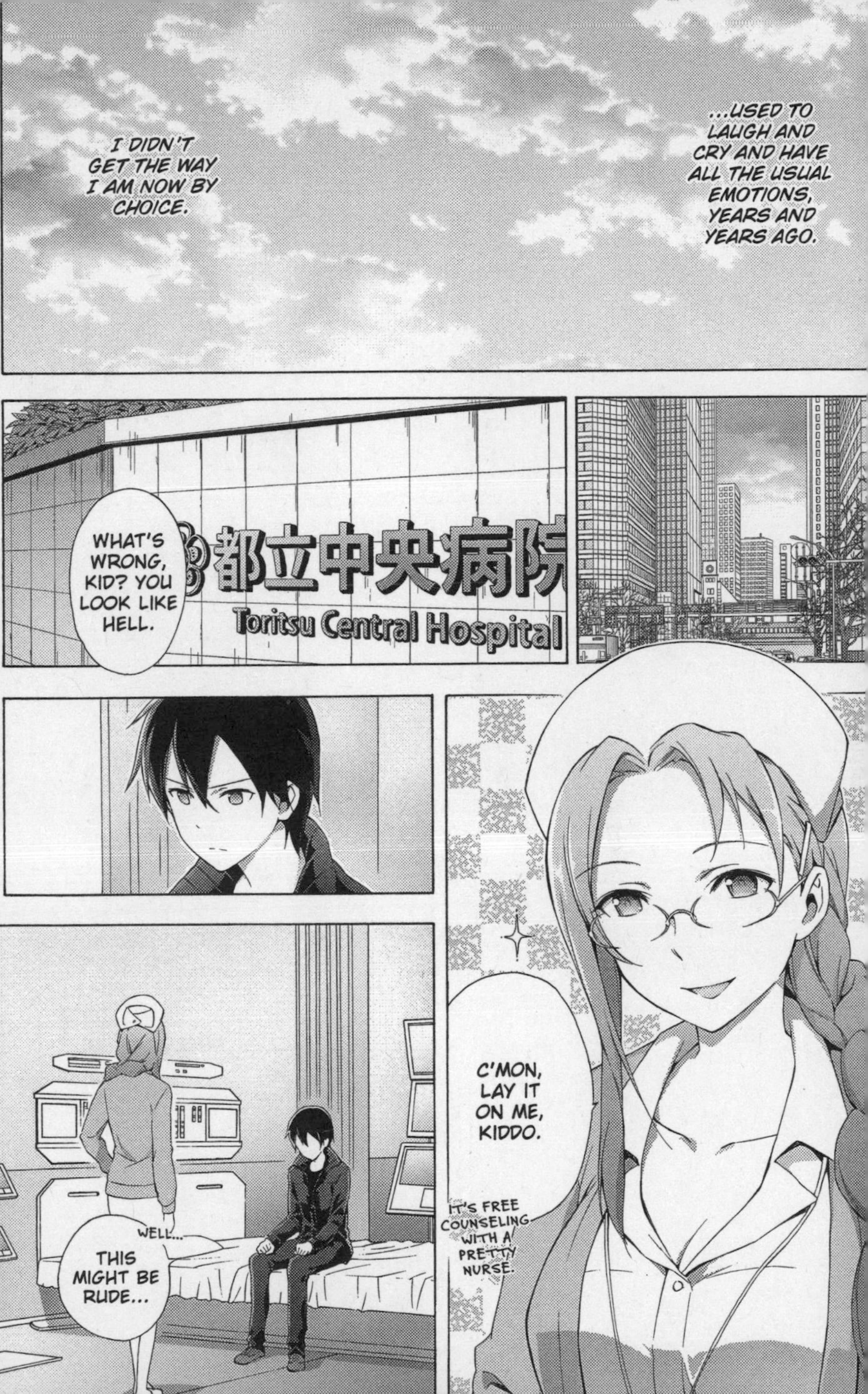
...USED TO LAUGH AND CRY AND HAVE ALL THE USUAL EMOTIONS, YEARS AND YEARS AGO.
I DIDN'T GET THE WAY I AM NOW BY CHOICE.
都立中央病院
Toritsu Central Hospital
WHAT'S WRONG, KID? YOU LOOK LIKE HELL.
C'MON, LAY IT ON ME, KIDDO.
IT'S FREE COUNSELING WITH A PRETTY NURSE.
WELL...
THIS MIGHT BE RUDE...

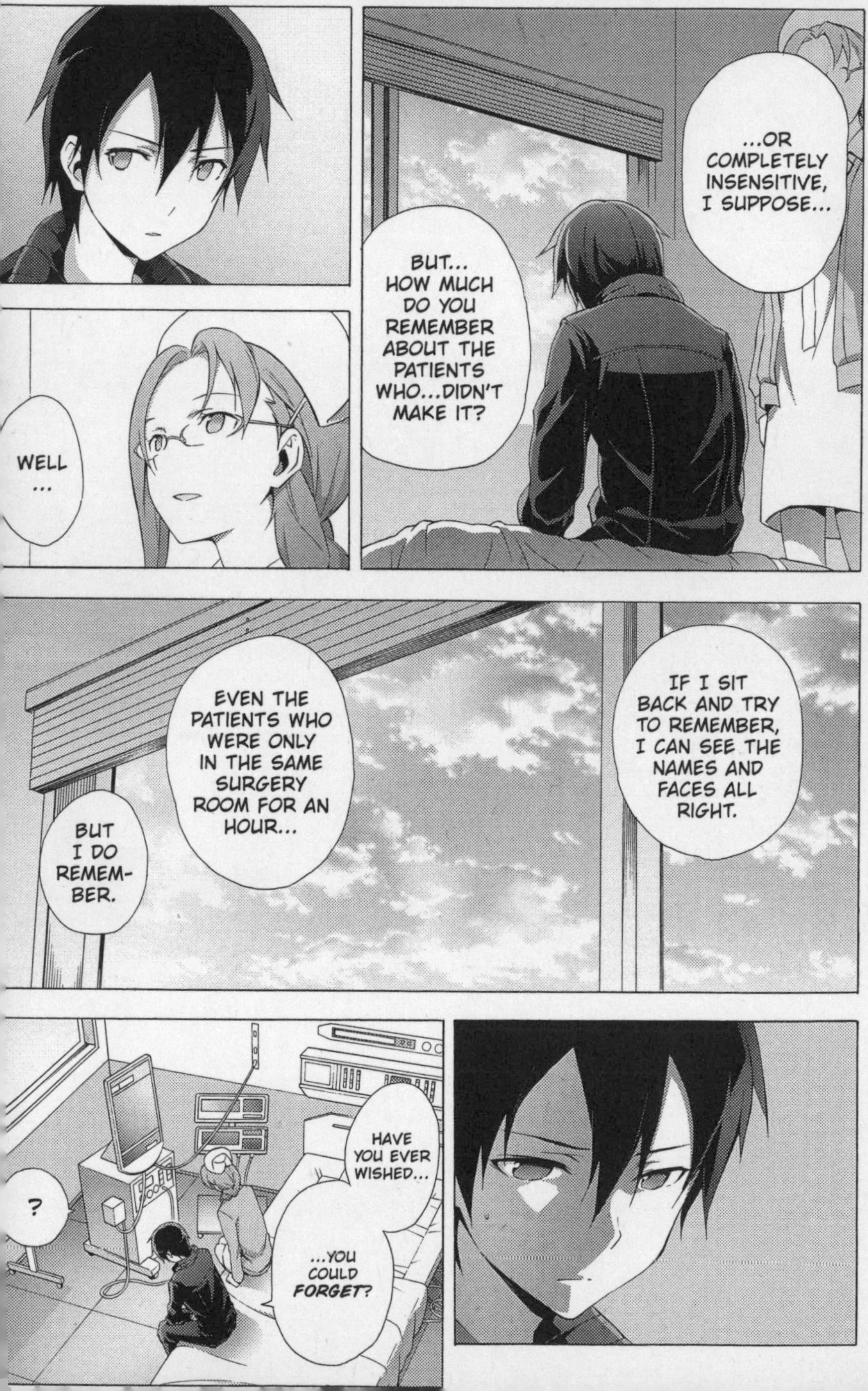
...OR COMPLETELY INSENSITIVE, I SUPPOSE...
BUT... HOW MUCH DO YOU REMEMBER ABOUT THE PATIENTS WHO...DIDN'T MAKE IT?
WELL ...
IF I SIT BACK AND TRY TO REMEMBER, I CAN SEE THE NAMES AND FACES ALL RIGHT.
EVEN THE PATIENTS WHO WERE ONLY IN THE SAME SURGERY ROOM FOR AN HOUR...
BUT I DO REMEMBER.
HAVE YOU EVER WISHED...
...YOU COULD *FORGET*?
?

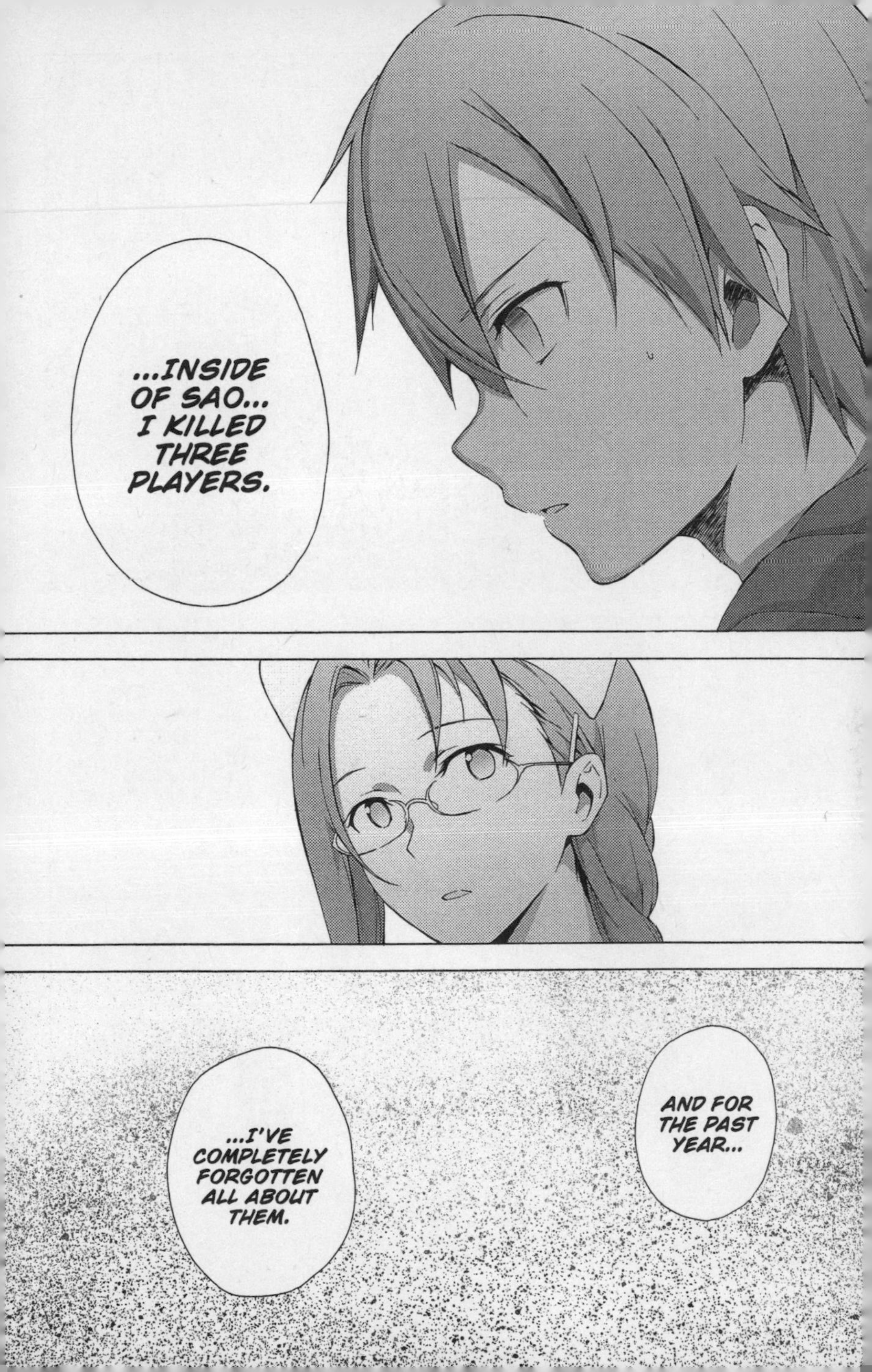
...INSIDE OF SAO... I KILLED THREE PLAYERS.
AND FOR THE PAST YEAR...
...I'VE COMPLETELY FORGOTTEN ALL ABOUT THEM.

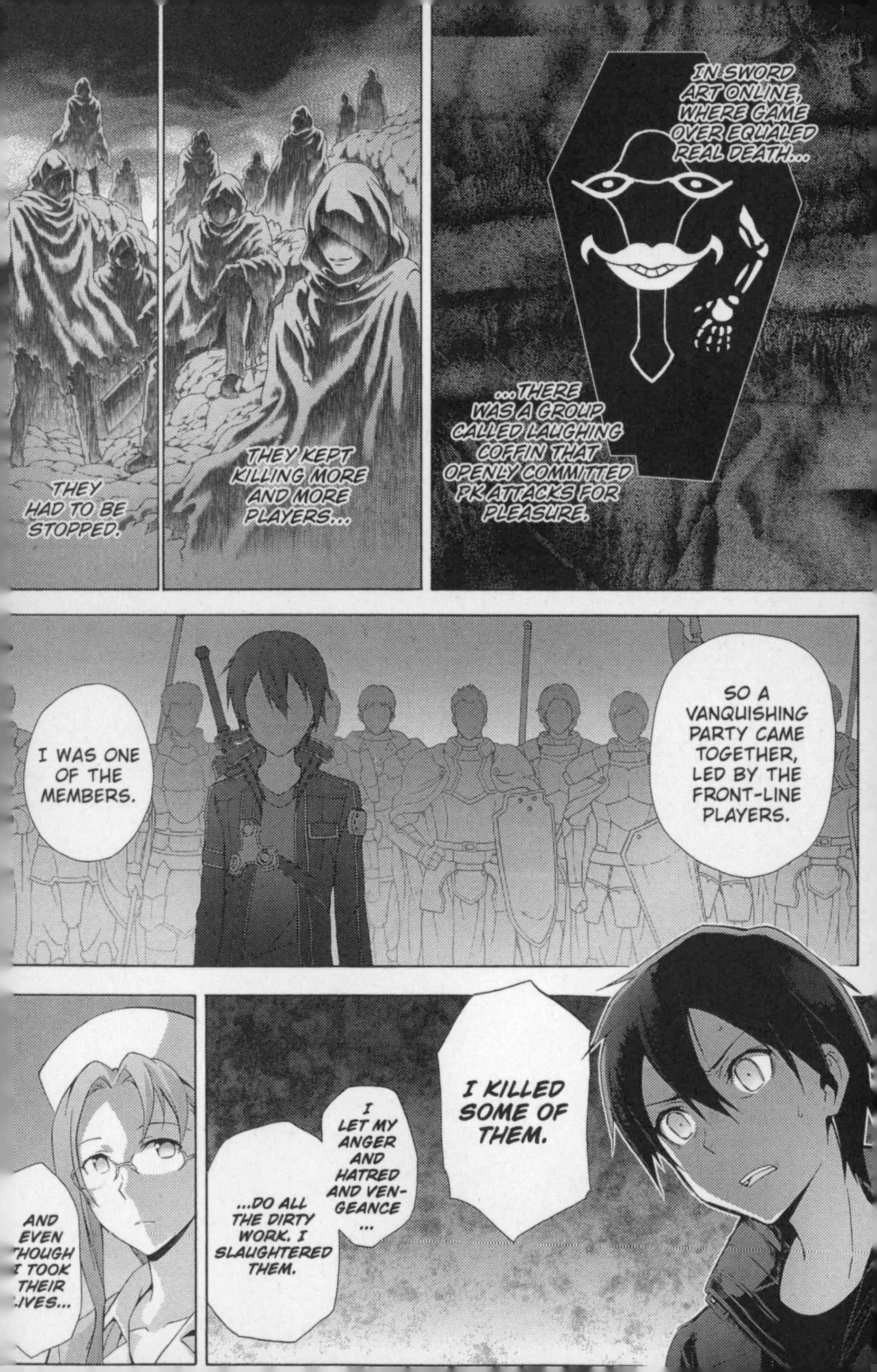
IN SWORD ART ONLINE, WHERE GAME OVER EQUALED REAL DEATH...
...THERE WAS A GROUP CALLED LAUGHING COFFIN THAT OPENLY COMMITTED PK ATTACKS FOR PLEASURE.
THEY KEPT KILLING MORE AND MORE PLAYERS...
THEY HAD TO BE STOPPED.
SO A VANQUISHING PARTY CAME TOGETHER, LED BY THE FRONT-LINE PLAYERS.
I WAS ONE OF THE MEMBERS.
I KILLED SOME OF THEM.
I LET MY ANGER AND HATRED AND VENGEANCE...
...DO ALL THE DIRTY WORK. I SLAUGHTERED THEM.
AND EVEN THOUGH I TOOK THEIR LIVES...

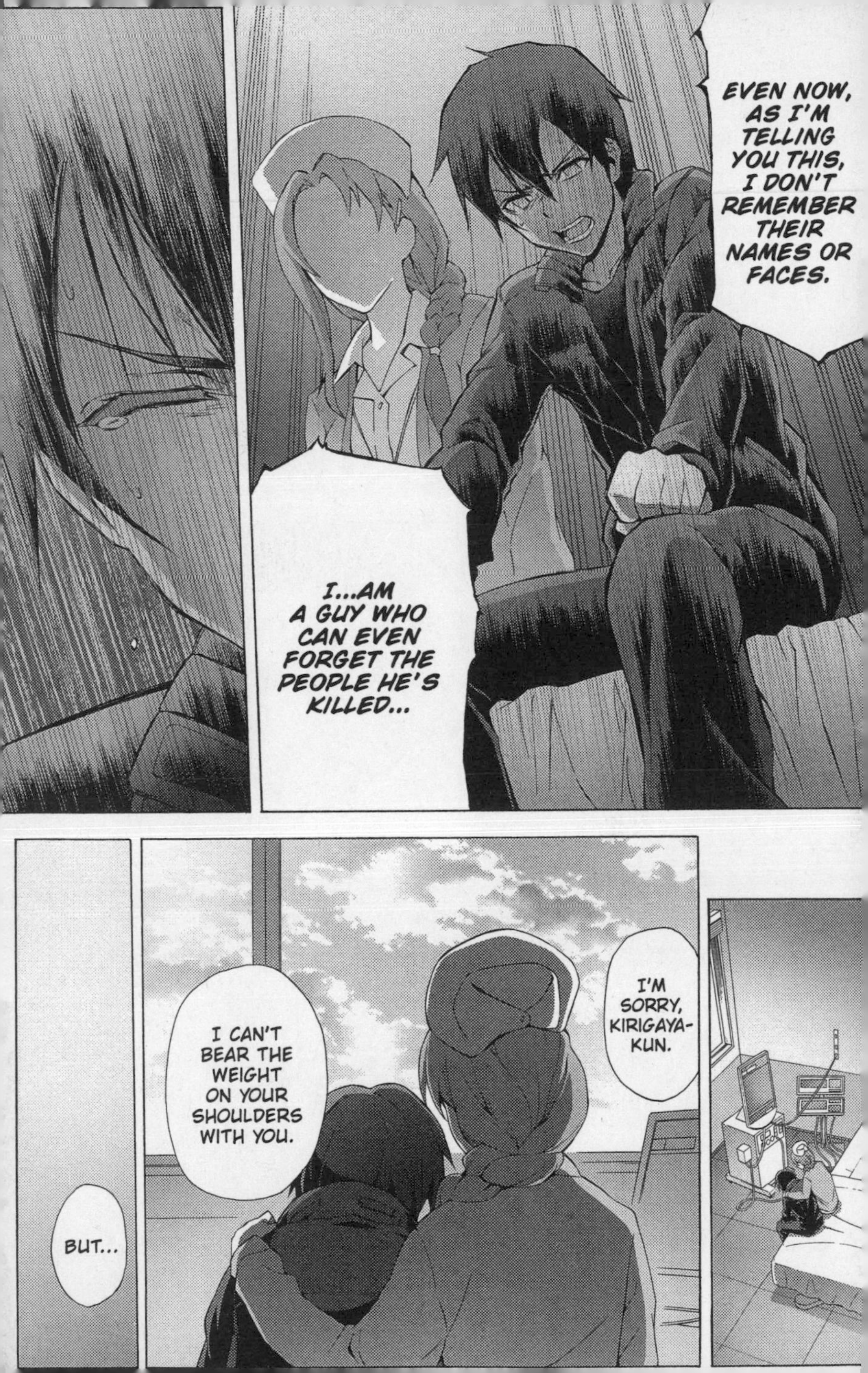
EVEN NOW, AS I'M TELLING YOU THIS, I DON'T REMEMBER THEIR NAMES OR FACES.
I...AM A GUY WHO CAN EVEN FORGET THE PEOPLE HE'S KILLED...
I'M SORRY, KIRIGAYA-KUN.
I CAN'T BEAR THE WEIGHT ON YOUR SHOULDERS WITH YOU.
BUT...

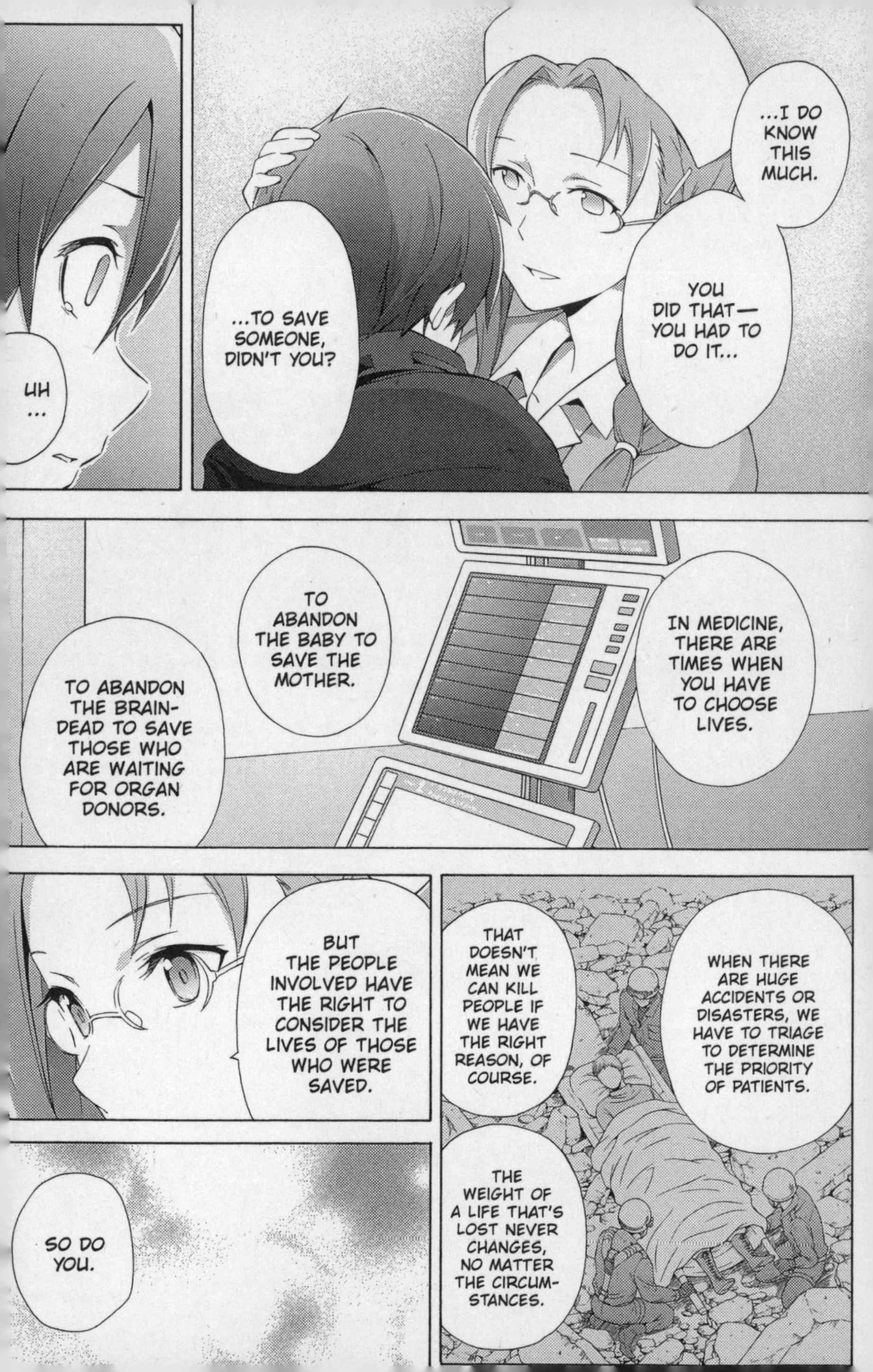
...I DO KNOW THIS MUCH.
YOU DID THAT— YOU HAD TO DO IT...
...TO SAVE SOMEONE, DIDN'T YOU?
UH ...
IN MEDICINE, THERE ARE TIMES WHEN YOU HAVE TO CHOOSE LIVES.
TO ABANDON THE BABY TO SAVE THE MOTHER.
TO ABANDON THE BRAIN-DEAD TO SAVE THOSE WHO ARE WAITING FOR ORGAN DONORS.
WHEN THERE ARE HUGE ACCIDENTS OR DISASTERS, WE HAVE TO TRIAGE TO DETERMINE THE PRIORITY OF PATIENTS.
THAT DOESN'T MEAN WE CAN KILL PEOPLE IF WE HAVE THE RIGHT REASON, OF COURSE.
THE WEIGHT OF A LIFE THAT'S LOST NEVER CHANGES, NO MATTER THE CIRCUM-STANCES.
BUT THE PEOPLE INVOLVED HAVE THE RIGHT TO CONSIDER THE LIVES OF THOSE WHO WERE SAVED.
SO DO YOU.

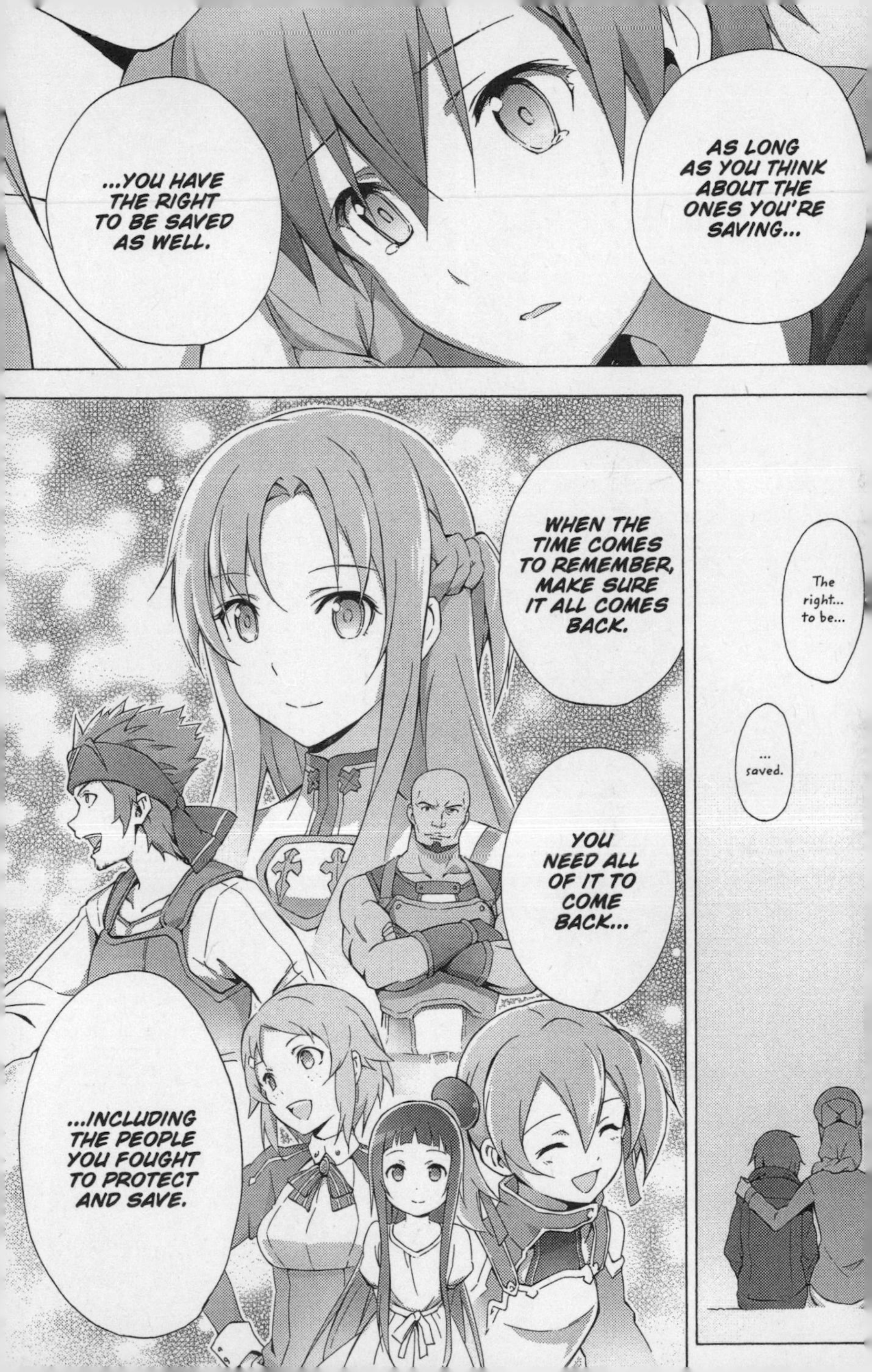
AS LONG AS YOU THINK ABOUT THE ONES YOU'RE SAVING...
...YOU HAVE THE RIGHT TO BE SAVED AS WELL.
The right... to be...
... saved.
WHEN THE TIME COMES TO REMEMBER, MAKE SURE IT ALL COMES BACK.
YOU NEED ALL OF IT TO COME BACK...
...INCLUDING THE PEOPLE YOU FOUGHT TO PROTECT AND SAVE.

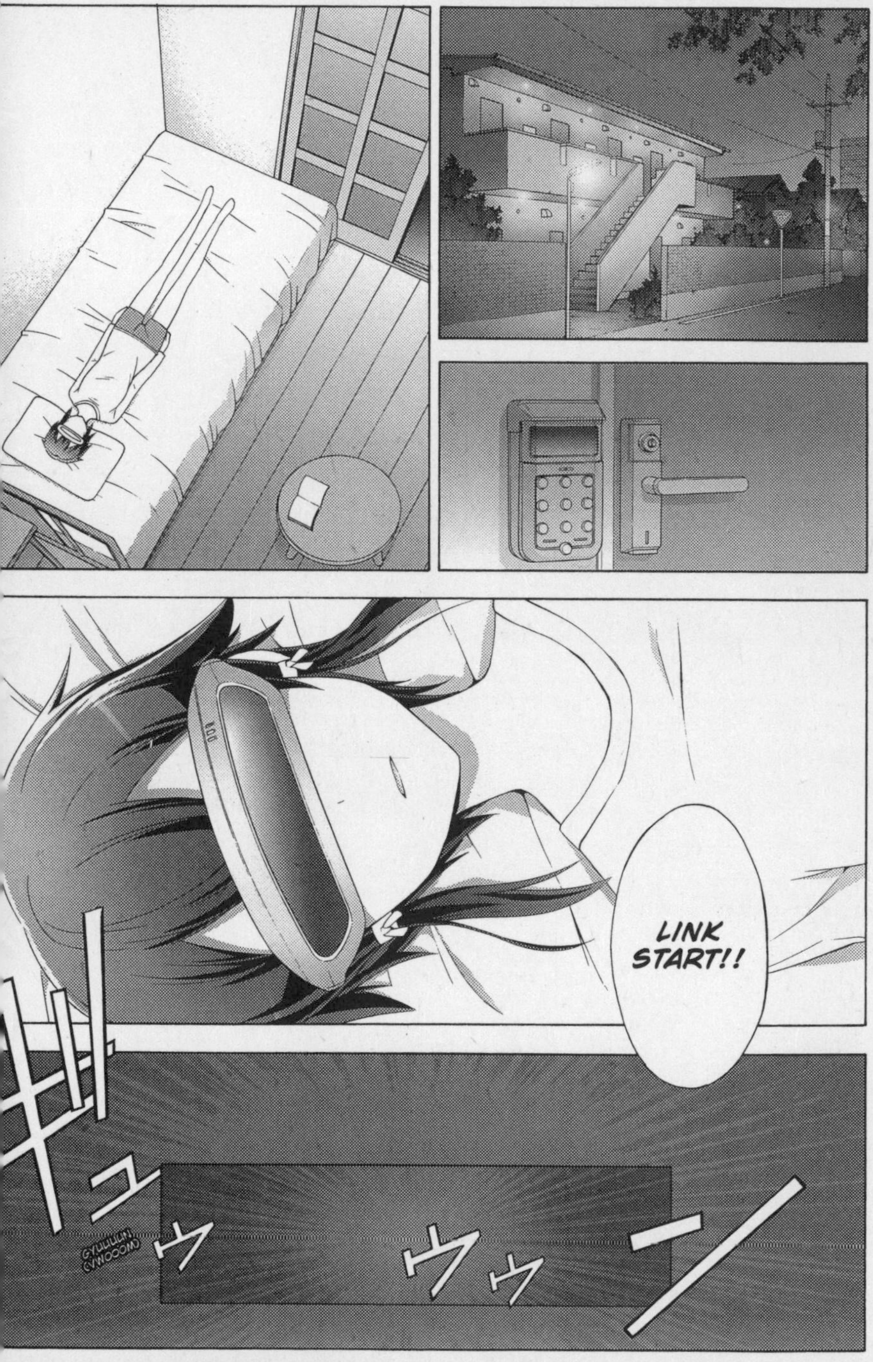
LINK START!!
ギュウウウーン
GYUUUUN (VWOOOOM)

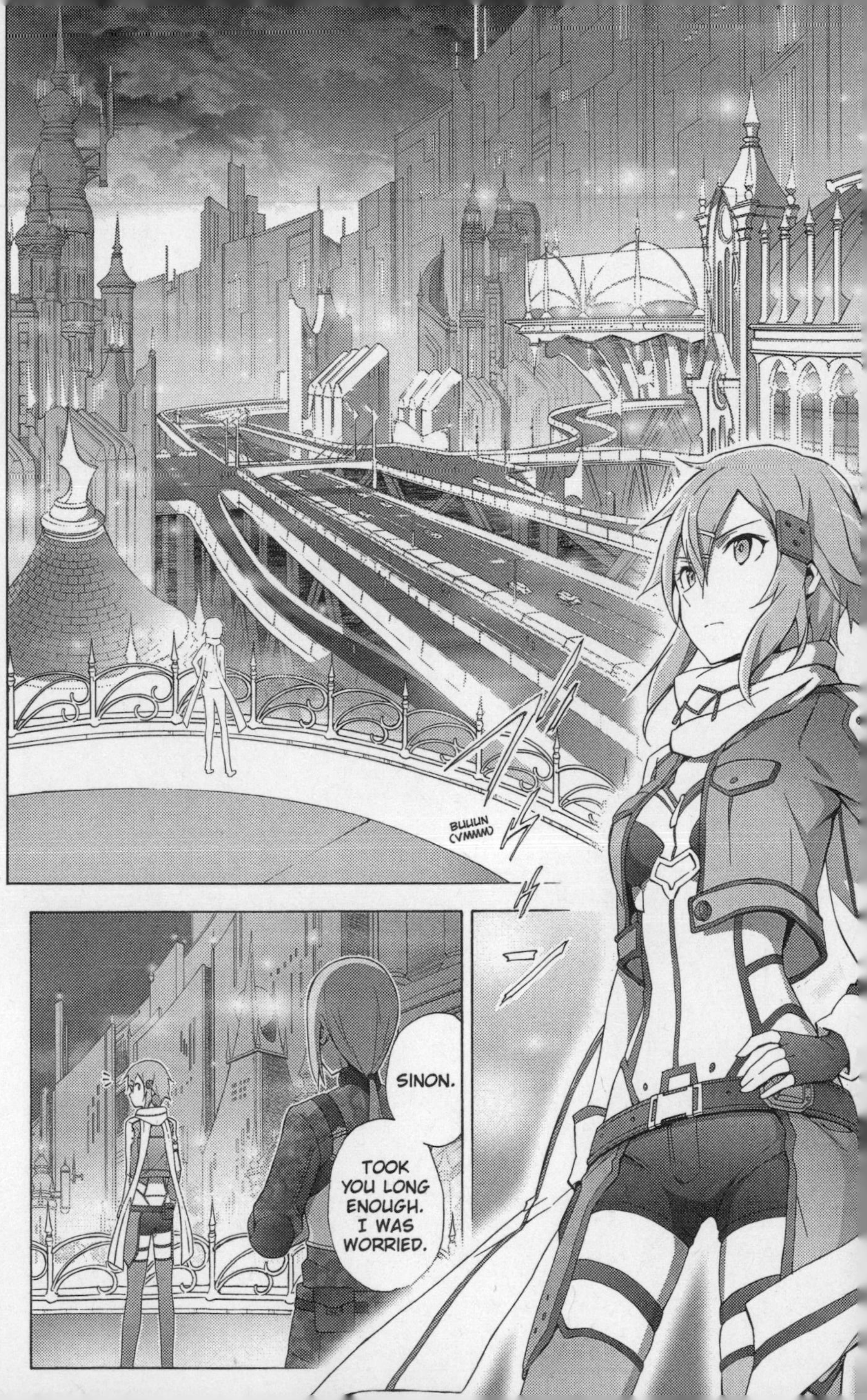
BUUUN (VMMM)
SINON.
TOOK YOU LONG ENOUGH. I WAS WORRIED.

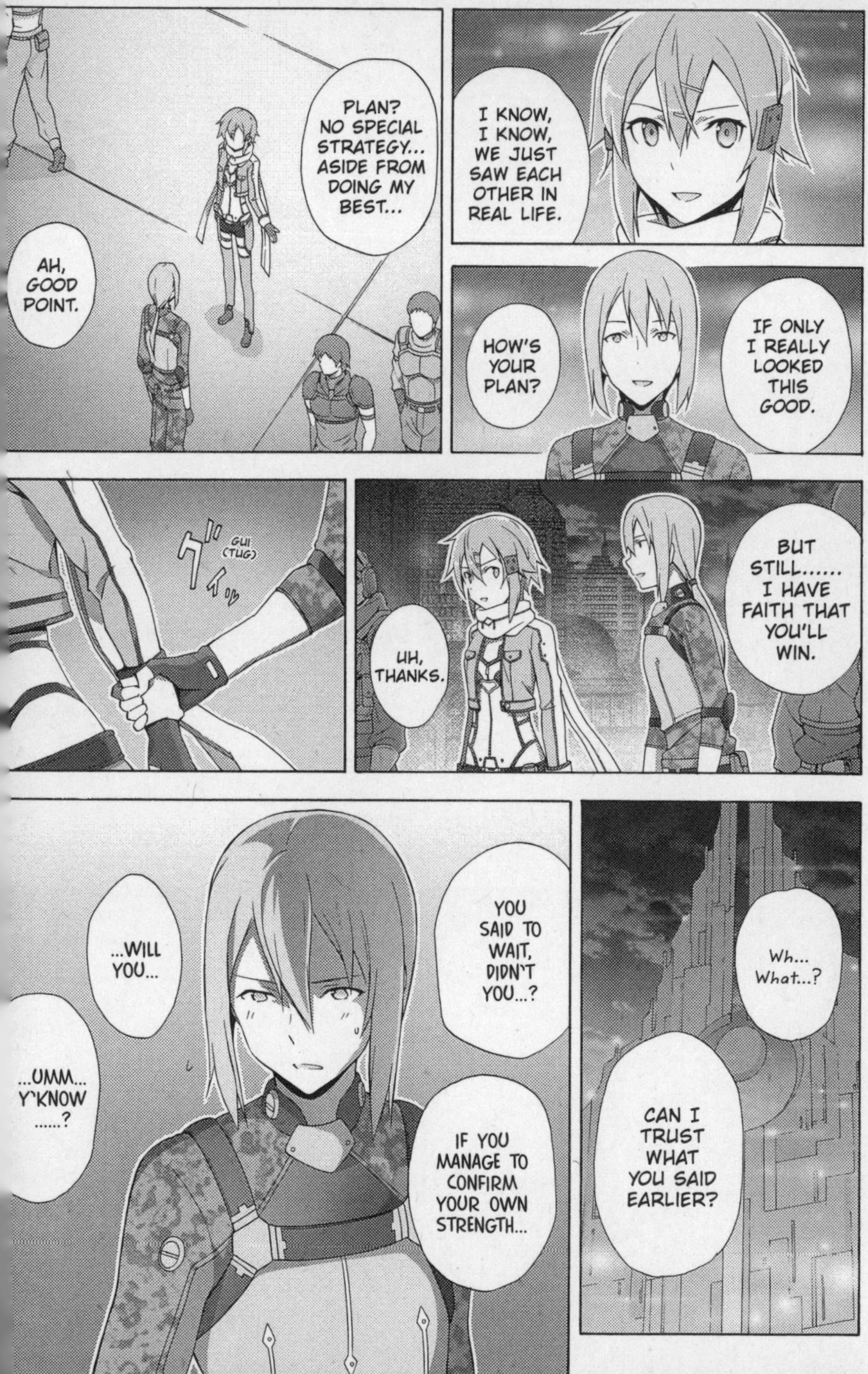
I KNOW, I KNOW, WE JUST SAW EACH OTHER IN REAL LIFE.
IF ONLY I REALLY LOOKED THIS GOOD.
HOW'S YOUR PLAN?
PLAN? NO SPECIAL STRATEGY... ASIDE FROM DOING MY BEST...
AH, GOOD POINT.
BUT STILL...... I HAVE FAITH THAT YOU'LL WIN.
UH, THANKS.
GUI (TUG)
Wh... What...?
CAN I TRUST WHAT YOU SAID EARLIER?
YOU SAID TO WAIT, DIDN'T YOU...?
...WILL YOU...
IF YOU MANAGE TO CONFIRM YOUR OWN STRENGTH...
...UMM... Y'KNOW ......?

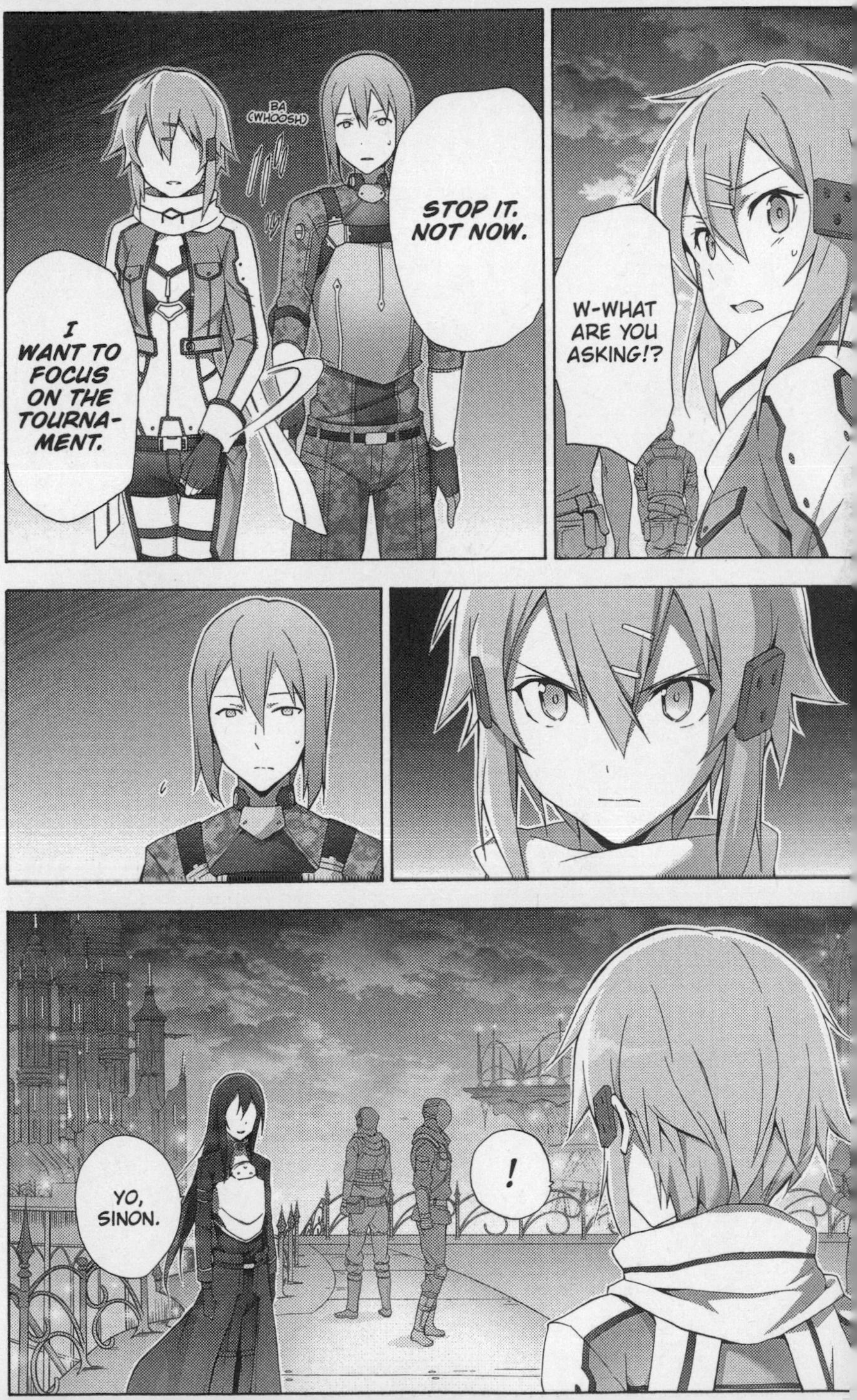
W-WHAT ARE YOU ASKING!?
STOP IT. NOT NOW.
BA (WHOOSH)
I WANT TO FOCUS ON THE TOURNAMENT.
!
YO, SINON.

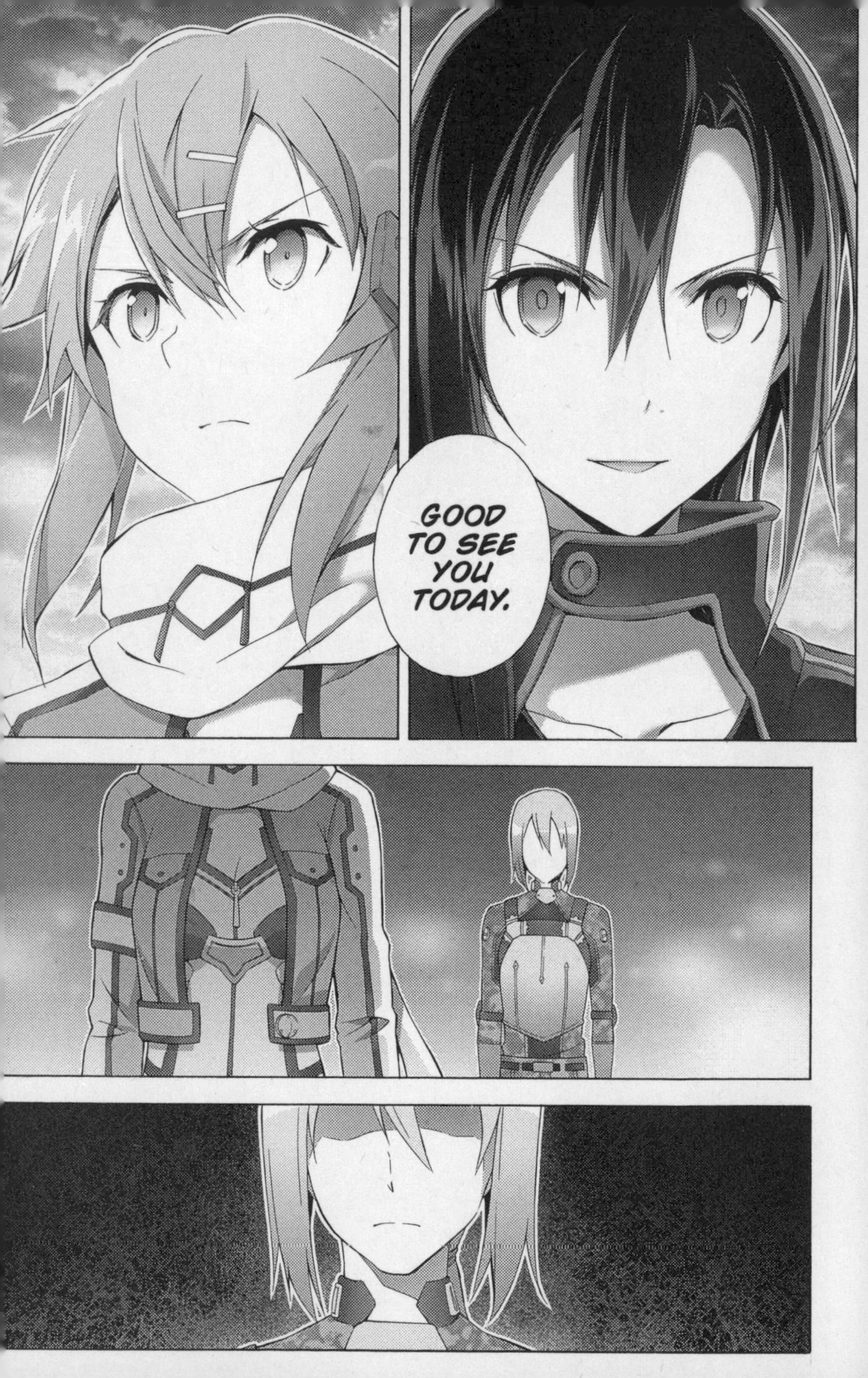
GOOD TO SEE YOU TODAY.

SWORD ART ONLINE
phantom bullet

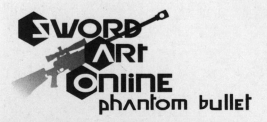

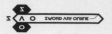

SWORD ART ONLINE
phantom bullet

check point! 001

THE BATTLE AGAINST LAUGHING COFFIN: WORLD

AN INCIDENT THAT OCCURRED WITHIN SAO IN AUGUST 2024. THE KNIGHTS OF THE BLOOD AND OTHER MAJOR GUILDS BANDED TOGETHER AGAINST THE MURDEROUS LAUGHING COFFIN GUILD, RAIDING THEIR HIDEOUT IN THE SAFE AREA OF A DUNGEON. BUT WORD LEAKED OUT, AND IT TURNED INTO A TERRIBLE BATTLE. IN THE END, THE RAID PARTY LOST ELEVEN MEMBERS, AND LAUGHING COFFIN LOST TWENTY-ONE. KIRITO WAS RESPONSIBLE FOR TWO LC DEATHS OUT OF SELF-DEFENSE. WHEN HE MENTIONED THAT HE HAD KILLED THREE IN THE PREVIOUS CHAPTER, IT WAS BECAUSE HE ALSO COUNTED KURADEEL, WHOM HE KILLED WHILE SAVING ASUNA.

KAZUTO'S ROOM: WORLD

KIRITO'S ROOM, AS SEEN MANY TIMES IN THE ANIME. IT'S A GAMER'S LAIR WITH A HARDCORE DESKTOP MACHINE AND THREE LCD MONITORS. HE'S OFTEN DEPICTED AS SLOPPY AND SLOVENLY WITHIN THE VRMMOS HE PLAYS, BUT IN REAL LIFE, HIS ROOM IS SURPRISINGLY TIDY. BECAUSE HIS MOTHER IS VERY BUSY AS A MAGAZINE EDITOR, IT'S POSSIBLE THAT HIS SISTER SUGUHA IS CLEANING UP AFTER HIM INSTEAD.

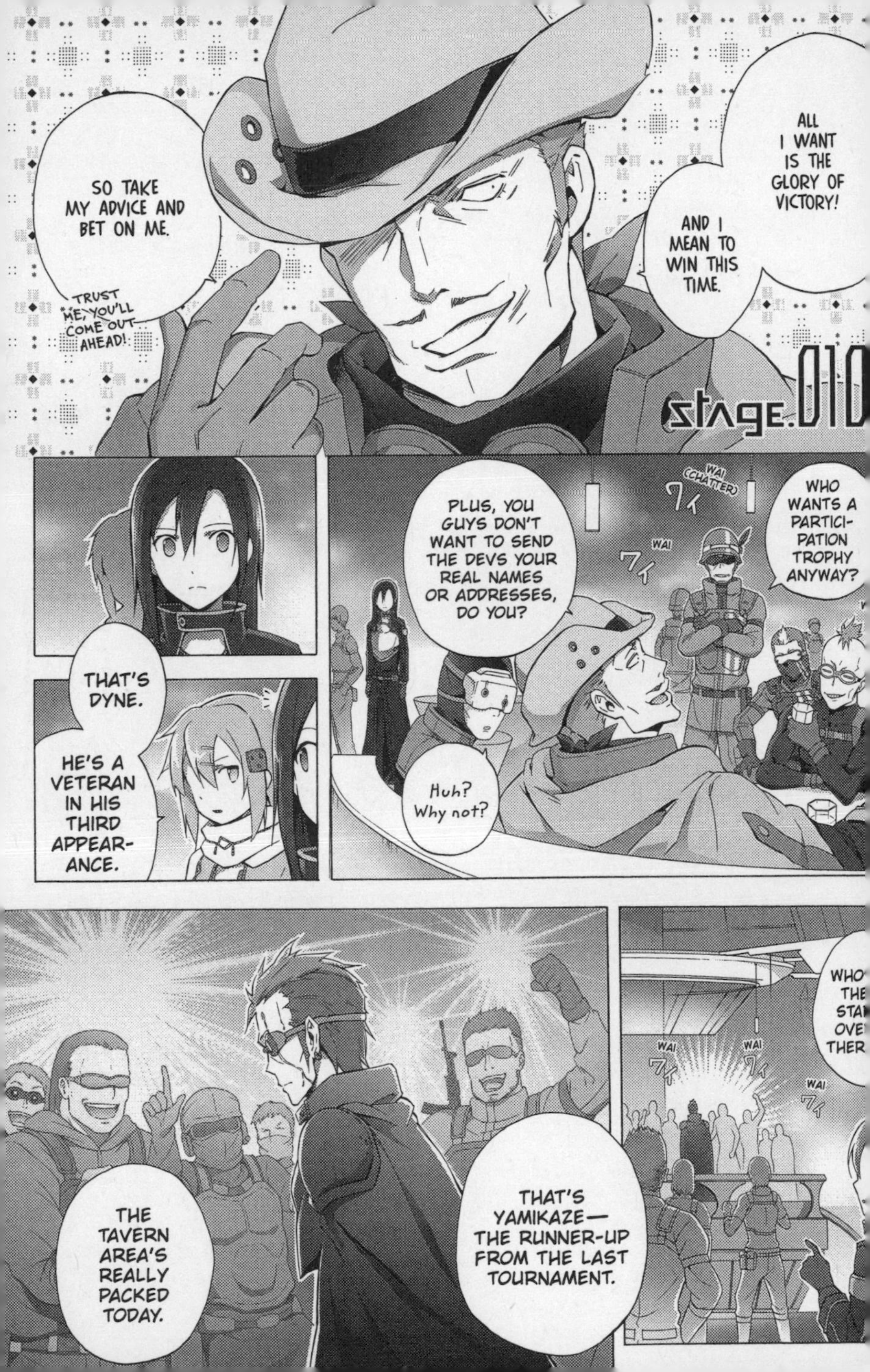
ALL I WANT IS THE GLORY OF VICTORY!
AND I MEAN TO WIN THIS TIME.
SO TAKE MY ADVICE AND BET ON ME.
TRUST ME, YOU'LL COME OUT AHEAD!
stage.010
WHO WANTS A PARTICIPATION TROPHY ANYWAY?
WAI (CHATTER)
WAI
PLUS, YOU GUYS DON'T WANT TO SEND THE DEVS YOUR REAL NAMES OR ADDRESSES, DO YOU?
Huh? Why not?
THAT'S DYNE.
HE'S A VETERAN IN HIS THIRD APPEARANCE.
WAI
WAI
WAI
THAT'S YAMIKAZE— THE RUNNER-UP FROM THE LAST TOURNAMENT.
THE TAVERN AREA'S REALLY PACKED TODAY.

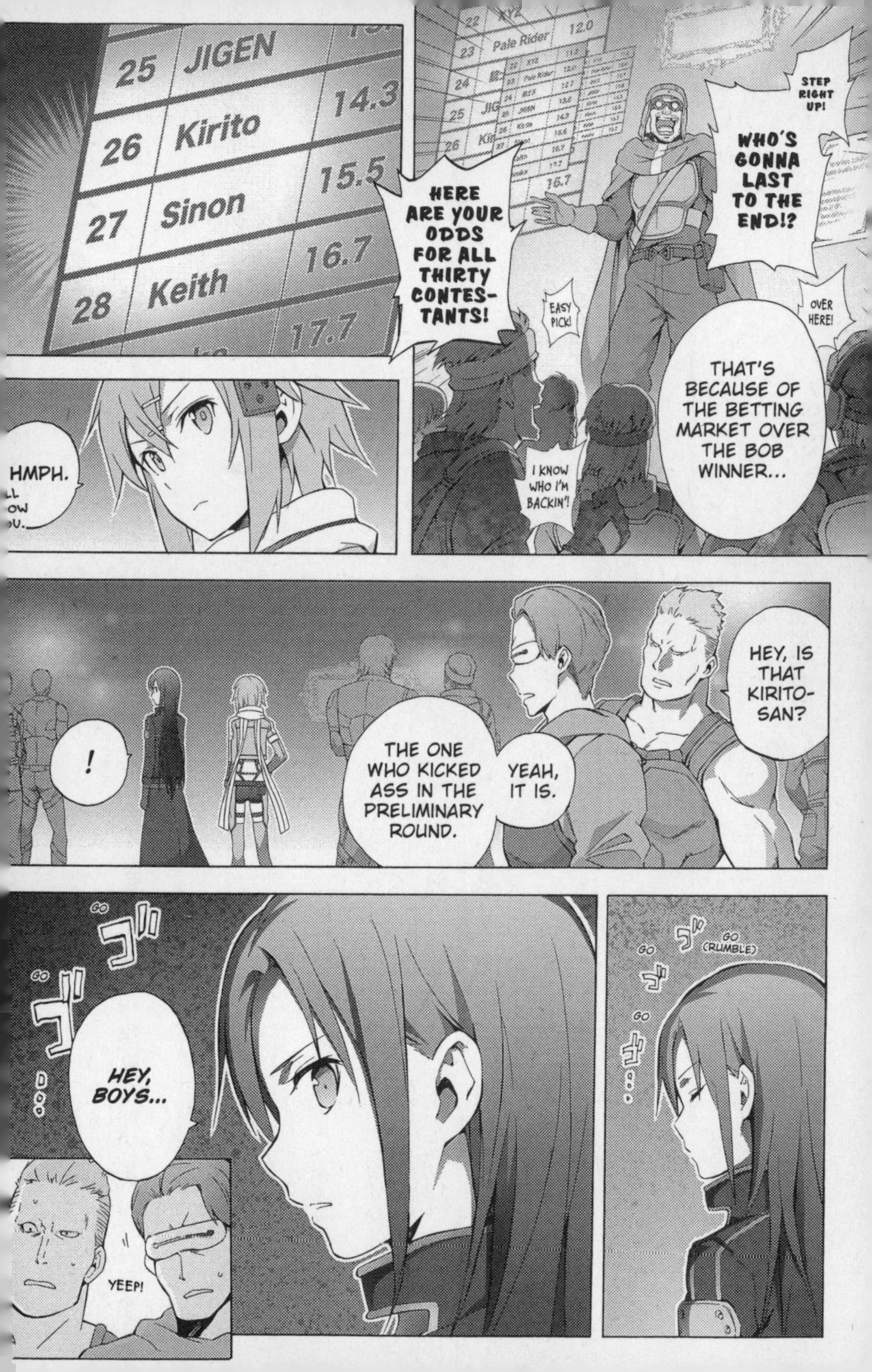
STEP RIGHT UP!
WHO'S GONNA LAST TO THE END!?
HERE ARE YOUR ODDS FOR ALL THIRTY CONTESTANTS!
22 XYZ
23 Pale Rider 12.0
OVER HERE!
EASY PICK!
THAT'S BECAUSE OF THE BETTING MARKET OVER THE BOB WINNER...
I KNOW WHO I'M BACKIN'!
25 JIGEN
14.3
26 Kirito
15.5
27 Sinon
16.7
28 Keith
17.7
HMPH.
HEY, IS THAT KIRITO-SAN?
YEAH, IT IS.
THE ONE WHO KICKED ASS IN THE PRELIMINARY ROUND.
!
GO
GO (RUMBLE)
GO
GO
GO
HEY, BOYS...
YEEP!

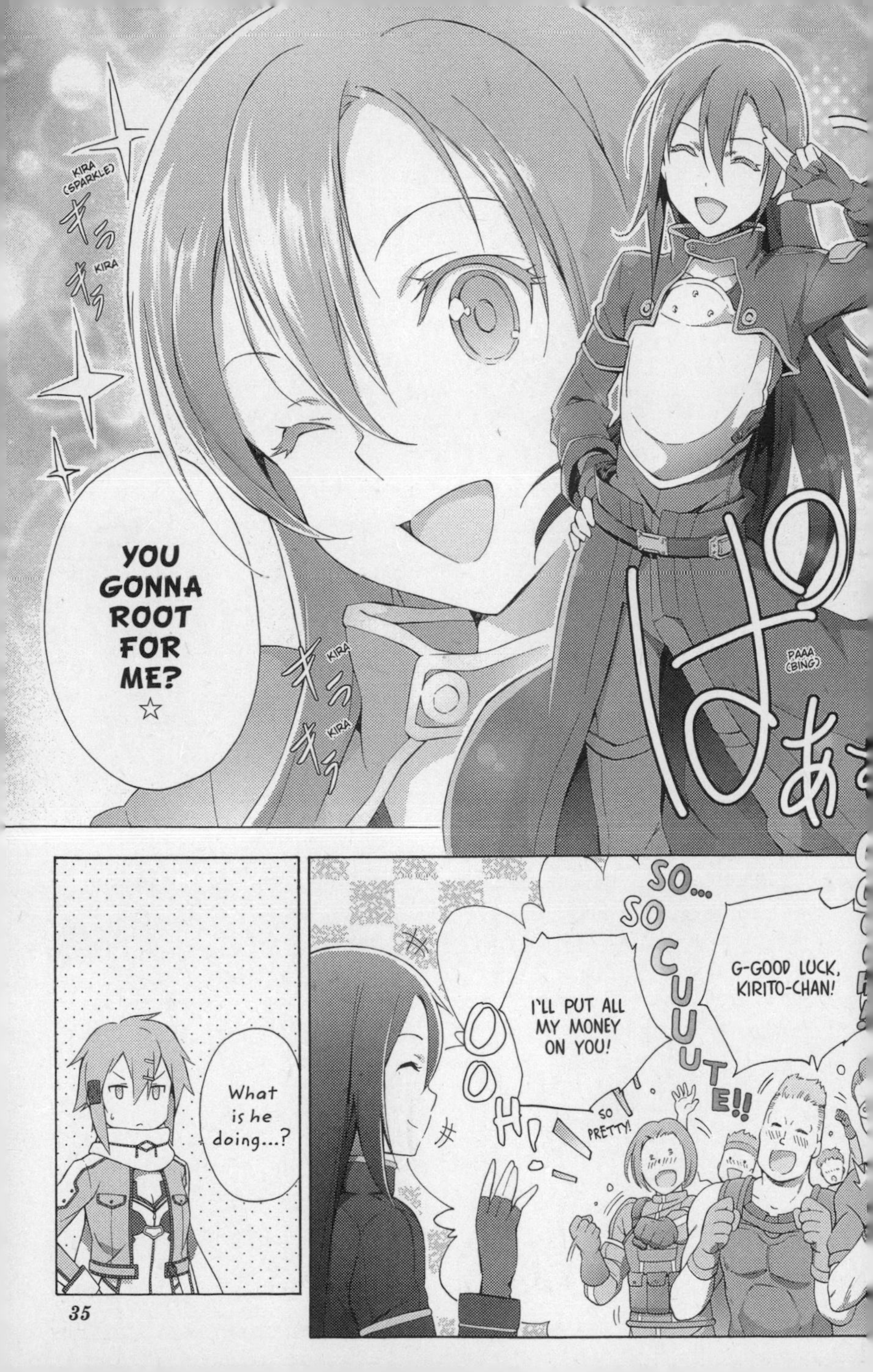
PAAA (BING)
KIRA (SPARKLE)
KIRA
YOU GONNA ROOT FOR ME? ☆
KIRA
KIRA
G-GOOD LUCK, KIRITO-CHAN!
SO... SO CUUUUTE!!
I'LL PUT ALL MY MONEY ON YOU!
OOOH!
SO PRETTY!
What is he doing...?

THANKS FOR ALL THE HELP.

WAI
WAI
WAI
WAI
WAI
WAI
((CHATTER))
WAI
WAI
WAI

SO ON THIS LIST OF THIRTY FINALISTS...

...WHICH NAMES DO YOU NOT RECOG-NIZE?

NOT RECOG-NIZE?

WHAT DO YOU MEAN BY THAT...?

PLEASE, TELL ME.

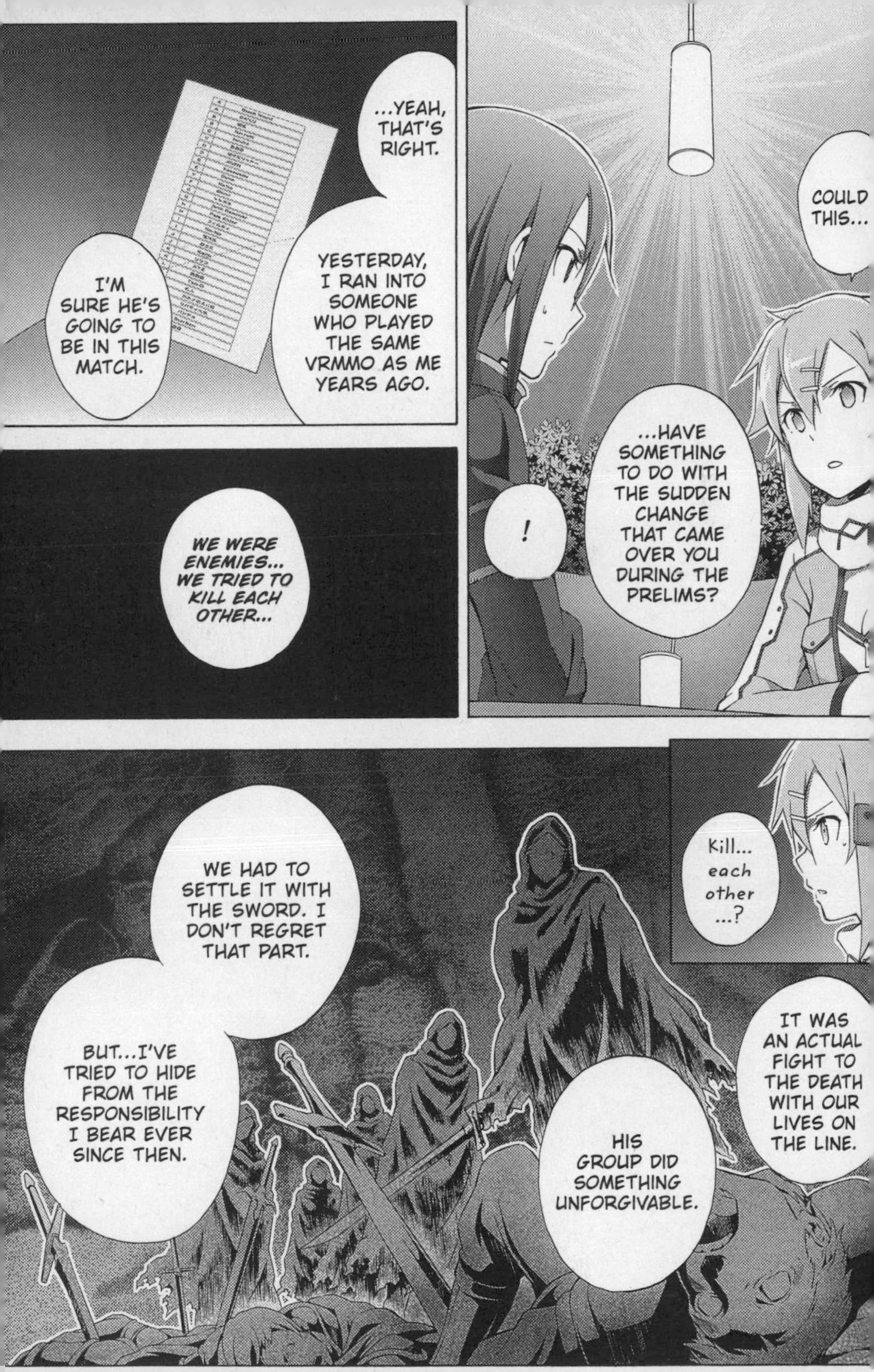
COULD THIS...
...HAVE SOMETHING TO DO WITH THE SUDDEN CHANGE THAT CAME OVER YOU DURING THE PRELIMS?
!
...YEAH, THAT'S RIGHT.
YESTERDAY, I RAN INTO SOMEONE WHO PLAYED THE SAME VRMMO AS ME YEARS AGO.
I'M SURE HE'S GOING TO BE IN THIS MATCH.
WE WERE ENEMIES... WE TRIED TO KILL EACH OTHER...
Kill... each other ...?
IT WAS AN ACTUAL FIGHT TO THE DEATH WITH OUR LIVES ON THE LINE.
HIS GROUP DID SOMETHING UNFORGIVABLE.
WE HAD TO SETTLE IT WITH THE SWORD. I DON'T REGRET THAT PART.
BUT...I'VE TRIED TO HIDE FROM THE RESPONSIBILITY I BEAR EVER SINCE THEN.

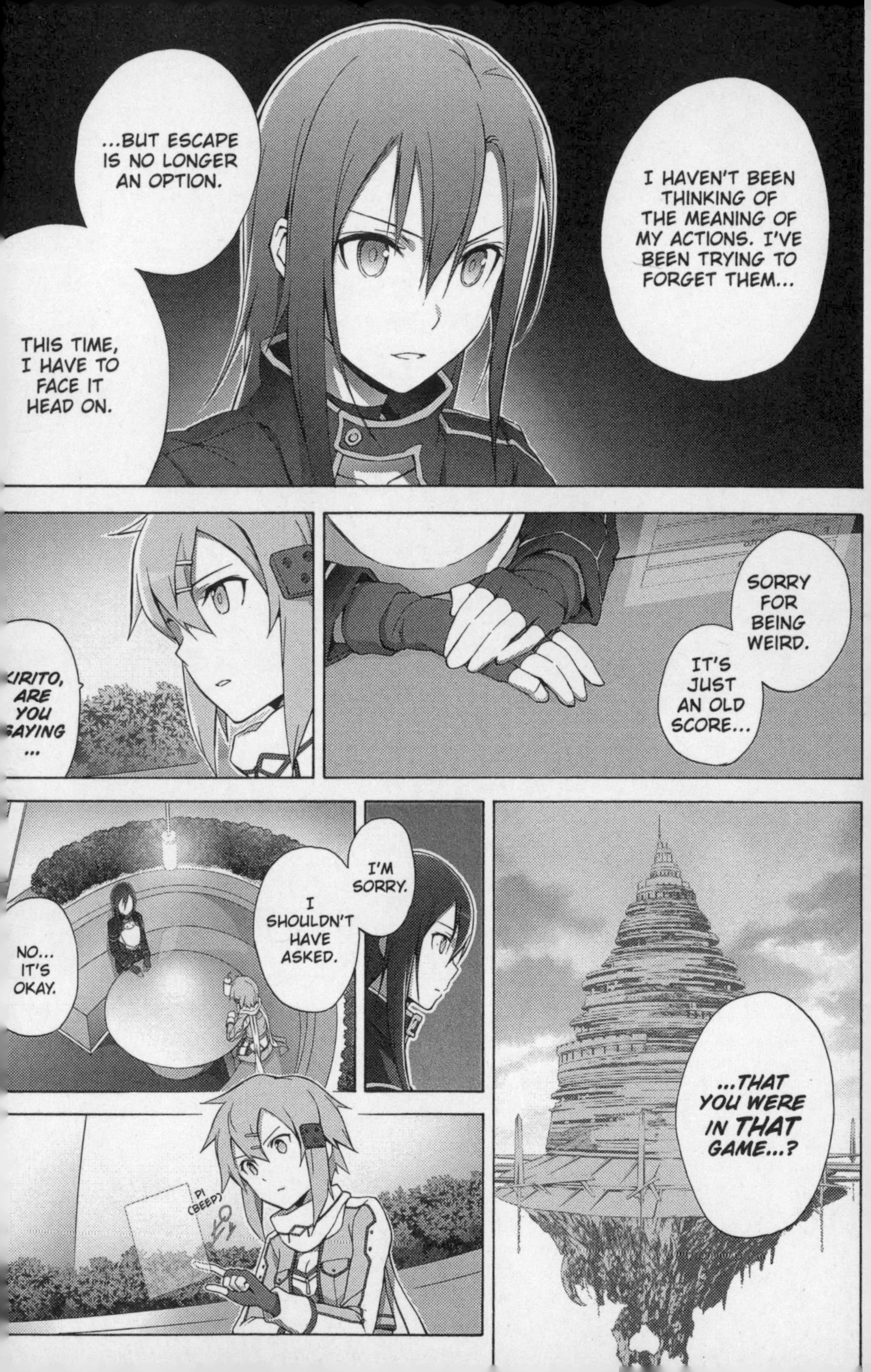
I HAVEN'T BEEN THINKING OF THE MEANING OF MY ACTIONS. I'VE BEEN TRYING TO FORGET THEM...
...BUT ESCAPE IS NO LONGER AN OPTION.
THIS TIME, I HAVE TO FACE IT HEAD ON.
SORRY FOR BEING WEIRD.
IT'S JUST AN OLD SCORE...
KIRITO, ARE YOU SAYING ...
...THAT YOU WERE IN THAT GAME...?
I'M SORRY.
I SHOULDN'T HAVE ASKED.
NO... IT'S OKAY.
PI (BEEP)

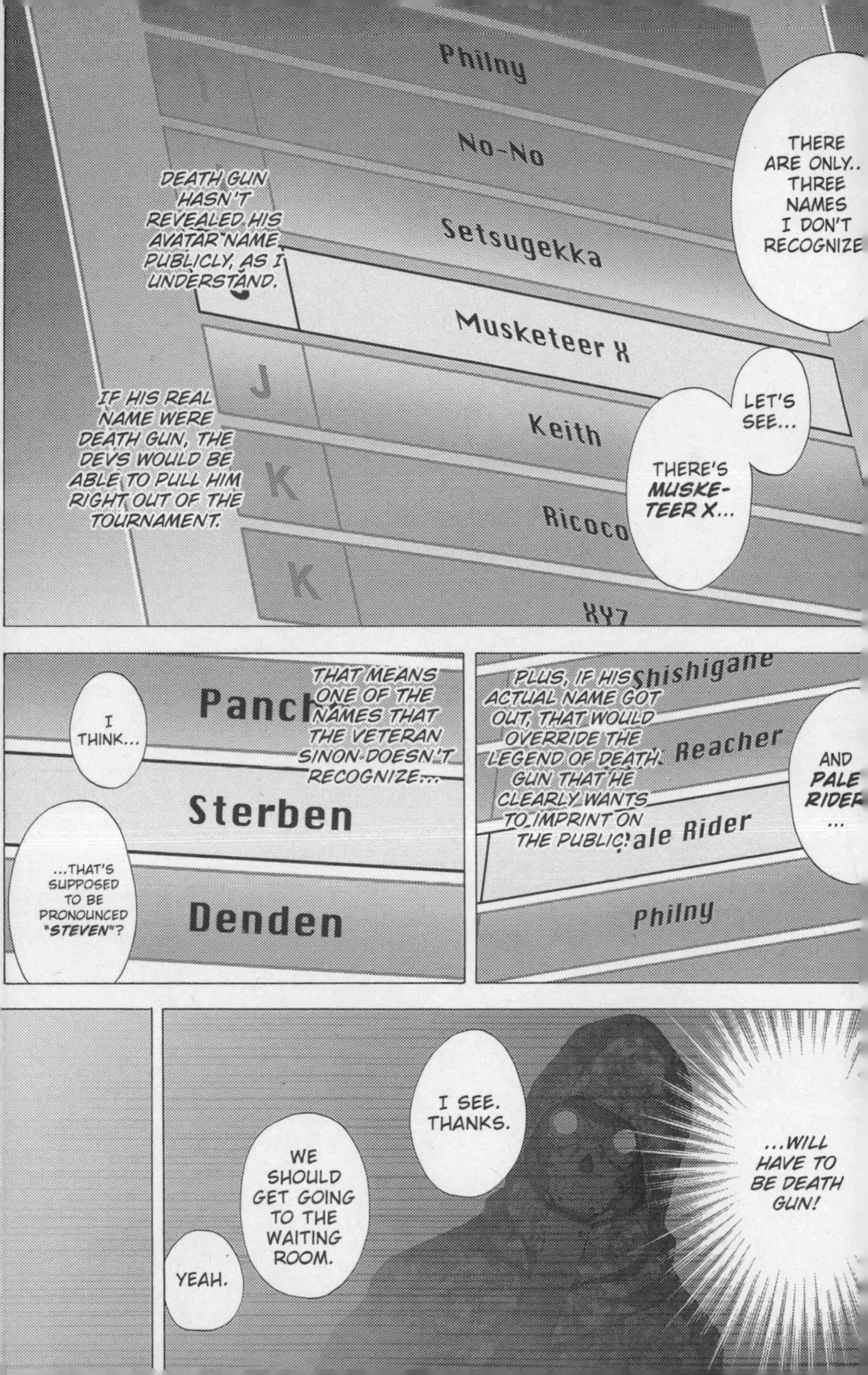
Philny
No-No
Setsugekka
Musketeer X
Keith
Ricoco
THERE ARE ONLY... THREE NAMES I DON'T RECOGNIZE
LET'S SEE...
THERE'S MUSKETEER X...
DEATH GUN HASN'T REVEALED HIS AVATAR NAME PUBLICLY, AS I UNDERSTAND.
IF HIS REAL NAME WERE DEATH GUN, THE DEVS WOULD BE ABLE TO PULL HIM RIGHT OUT OF THE TOURNAMENT.
Shishigane
Reacher
Philny
AND PALE RIDER...
PLUS, IF HIS ACTUAL NAME GOT OUT, THAT WOULD OVERRIDE THE LEGEND OF DEATH GUN THAT HE CLEARLY WANTS TO IMPRINT ON THE PUBLIC.
Sterben
Denden
THAT MEANS ONE OF THE NAMES THAT THE VETERAN SINON DOESN'T RECOGNIZE...
I THINK...
...THAT'S supposed TO BE pronounced "STEVEN"?
...WILL HAVE TO BE DEATH GUN!
I SEE. THANKS.
WE SHOULD GET GOING TO THE WAITING ROOM.
YEAH.

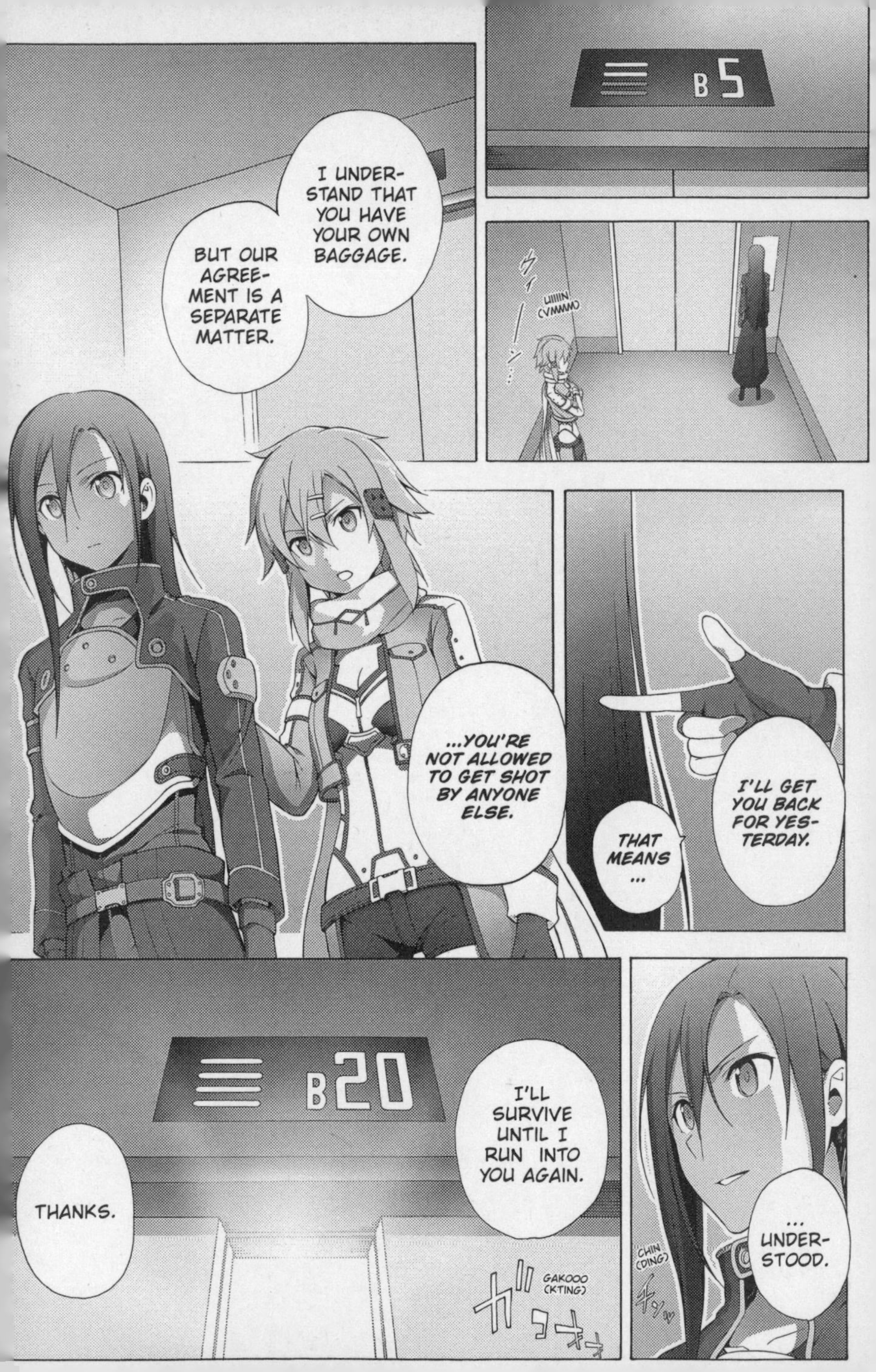
B 5
UIIIN (VMMMM)
I'LL GET YOU BACK FOR YES-TERDAY.
THAT MEANS ...
I UNDER-STAND THAT YOU HAVE YOUR OWN BAGGAGE.
BUT OUR AGREE-MENT IS A SEPARATE MATTER.
...YOU'RE NOT ALLOWED TO GET SHOT BY ANYONE ELSE.
... UNDER-STOOD.
CHIN (DING)
B 20
I'LL SURVIVE UNTIL I RUN INTO YOU AGAIN.
THANKS.
GAKOOO (KTING)

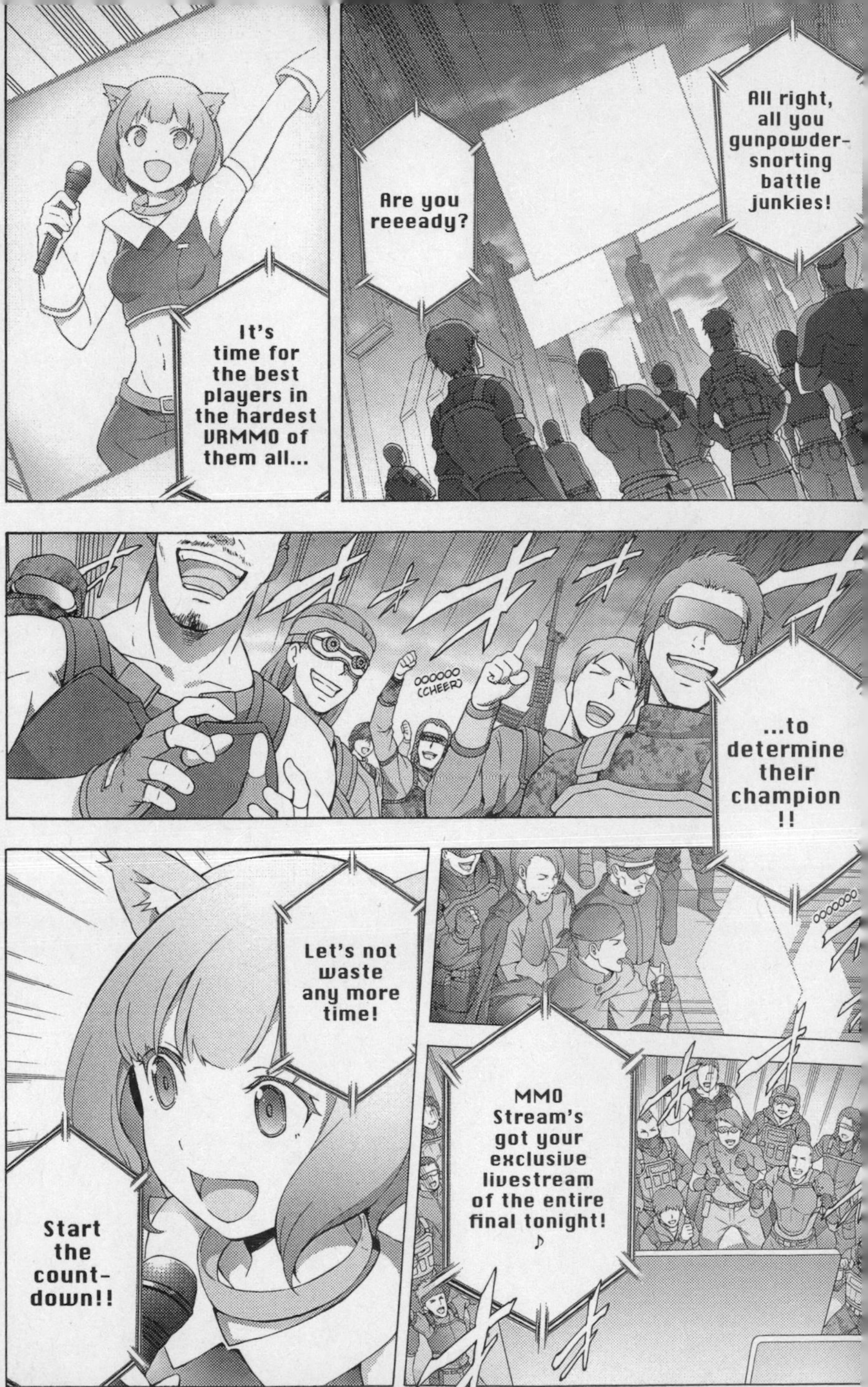
All right, all you gunpowder-snorting battle junkies!
Are you reeeady?
It's time for the best players in the hardest VRMMO of them all...
...to determine their champion!!
OOOOOO (CHEER)
OOOOOO
Let's not waste any more time!
MMO Stream's got your exclusive livestream of the entire final tonight! ♪
Start the countdown!!

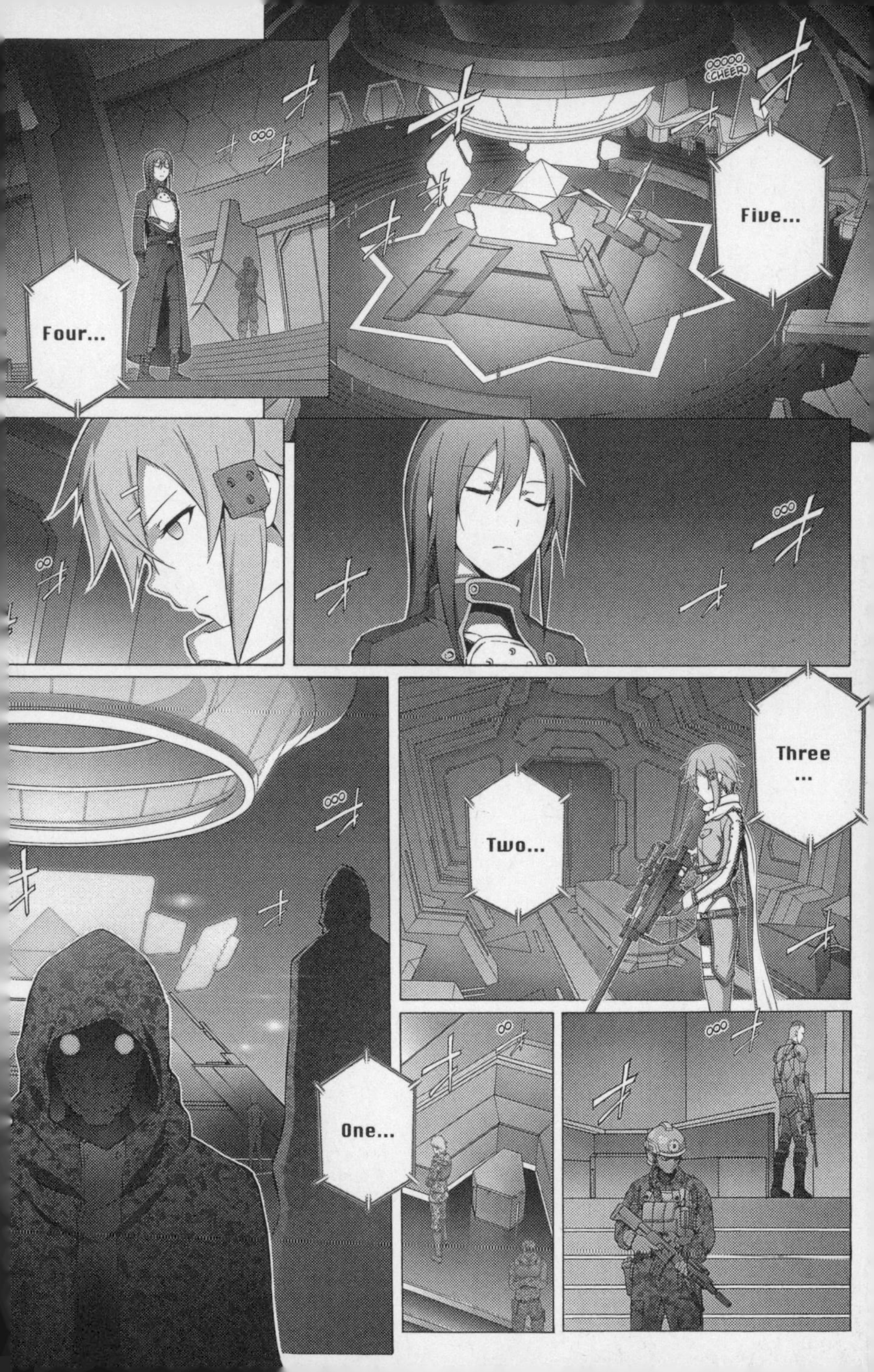
OOOOO (CHEER)
Five...
OOO
Four...
OOO
Three ...
Two...
OOO
One...

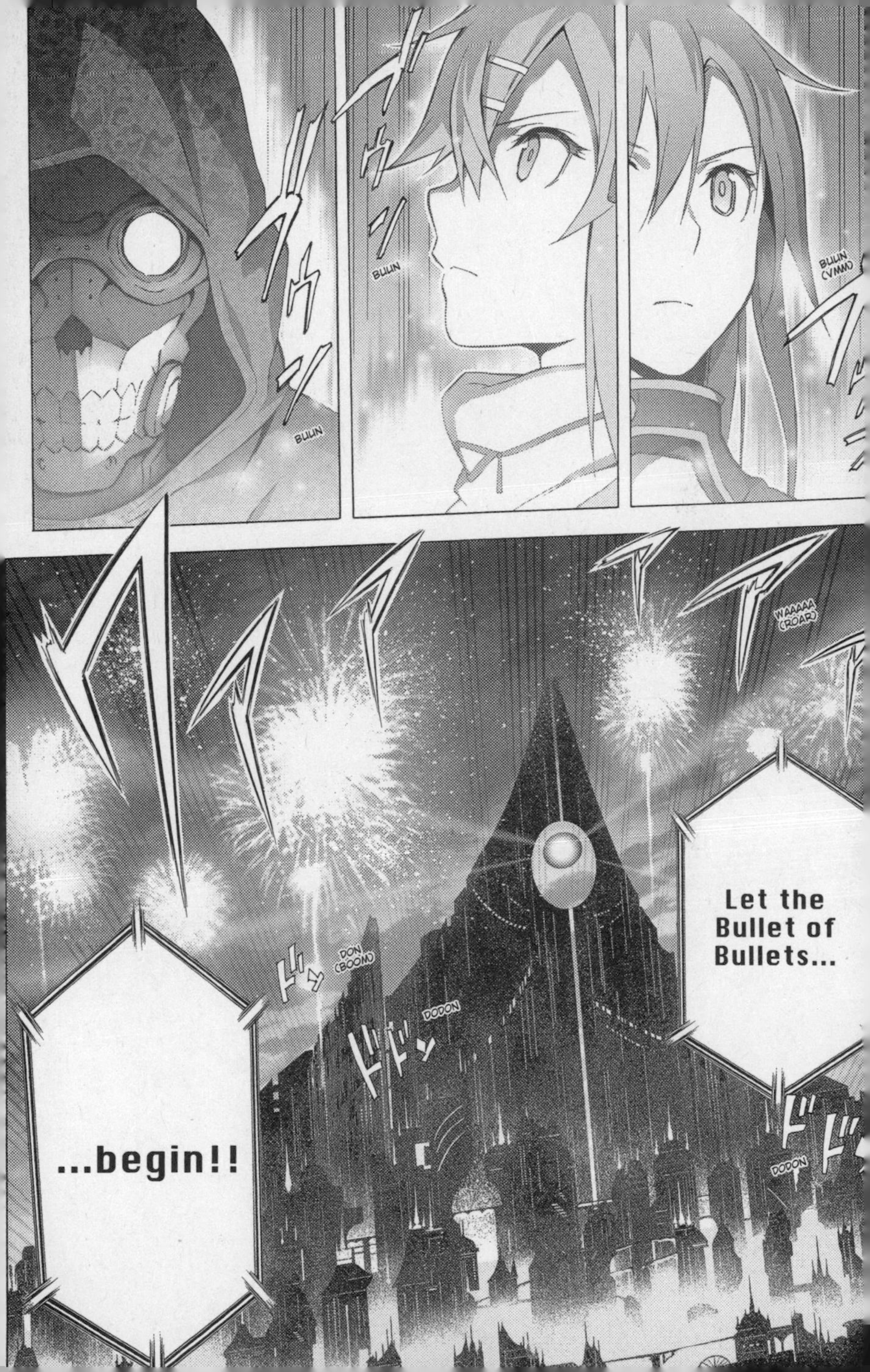
BULUN (VMM)
BULUN
BULUN
WAAAAA (ROAR)
Let the Bullet of Bullets...
DODON
DODON
DON (BOOM)
...begin!!

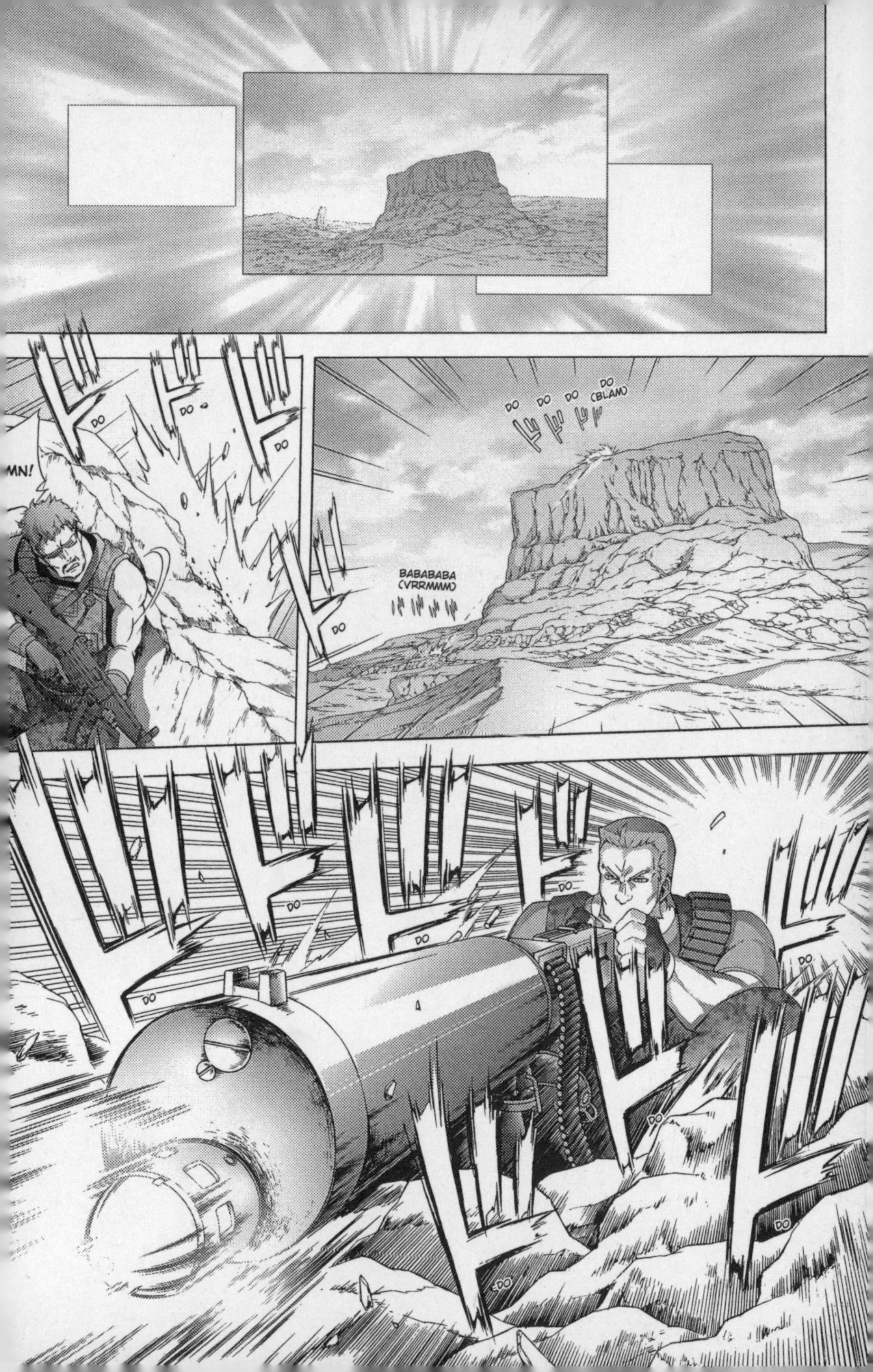
DO DO DO DO (BLAM)
BABABABA (VRRMMM)
MN!
DO
DO
DO
DO
DO
DO
DO
DO
DO
DO
DO
DO

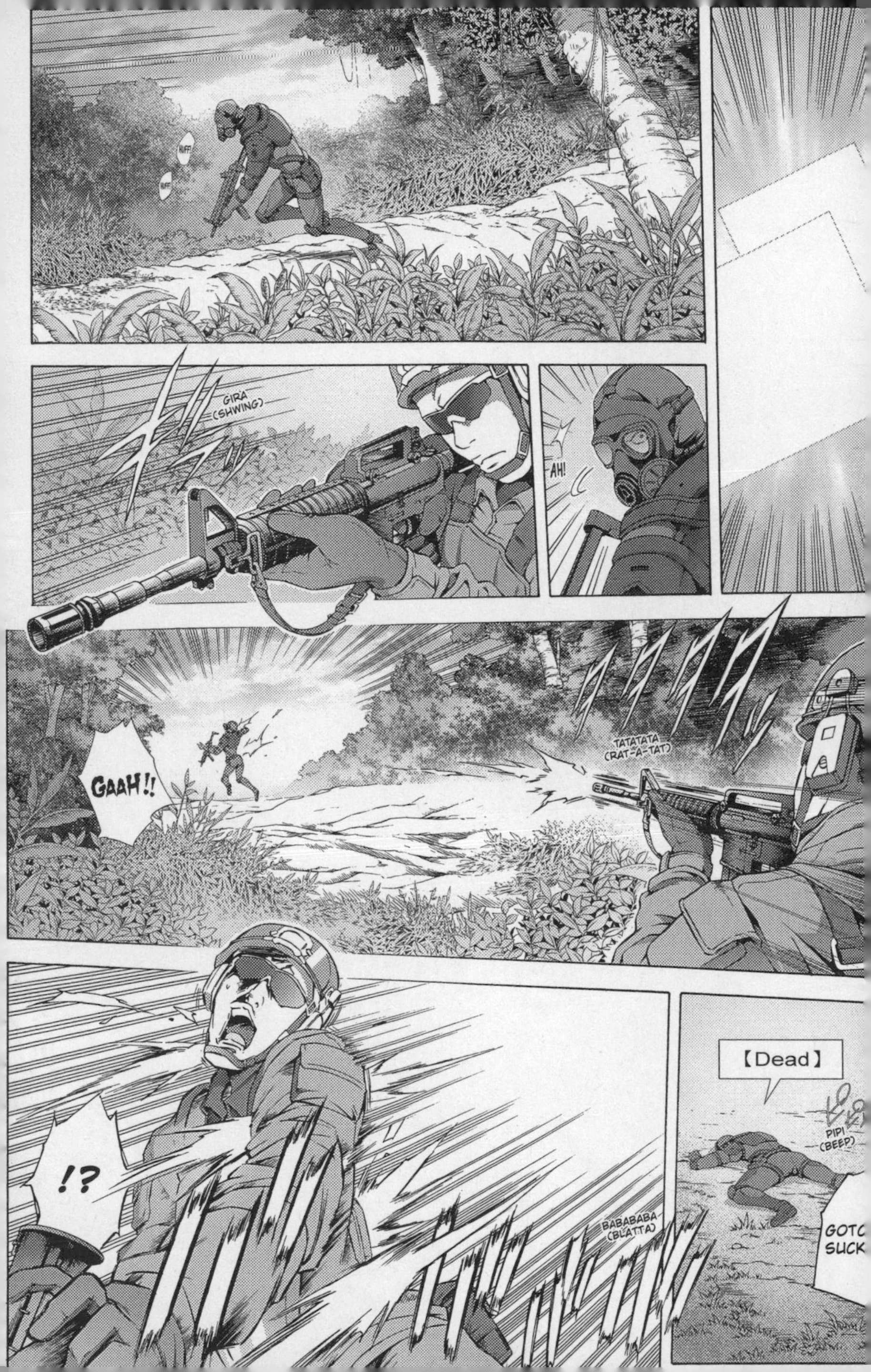
HUFF
HUFF
AH!
GIRA (SHWING)
TATATATA (RAT-A-TAT)
GAAH!!
【Dead】
PIPI (BEEP)
GOTC
SUCK
BABABABA (BLATTA)
!?

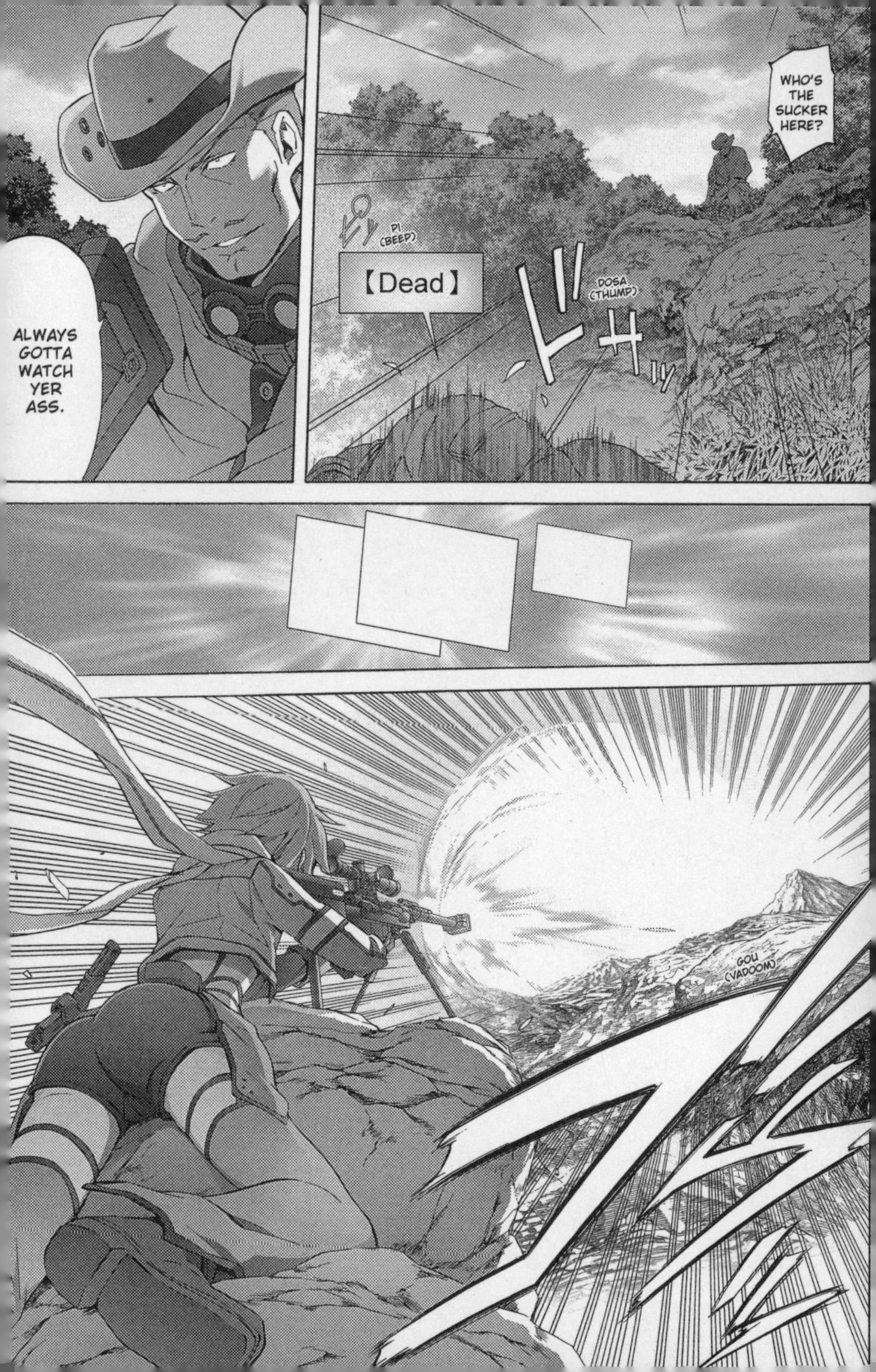
WHO'S THE SUCKER HERE?
PI (BEEP)
【Dead】
DOSA (THUMP)
ALWAYS GOTTA WATCH YER ASS.
GOU (VADOOM)

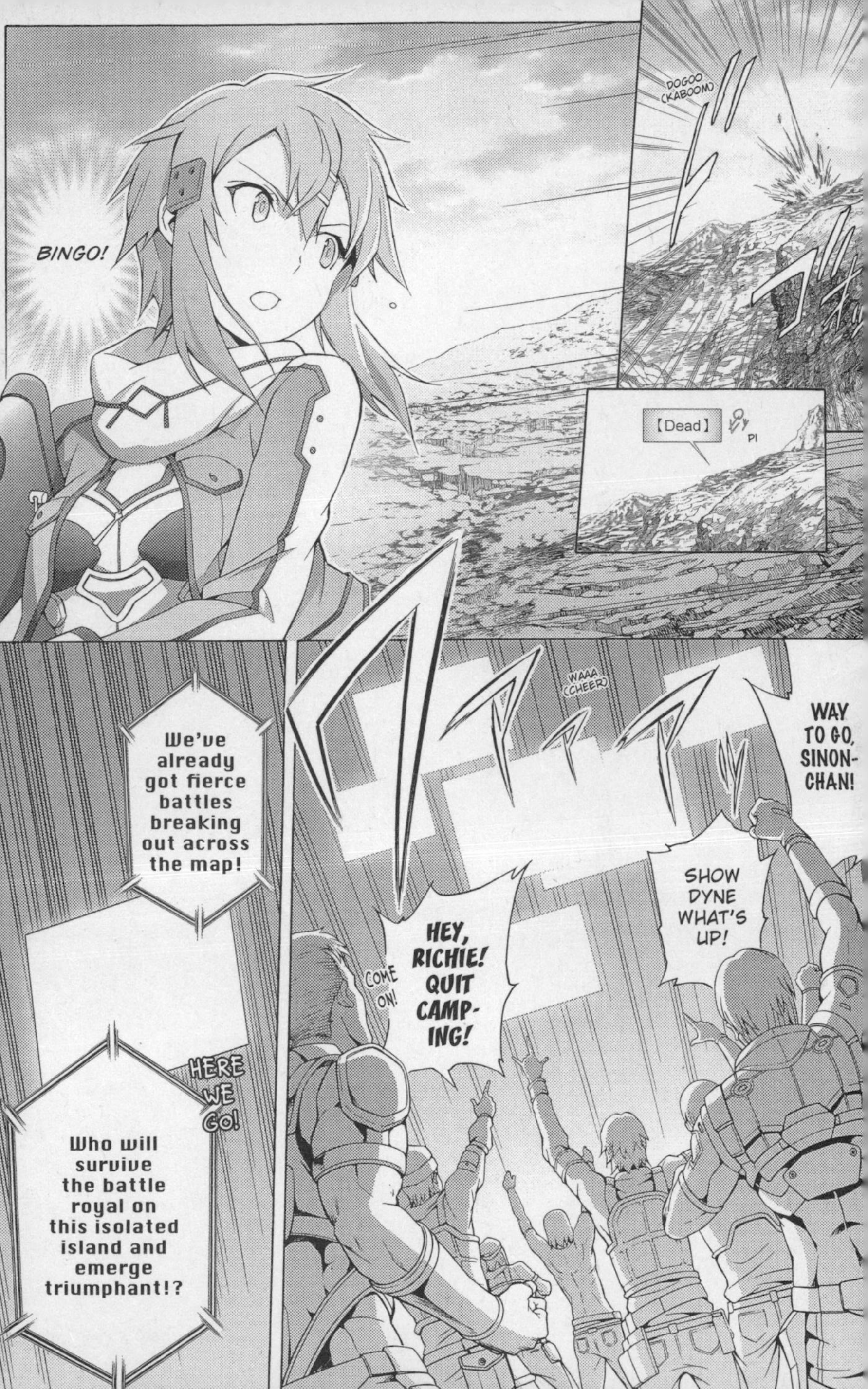
DOGOO (KABOOM)
【Dead】
PI
BINGO!
WAAA (CHEER)
WAY TO GO, SINON-CHAN!
SHOW DYNE WHAT'S UP!
HEY, RICHIE! QUIT CAMPING!
COME ON!
We've already got fierce battles breaking out across the map!
HERE WE GO!
Who will survive the battle royal on this isolated island and emerge triumphant!?

ISL Ragnarok

The setting of the third Bullet of Bullets tournament is this massive, ten-kilometer-wide island. Each avatar is placed at a random spot on the map at the start of the event.

All players are automatically given an item called a Satellite Scan Terminal. Every fifteen minutes, a satellite passes over the island, reading the coordinates of all players and relaying that information to all terminals.

In other words, fifteen minutes is the maximum amount of effective time to camp out before you have to worry about an ambush.

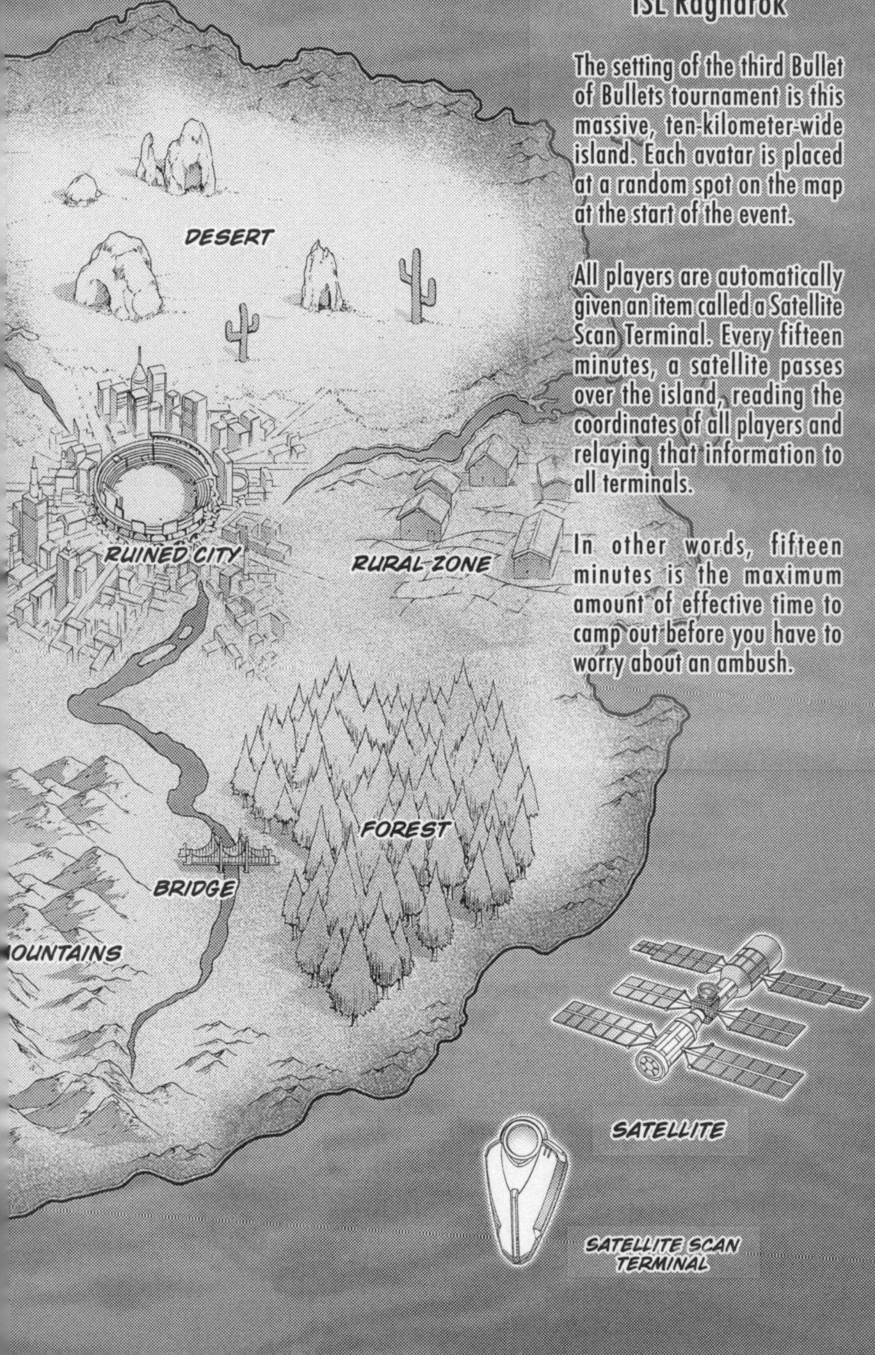
DESERT
RUINED CITY
RURAL ZONE
FOREST
BRIDGE
OUNTAINS
SATELLITE
SATELLITE SCAN TERMINAL

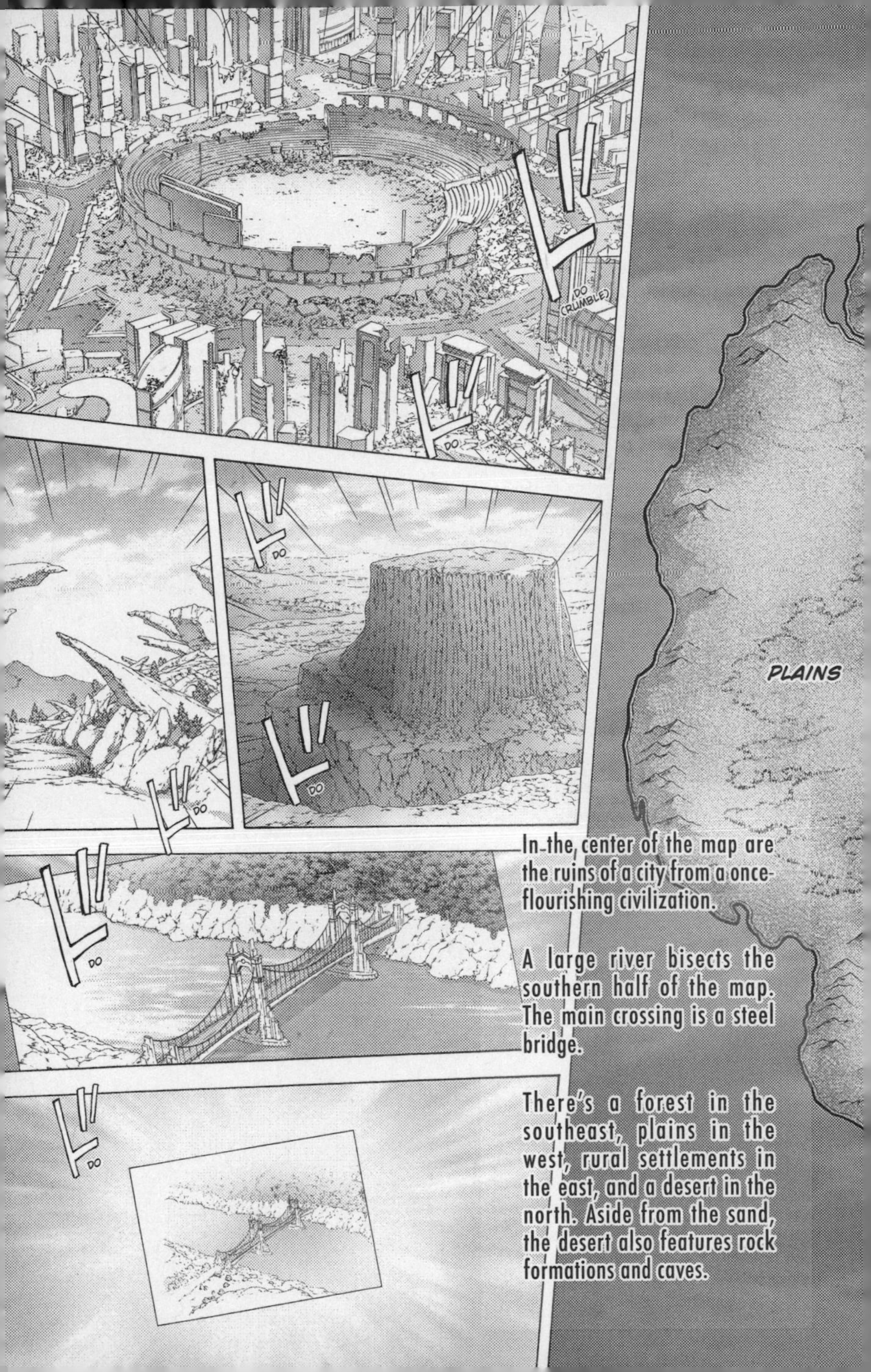
PLAINS
In the center of the map are the ruins of a city from a once-flourishing civilization.
A large river bisects the southern half of the map. The main crossing is a steel bridge.
There's a forest in the southeast, plains in the west, rural settlements in the east, and a desert in the north. Aside from the sand, the desert also features rock formations and caves.
DO (RUMBLE)
DO
DO
DO
DO
DO
DO

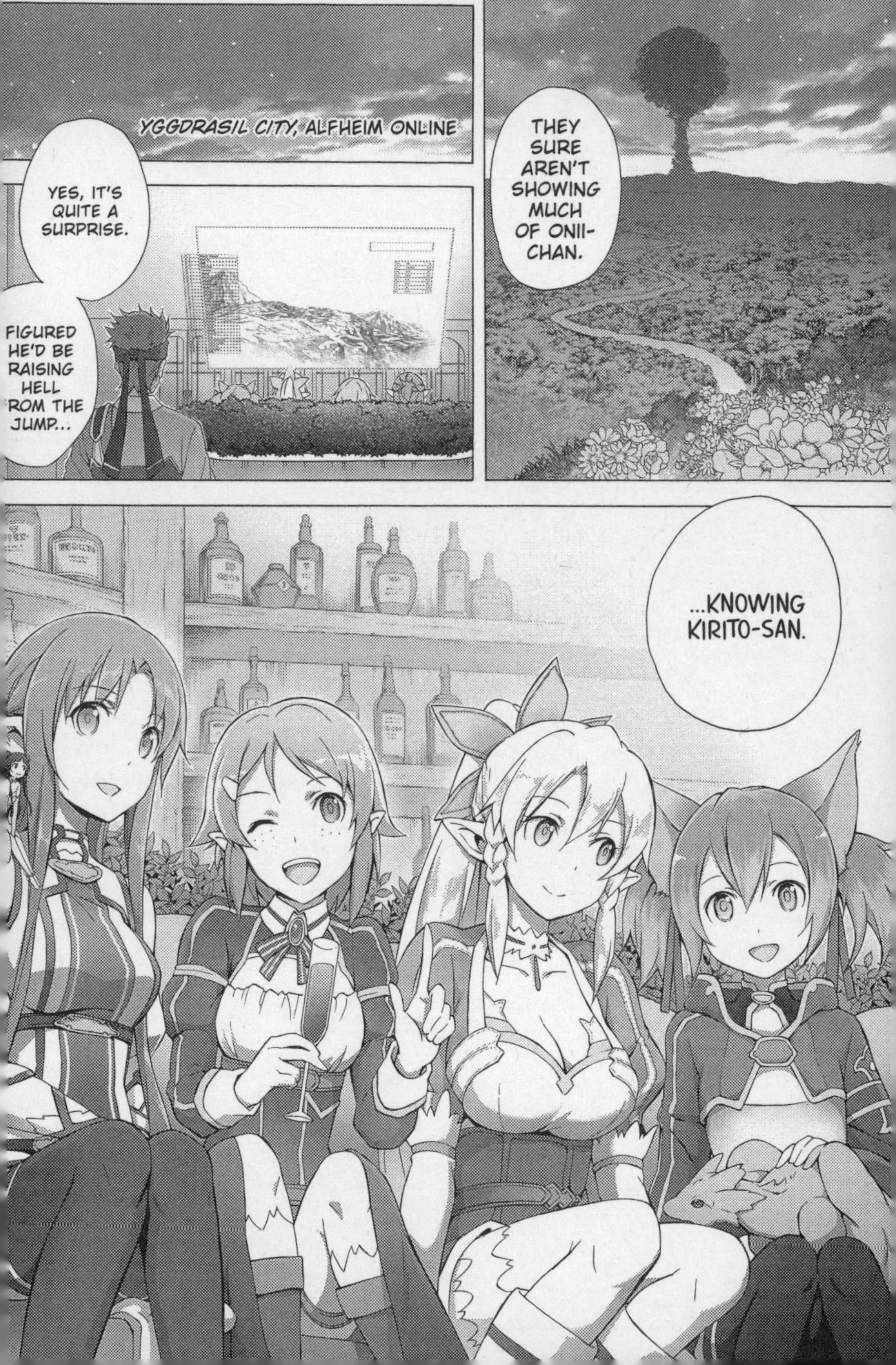
THEY SURE AREN'T SHOWING MUCH OF ONII-CHAN.
YGGDRASIL CITY, ALFHEIM ONLINE
YES, IT'S QUITE A SURPRISE.
FIGURED HE'D BE RAISING HELL FROM THE JUMP...
...KNOWING KIRITO-SAN.

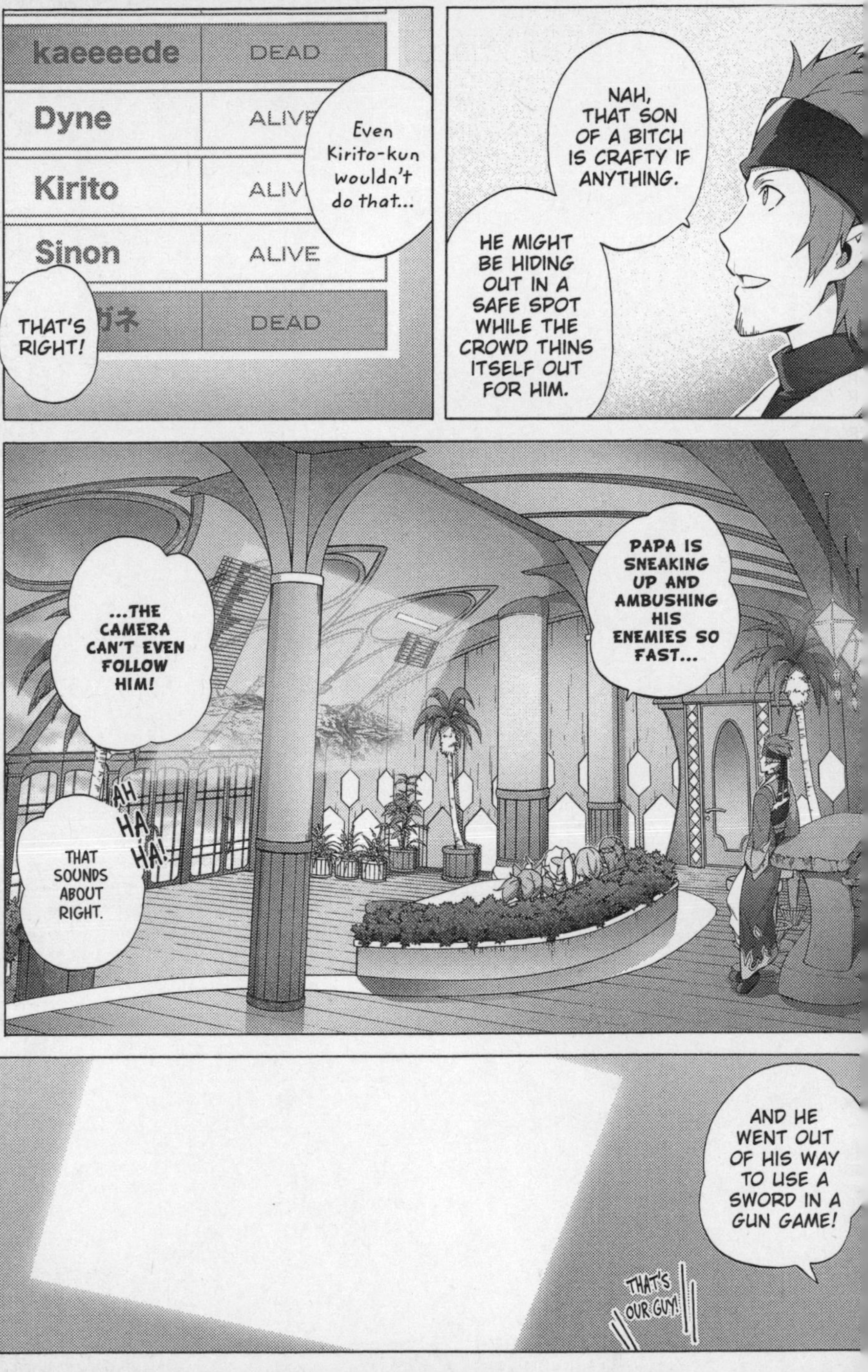
NAH, THAT SON OF A BITCH IS CRAFTY IF ANYTHING.
HE MIGHT BE HIDING OUT IN A SAFE SPOT WHILE THE CROWD THINS ITSELF OUT FOR HIM.
kaeeeede DEAD
Dyne ALIVE
Kirito ALIVE
Sinon ALIVE
DEAD
Even Kirito-kun wouldn't do that...
THAT'S RIGHT!
PAPA IS SNEAKING UP AND AMBUSHING HIS ENEMIES SO FAST...
...THE CAMERA CAN'T EVEN FOLLOW HIM!
AH HA HA!
THAT SOUNDS ABOUT RIGHT.
AND HE WENT OUT OF HIS WAY TO USE A SWORD IN A GUN GAME!
THAT'S OUR GUY!

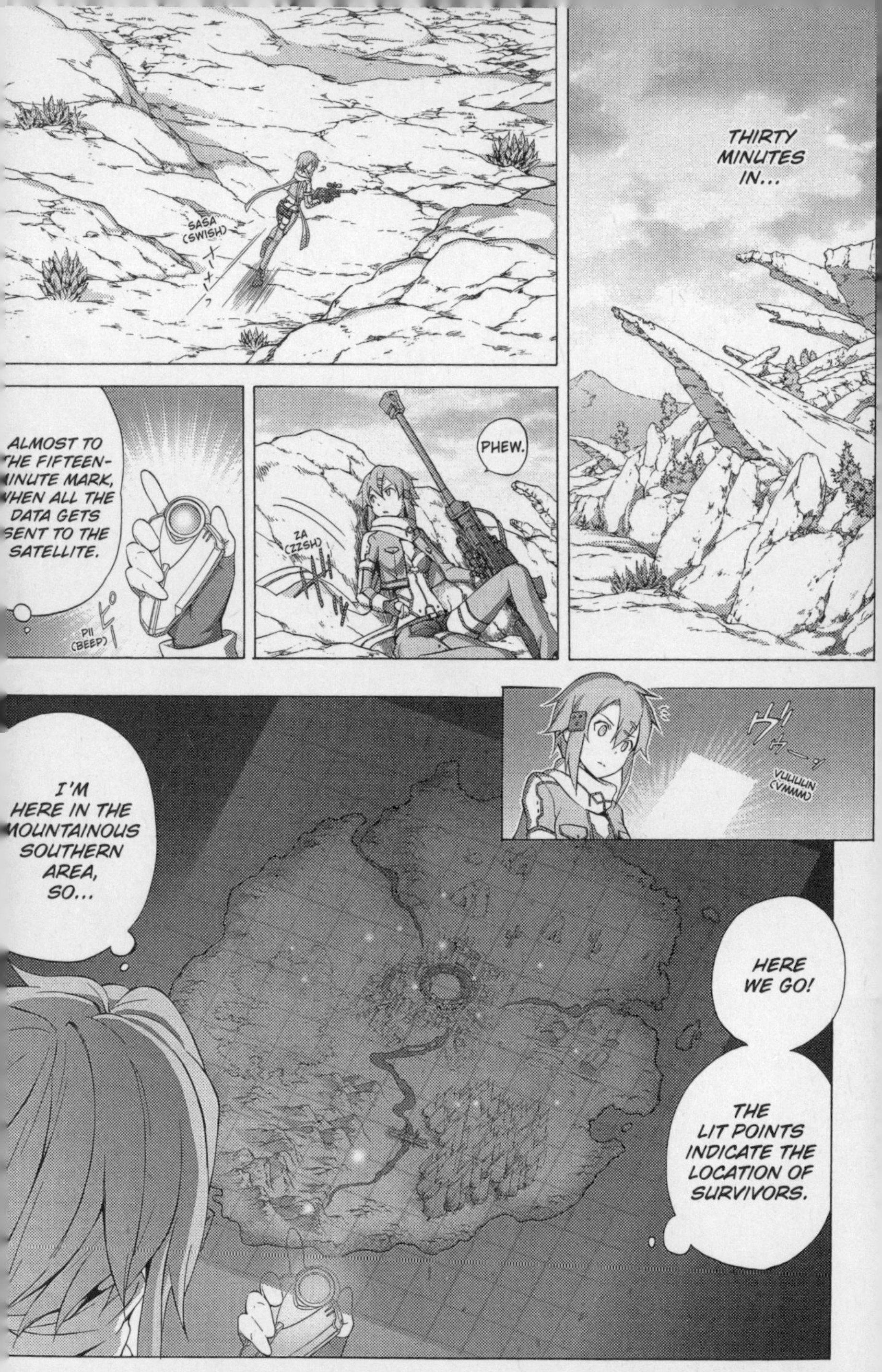
THIRTY MINUTES IN...
SASA (SWISH)
PHEW.
ZA (ZZSH)
ALMOST TO HE FIFTEEN-INUTE MARK, HEN ALL THE DATA GETS SENT TO THE SATELLITE.
PII (BEEP)
VUUUUN (VMMM)
I'M HERE IN THE OUNTAINOUS SOUTHERN AREA, SO...
HERE WE GO!
THE LIT POINTS INDICATE THE LOCATION OF SURVIVORS.

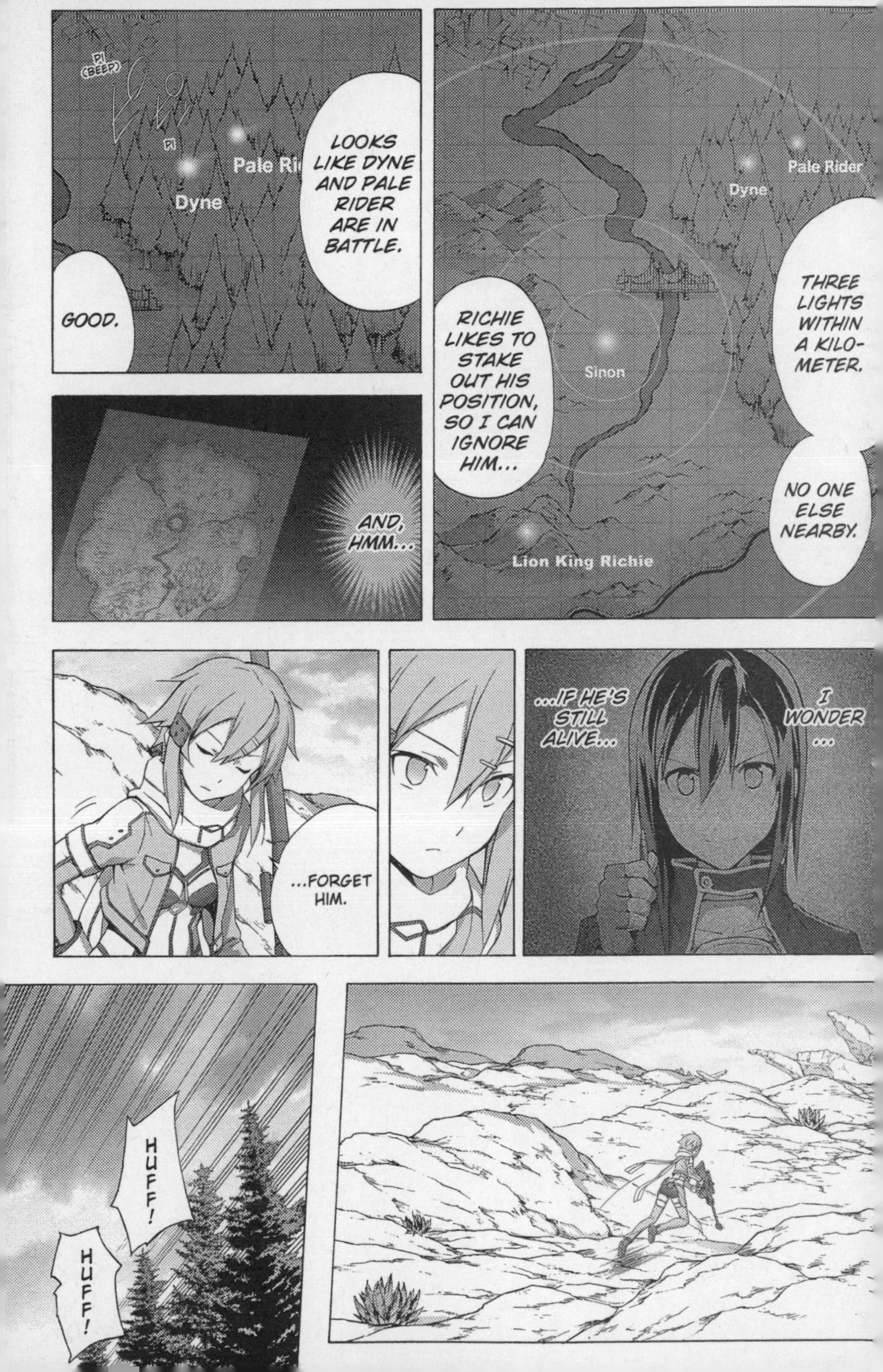
Pale Rider
Dyne
THREE LIGHTS WITHIN A KILO-METER.
NO ONE ELSE NEARBY.
RICHIE LIKES TO STAKE OUT HIS POSITION, SO I CAN IGNORE HIM...
Sinon
Lion King Richie
PI (BEEP)
PI
Pale Ri
Dyne
LOOKS LIKE DYNE AND PALE RIDER ARE IN BATTLE.
GOOD.
AND, HMM...
I WONDER...
...IF HE'S STILL ALIVE...
...FORGET HIM.
HUFF!
HUFF!

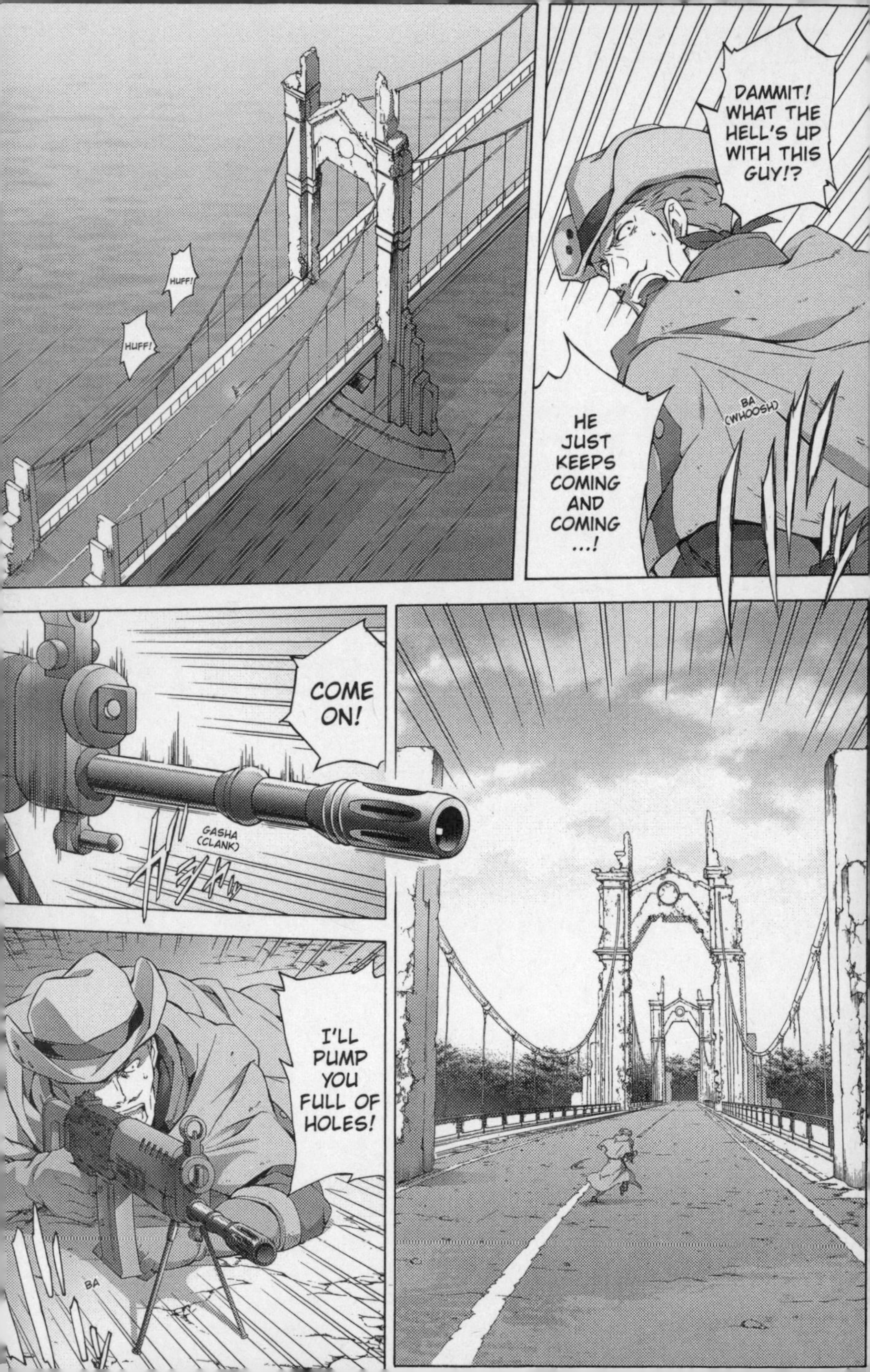
DAMMIT! WHAT THE HELL'S UP WITH THIS GUY!?
HE JUST KEEPS COMING AND COMING ...!
BA (WHOOSH)
HUFF!
HUFF!
COME ON!
GASHA (CLANK)
I'LL PUMP YOU FULL OF HOLES!
BA

...DYNE-KUN.

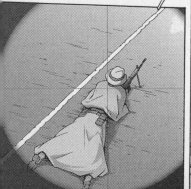

oooo
(WHOOSH)

CHECK YOUR SIX AT ALL TIMES...

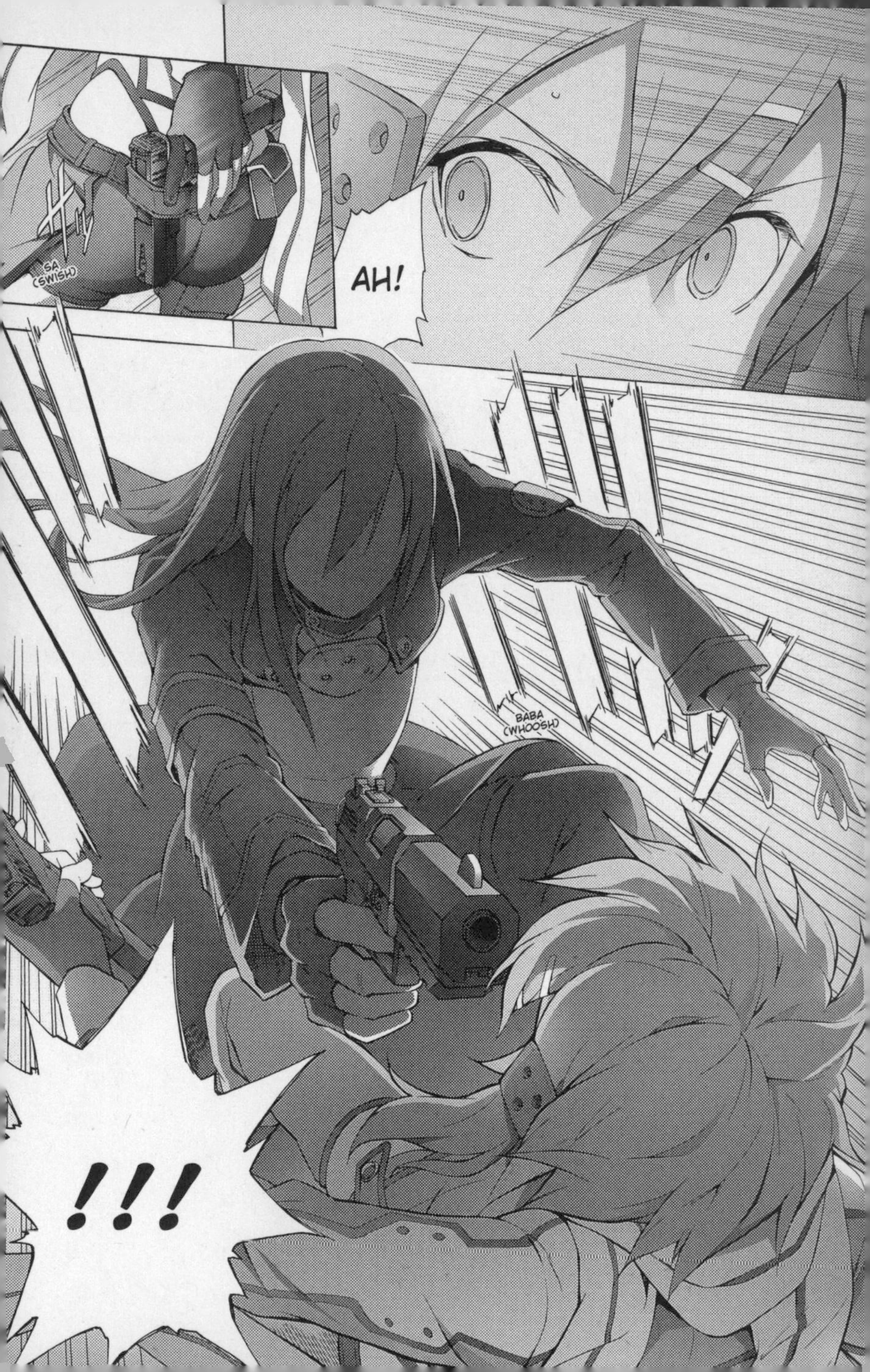
AH!
SA (SWISH)
BABA (WHOOSH)
!!!

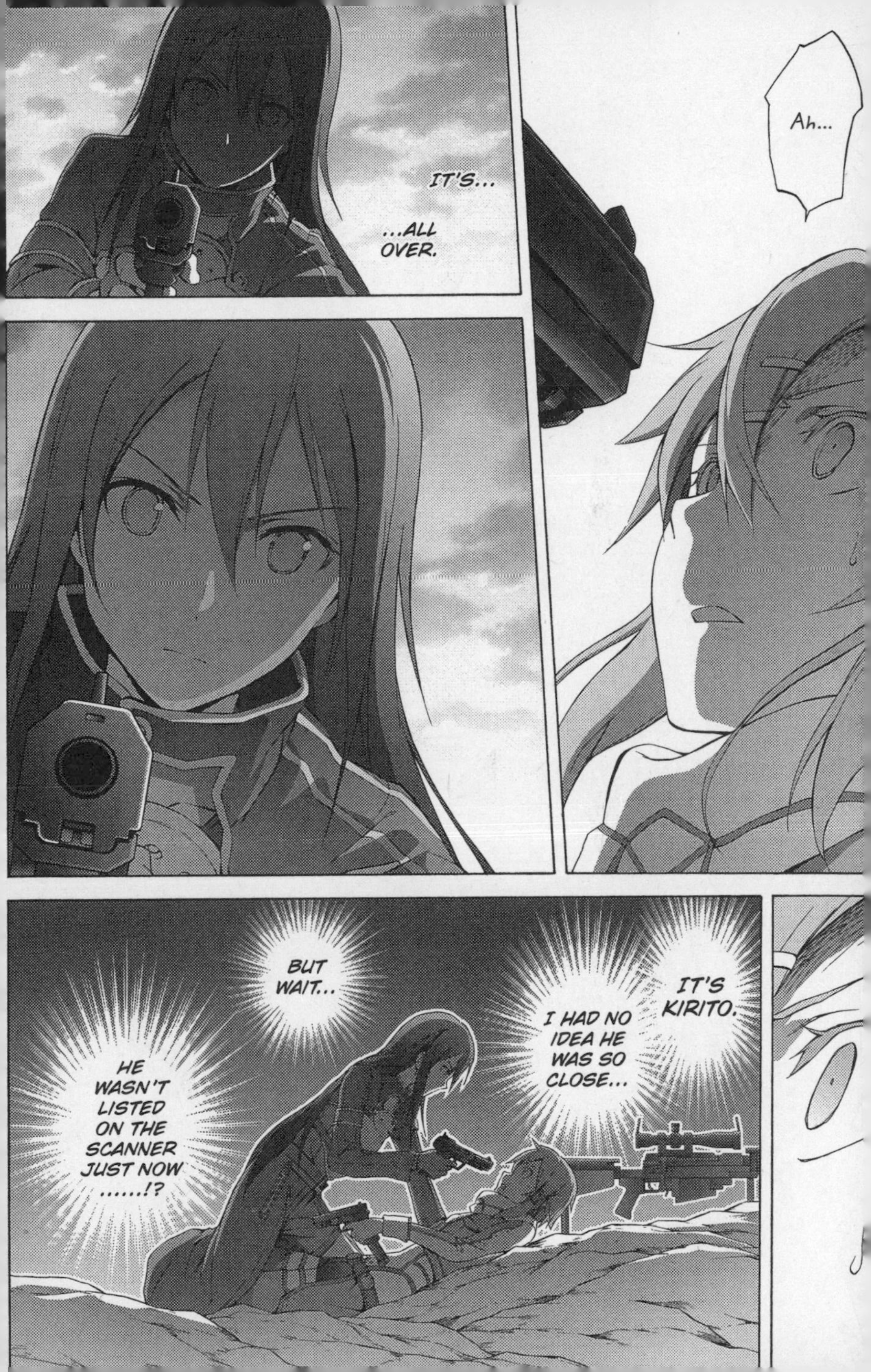
Ah...
IT'S...
...ALL OVER.
IT'S KIRITO.
I HAD NO IDEA HE WAS SO CLOSE...
BUT WAIT...
HE WASN'T LISTED ON THE SCANNER JUST NOW ......!?

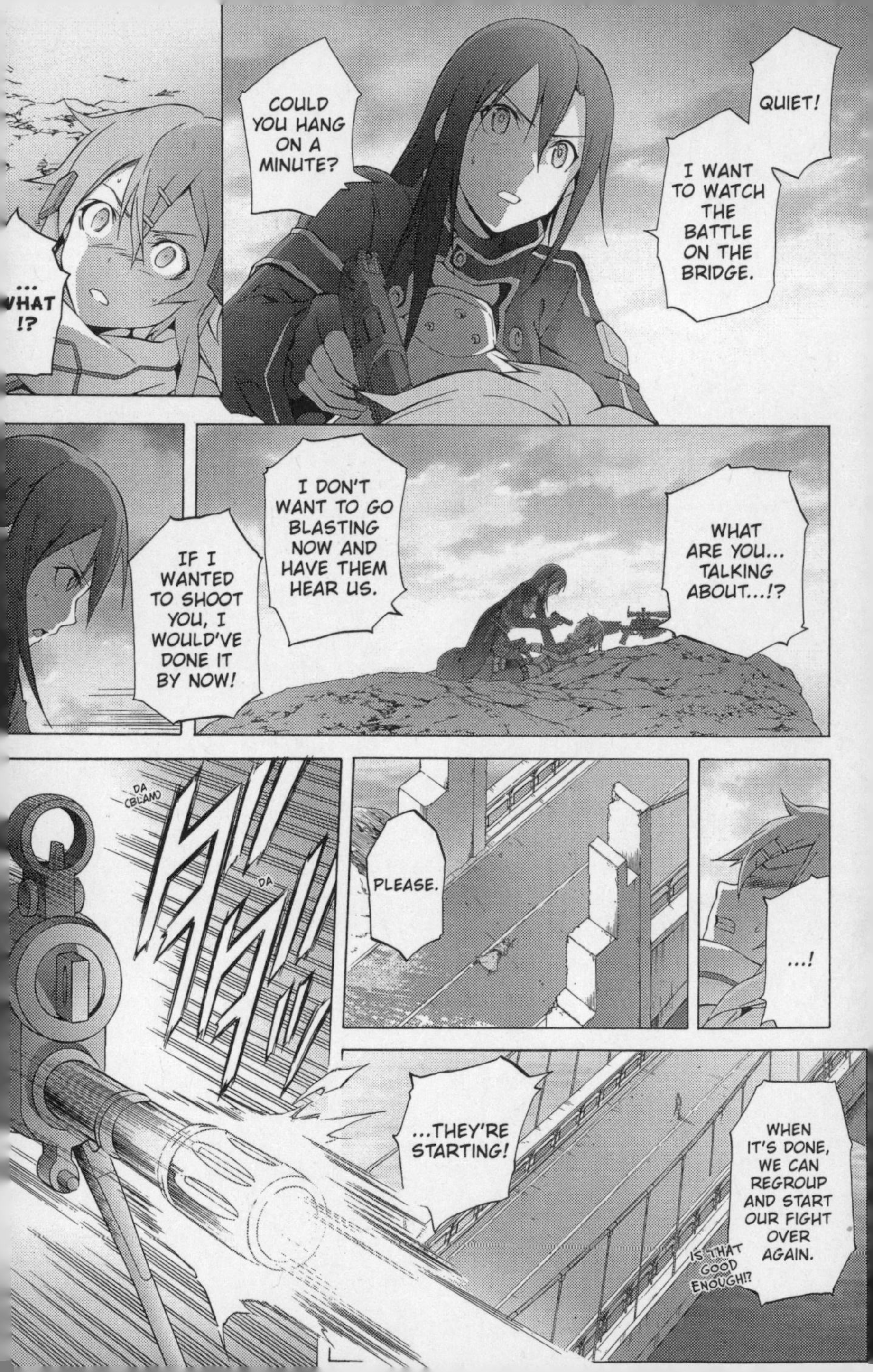
QUIET!
I WANT TO WATCH THE BATTLE ON THE BRIDGE.
COULD YOU HANG ON A MINUTE?
...WHAT!?
WHAT ARE YOU... TALKING ABOUT...!?
I DON'T WANT TO GO BLASTING NOW AND HAVE THEM HEAR US.
IF I WANTED TO SHOOT YOU, I WOULD'VE DONE IT BY NOW!
...!
PLEASE.
DA (BLAM)
DA
WHEN IT'S DONE, WE CAN REGROUP AND START OUR FIGHT OVER AGAIN.
IS THAT GOOD ENOUGH!?
...THEY'RE STARTING!

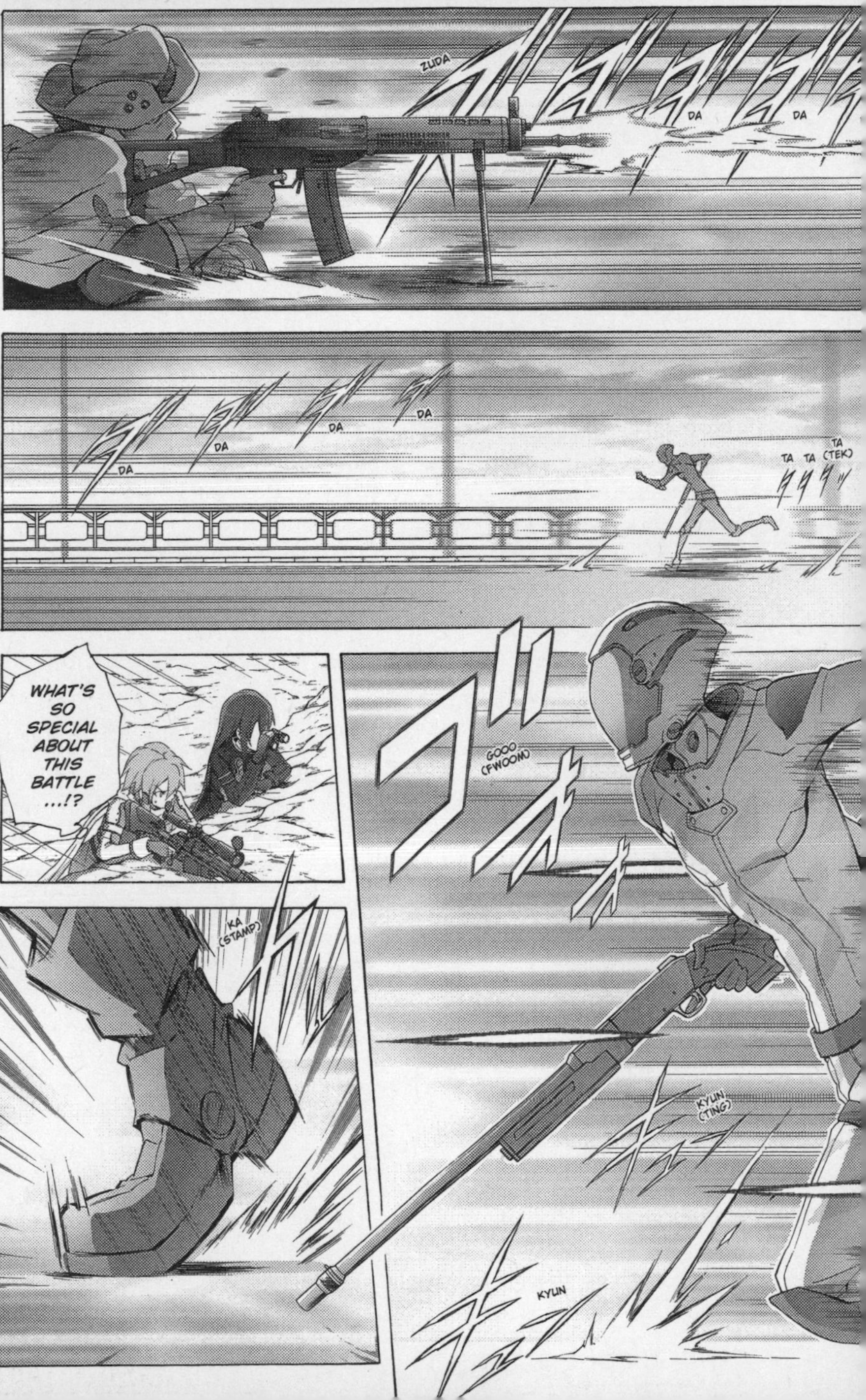

ZUDA
DA
DA
TA TA TA (TEK)
DA
DA
DA
DA
GOOO (FWOOM)
KYUN (TING)
KYUN
WHAT'S SO SPECIAL ABOUT THIS BATTLE ...!?
KA (STAMP)

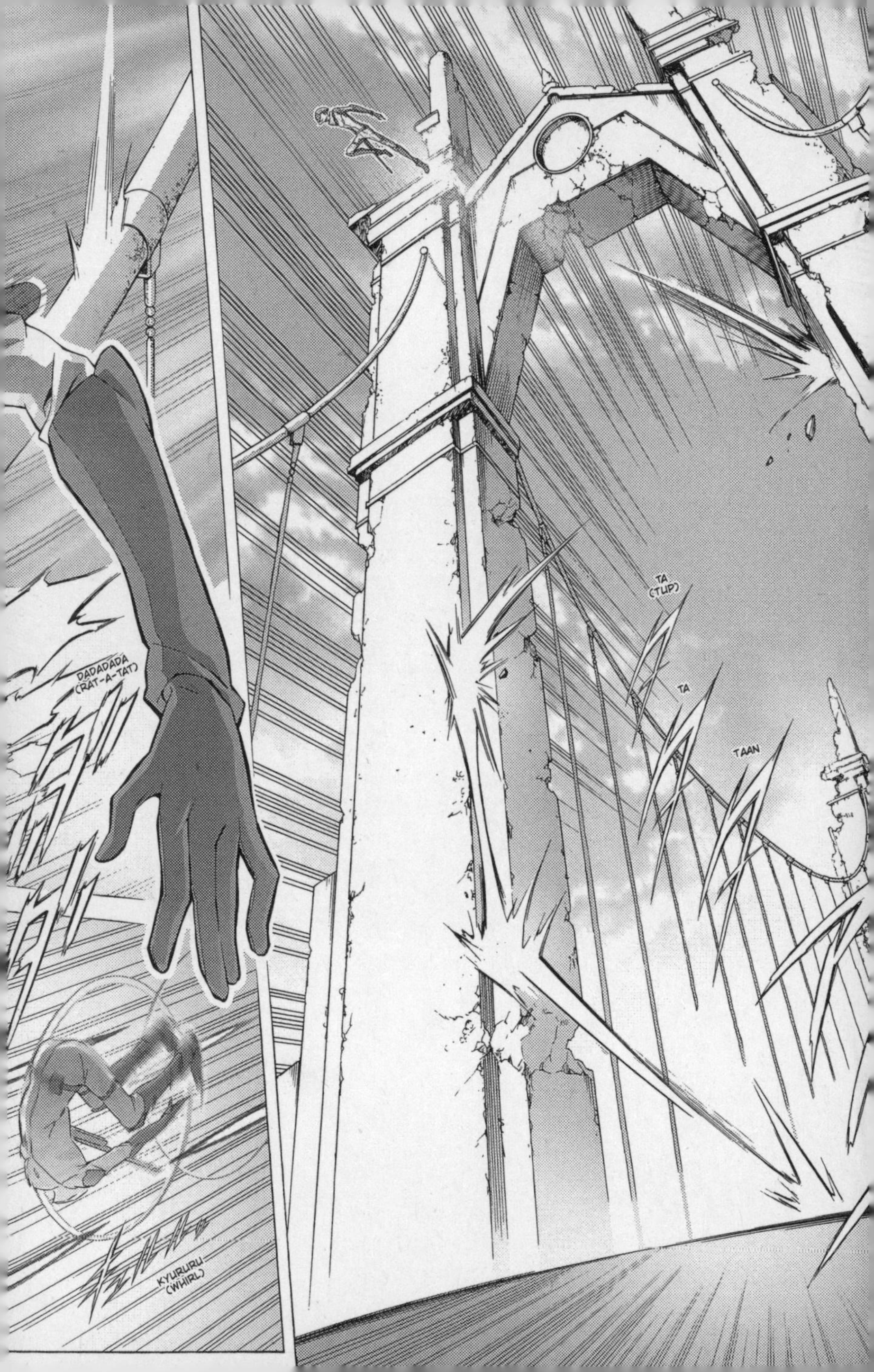
TA (TUP)
TA
TAAN
DADADADA (RAT-A-TAT)
KYURURU (WHIRL)

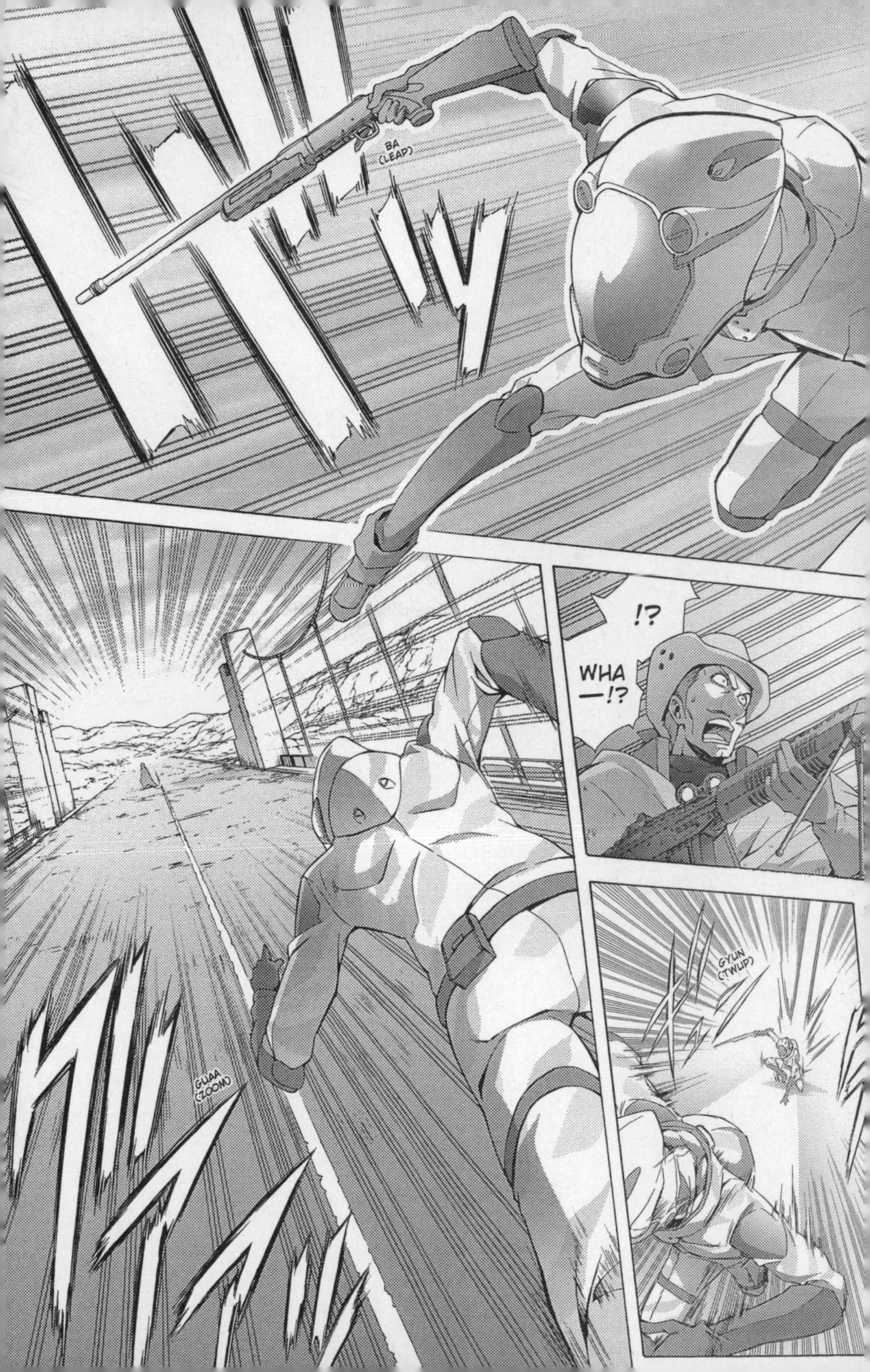
BA (LEAP)
!?
WHA —!?
GYUN (TWUP)
GUAA (ZOOM)

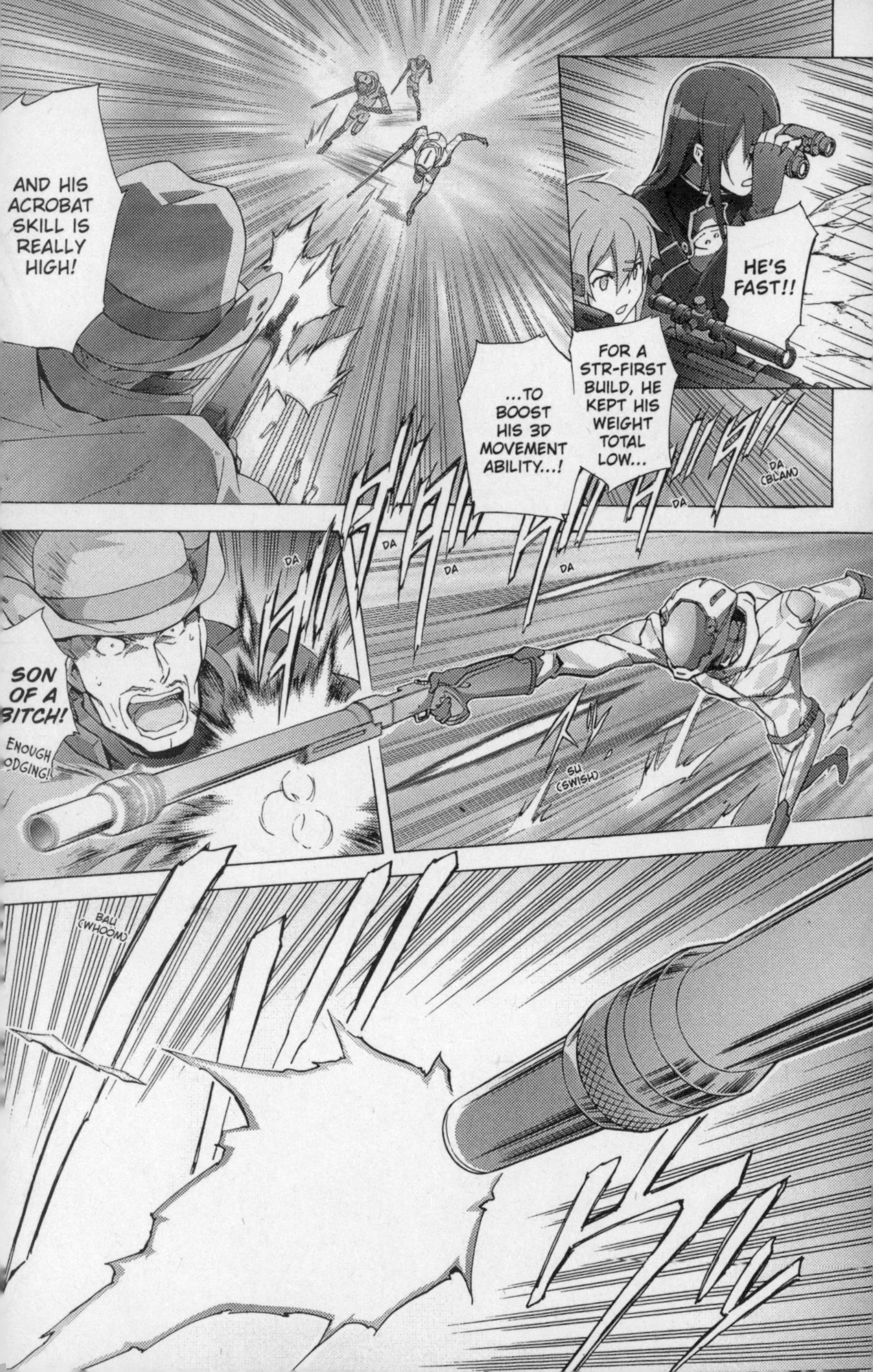
HE'S FAST!!
FOR A STR-FIRST BUILD, HE KEPT HIS WEIGHT TOTAL LOW...
...TO BOOST HIS 3D MOVEMENT ABILITY...!
DA (BLAM)
DA
DA
DA
DA
DA
AND HIS ACROBAT SKILL IS REALLY HIGH!
SU (SWISH)
SON OF A BITCH!
ENOUGH DODGING!
BAU (WHOOM)

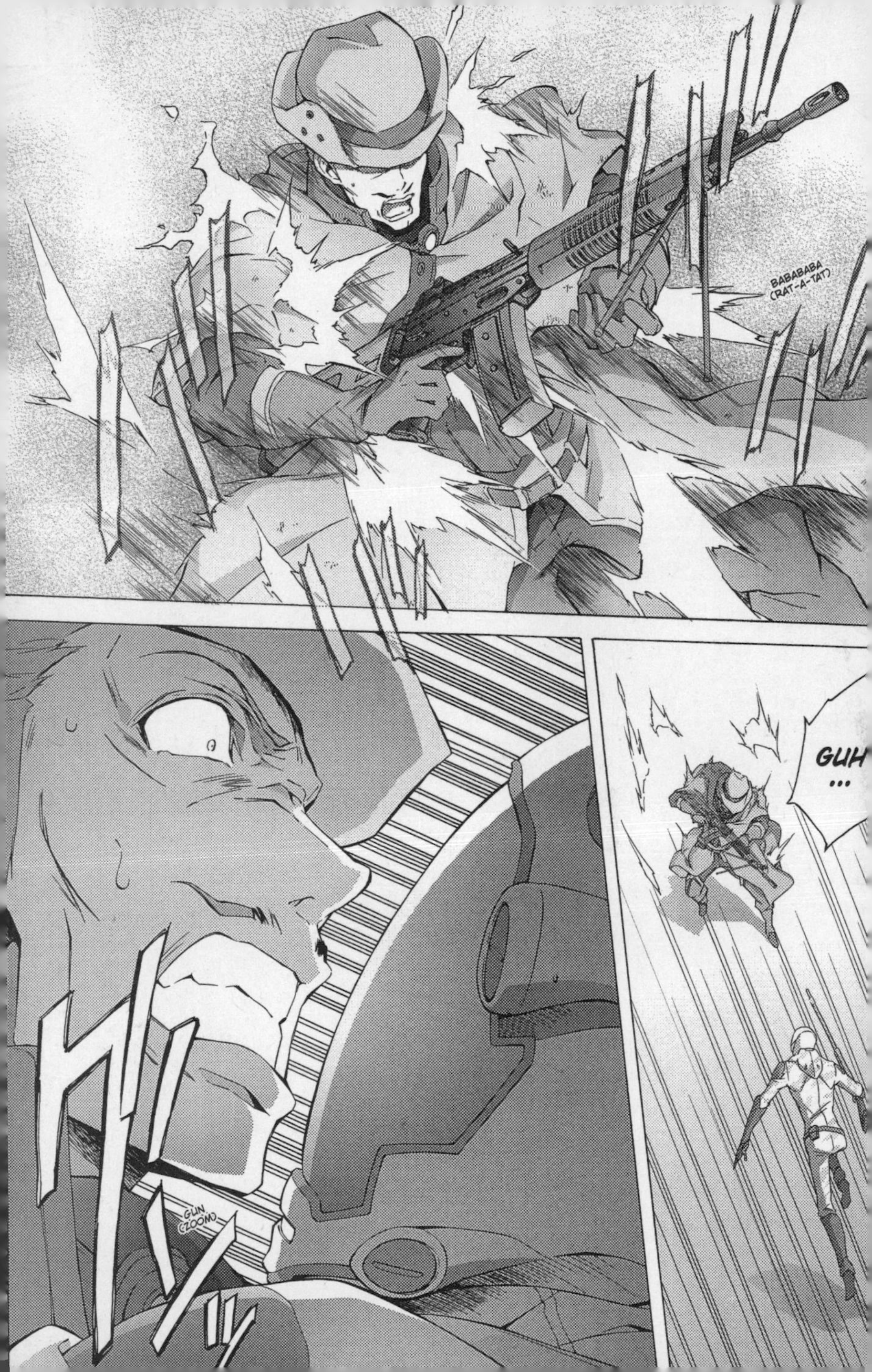
BABABABA (RAT-A-TAT)
GUH ...
GUN (ZOOM)

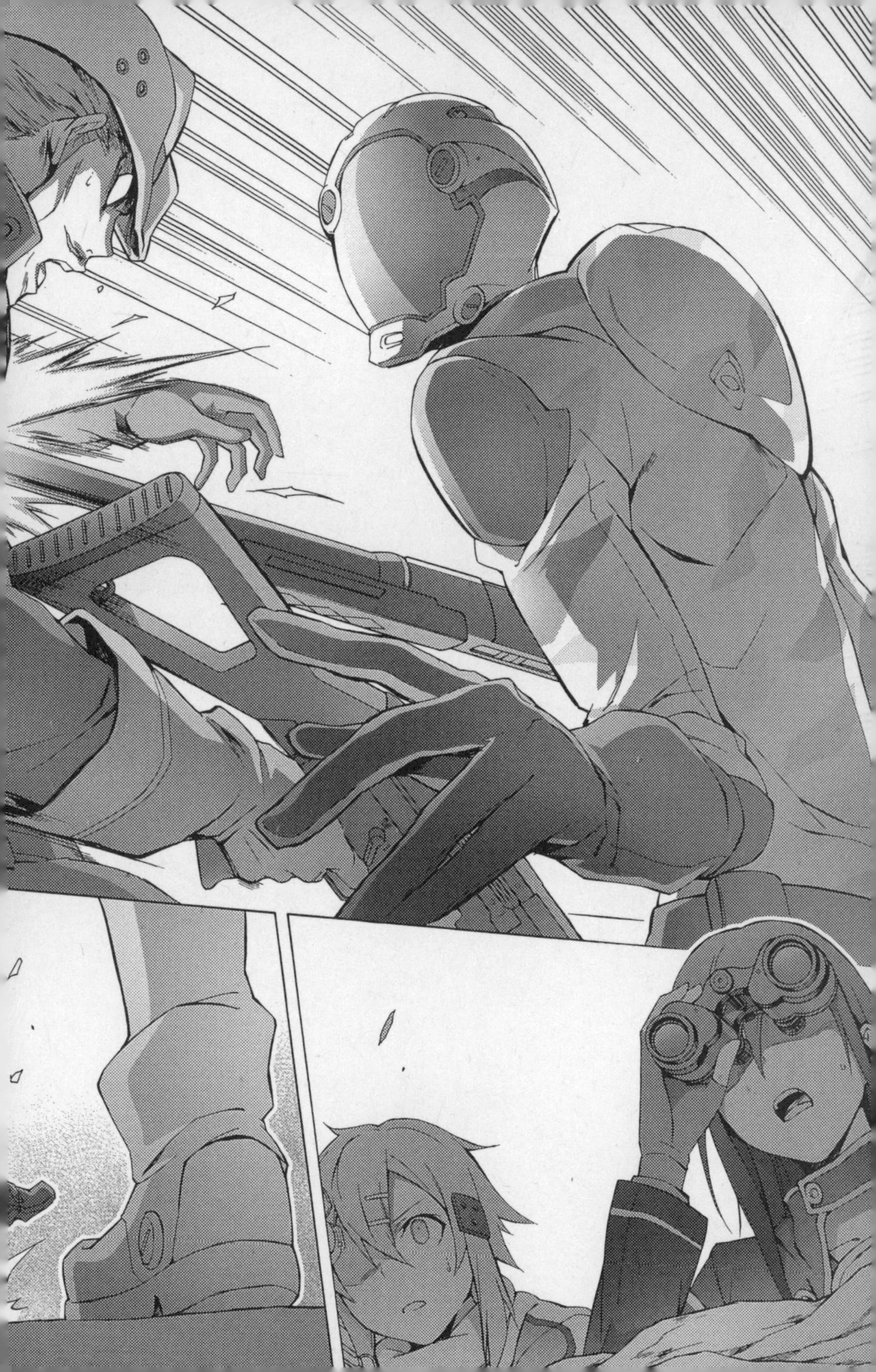

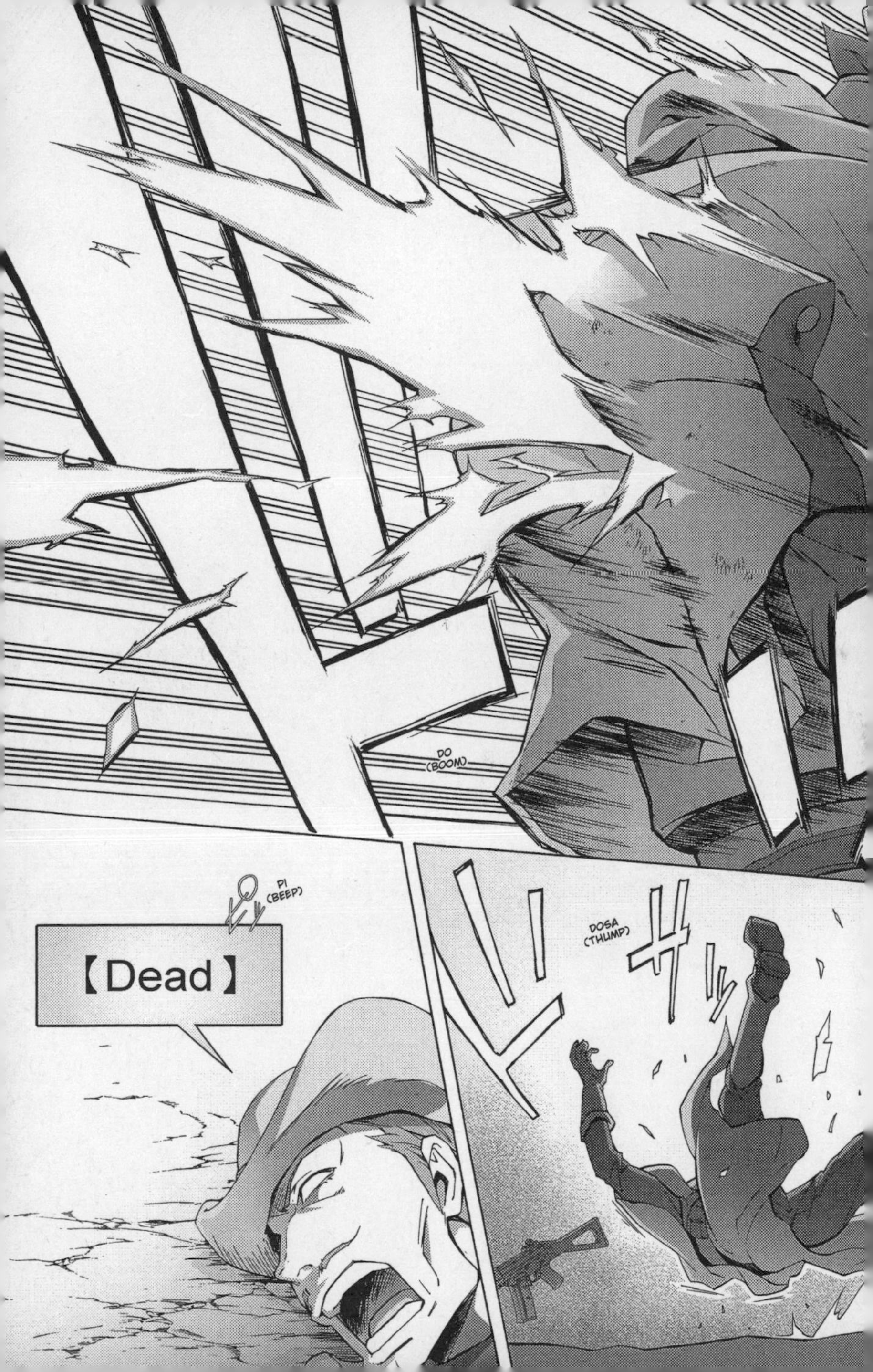
DO (BOOM)
DOSA (THUMP)
PI (BEEP)
【Dead】

IS HE THE CLOAKED PLAYER ...?

PALE RIDER...

HE'S GOOD.

......

I'M GONNA SHOOT HIM.

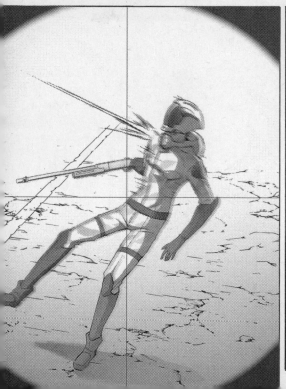

SURE... ......

BUT IF HE'S REALLY THE GUY ......

YOU THINK HE'S GOING TO DODGE MY SHOT AT THIS CLOSE RANGE?

YOU MUST BE JOKING.

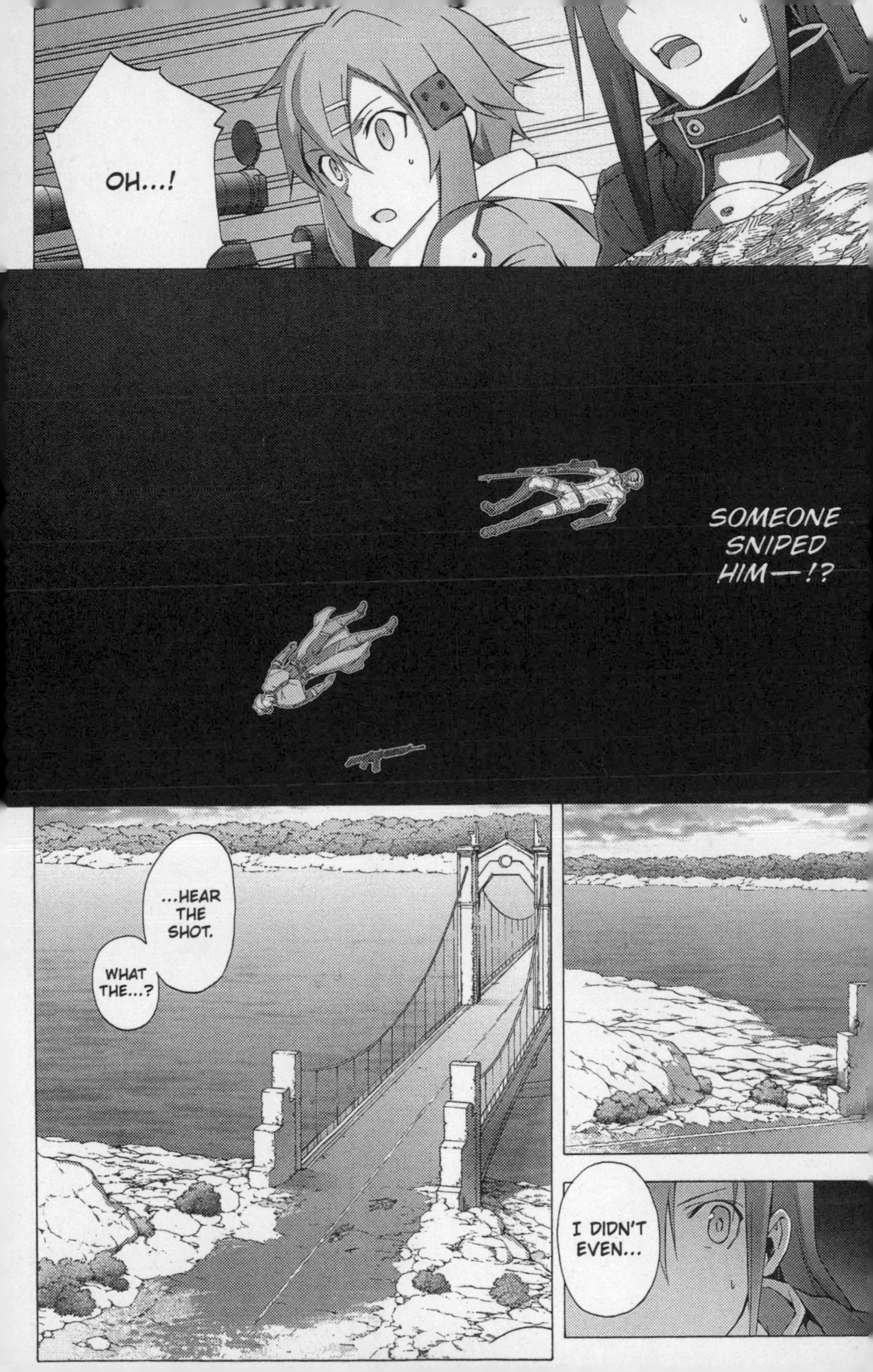
OH...!
SOMEONE SNIPED HIM—!?
I DIDN'T EVEN...
...HEAR THE SHOT.
WHAT THE...?

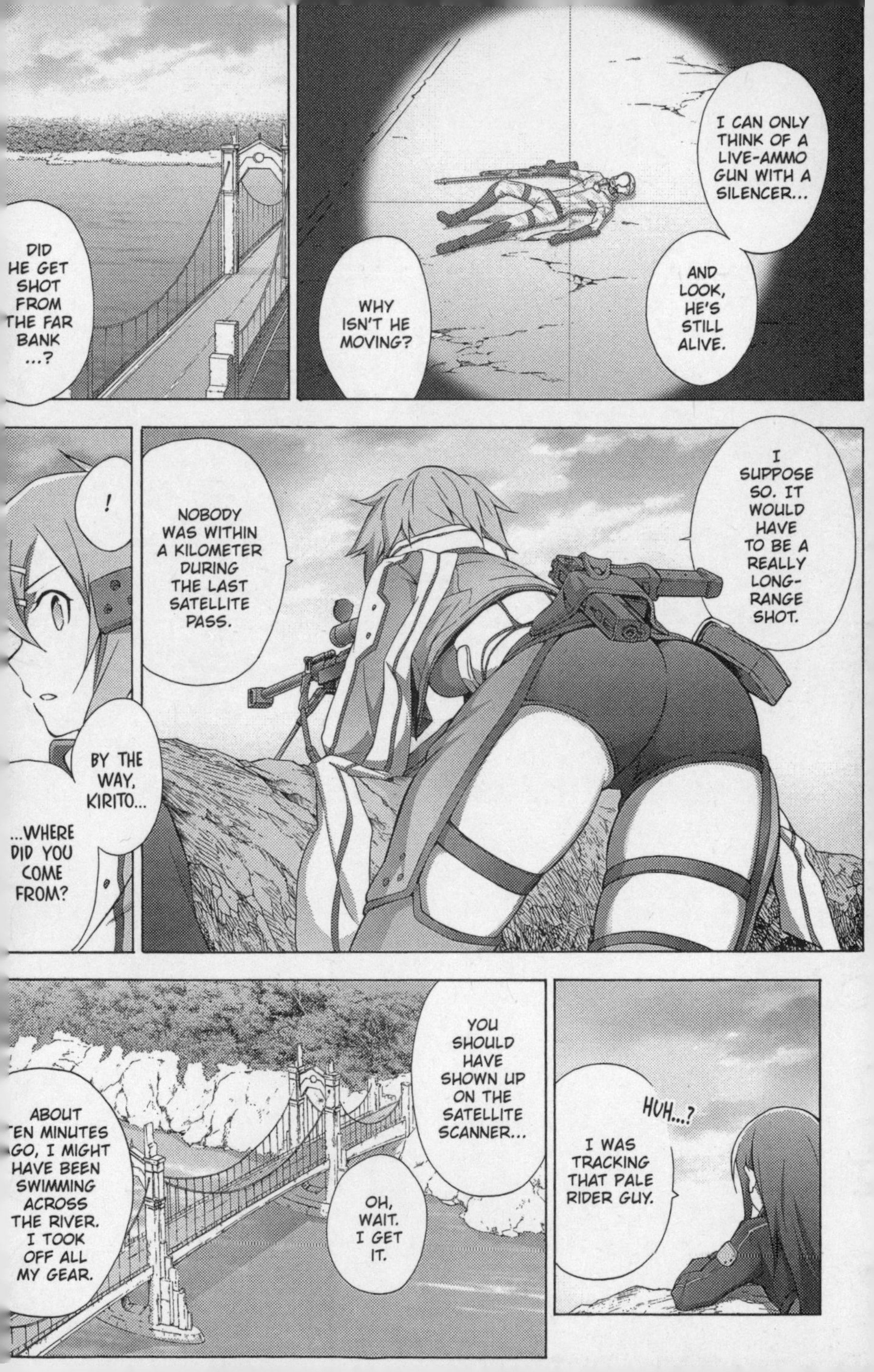
I CAN ONLY THINK OF A LIVE-AMMO GUN WITH A SILENCER...
AND LOOK, HE'S STILL ALIVE.
WHY ISN'T HE MOVING?
DID HE GET SHOT FROM THE FAR BANK ...?
I SUPPOSE SO. IT WOULD HAVE TO BE A REALLY LONG-RANGE SHOT.
NOBODY WAS WITHIN A KILOMETER DURING THE LAST SATELLITE PASS.
!
BY THE WAY, KIRITO...
...WHERE DID YOU COME FROM?
HUH...?
I WAS TRACKING THAT PALE RIDER GUY.
YOU SHOULD HAVE SHOWN UP ON THE SATELLITE SCANNER...
OH, WAIT. I GET IT.
ABOUT TEN MINUTES GO, I MIGHT HAVE BEEN SWIMMING ACROSS THE RIVER. I TOOK OFF ALL MY GEAR.

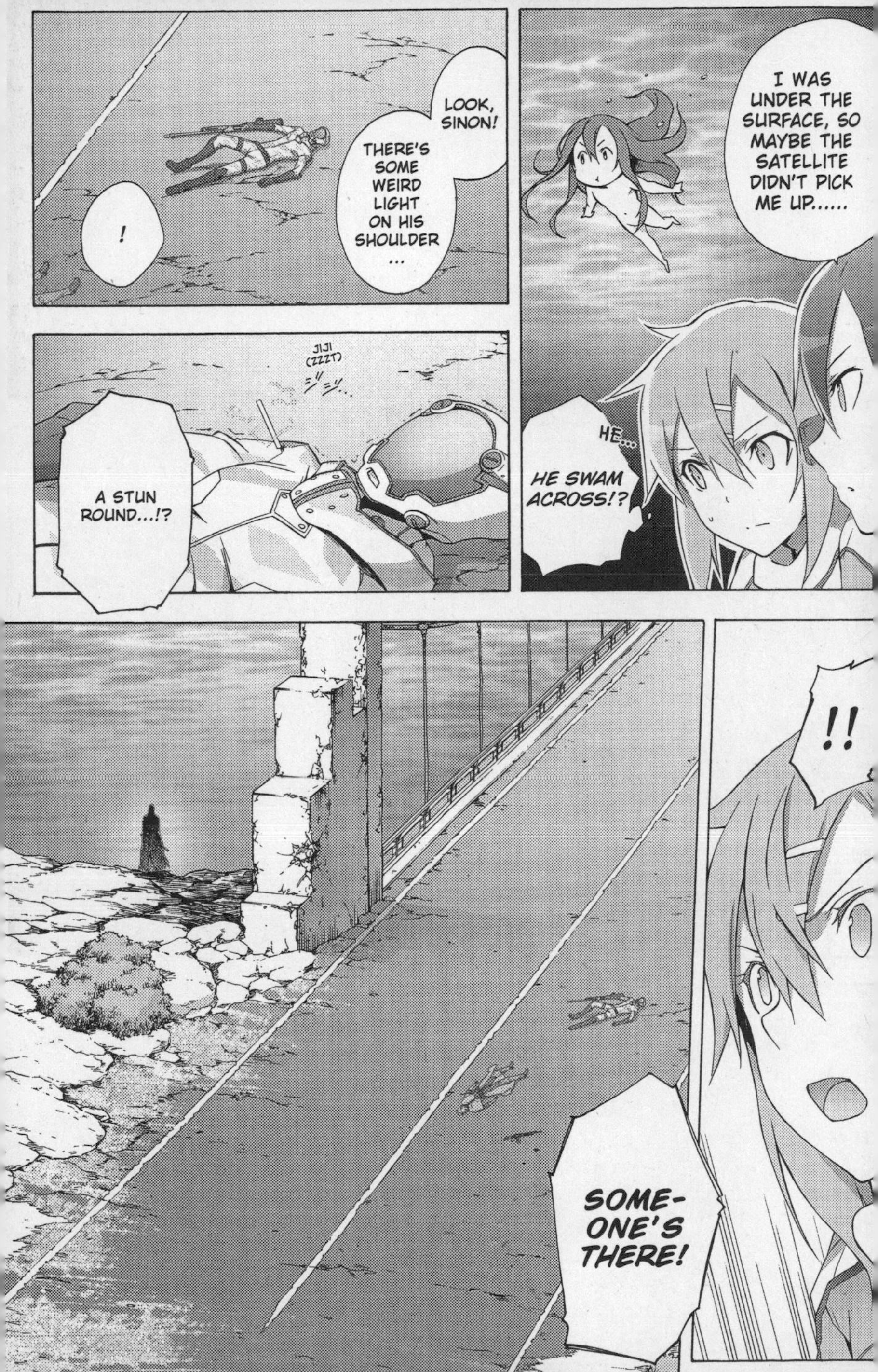
I WAS UNDER THE SURFACE, SO MAYBE THE SATELLITE DIDN'T PICK ME UP......
HE...
HE SWAM ACROSS!?
LOOK, SINON!
THERE'S SOME WEIRD LIGHT ON HIS SHOULDER ...
!
JIJI (ZZZT)
A STUN ROUND...!?
!!
SOME-ONE'S THERE!

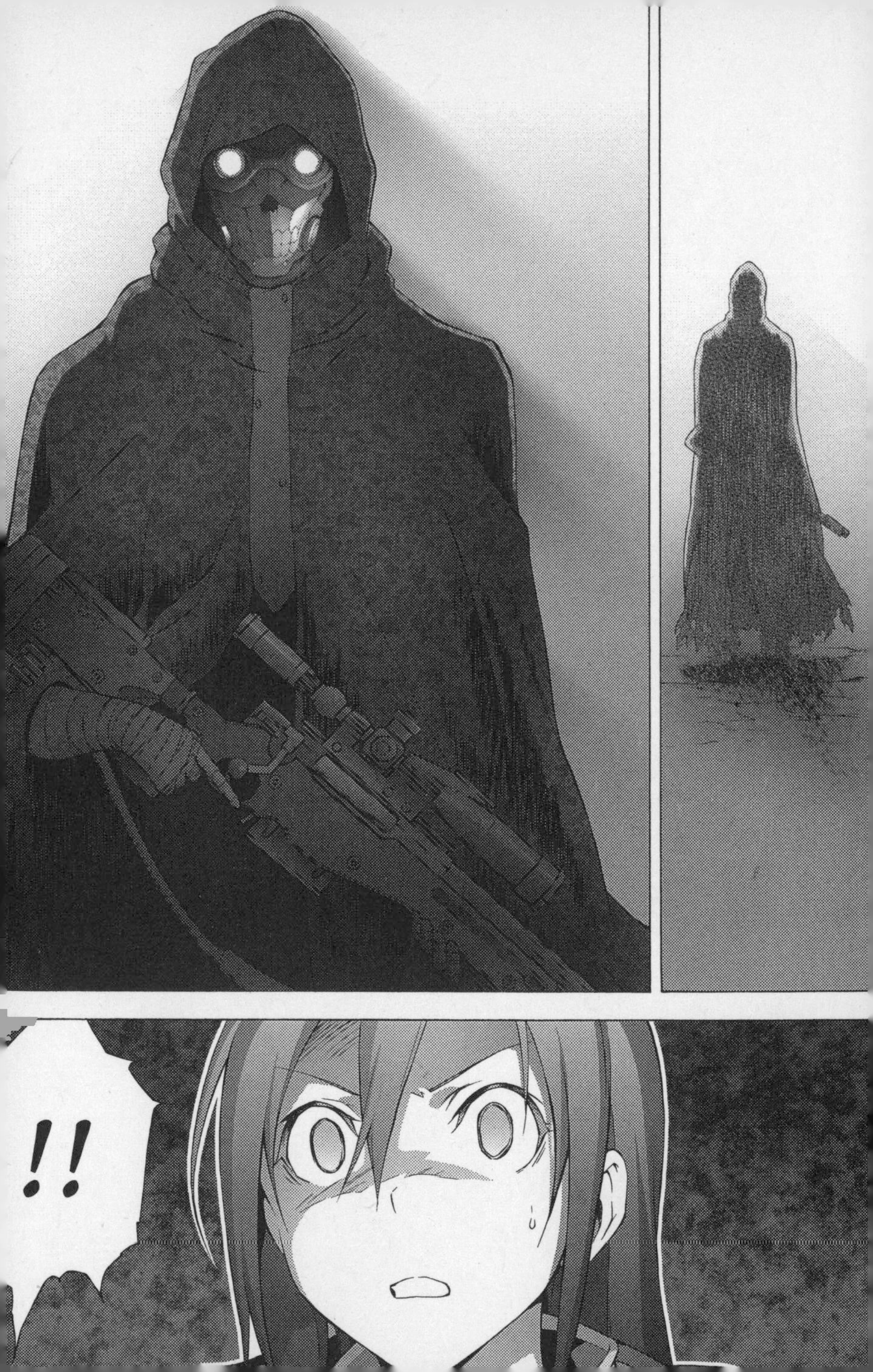
!!

SWORD ART ONLINE
phantom bullet

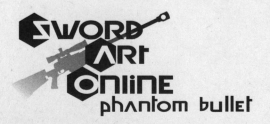

SWORD ART ONLINE
phantom bullet
check point! 002

BoB FINAL: WORLD

JUST THIRTY CONTESTANTS FIGHT IN THE BoB FINAL MATCH ON A TEN-KILOMETER-WIDE BATTLEFIELD. THANKS TO THE PERIODIC EXPOSURE OF INFORMATION THROUGH THE SATELLITE SCAN, PLAYERS MUST ENGAGE IN HIGHLY TACTICAL BATTLES—SEARCHING FOR TARGETS, MOVING, AND TAKING ADVANTAGE OF TERRAIN. THE *SAO ALTERNATIVE GUN GALE ONLINE* SPINOFF BY KEIICHI SIGSAWA FEATURES A "SQUAD JAM" BATTLE SYSTEM THAT IS BASED ON THE BoB FINAL, INVOLVING ONLY TEAM PLAY INSTEAD OF A FREE-FOR-ALL. HIGHLY RECOMMENDED IF YOU WANT TO EXPERIENCE STRATEGIC GUN BATTLES.

DYNE'S SG 550: ITEM

AN ASSAULT RIFLE MANUFACTURED BY THE SWISS COMPANY SIG. ITS EXTREMELY TOUGH STRUCTURE IS DESIGNED FOR USE IN THE COLD, RUGGED SWISS ALPS, AND IT'S ACCURATE ENOUGH TO HIT A TARGET AT 400 METERS WITHOUT A SCOPE. THESE QUALITY SPECS MAKE IT A POPULAR GUN FOR SPECIAL FORCES AROUND THE WORLD. AS A NEUTRAL NATION, SWITZERLAND PROTECTS ITSELF BY CONSCRIPTING CITIZENS. THIS RIFLE IS DISTRIBUTED TO THOSE SOLDIERS TO KEEP AT HOME (ALTHOUGH AMMUNITION IS DISTRIBUTED ONLY IF NEEDED). IT'S QUITE A REMARKABLE COUNTRY.

COURTESY OF: A-1 PICTURES

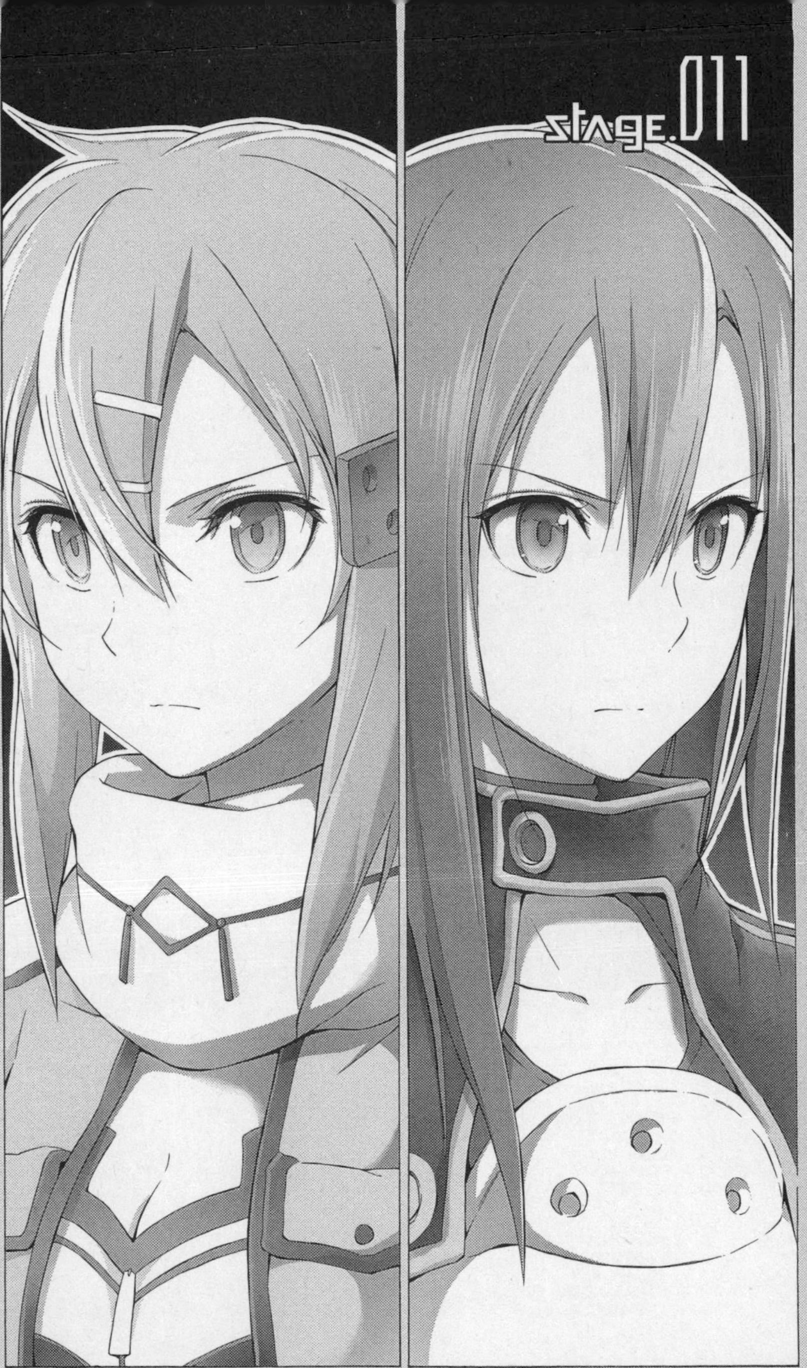
stage.011

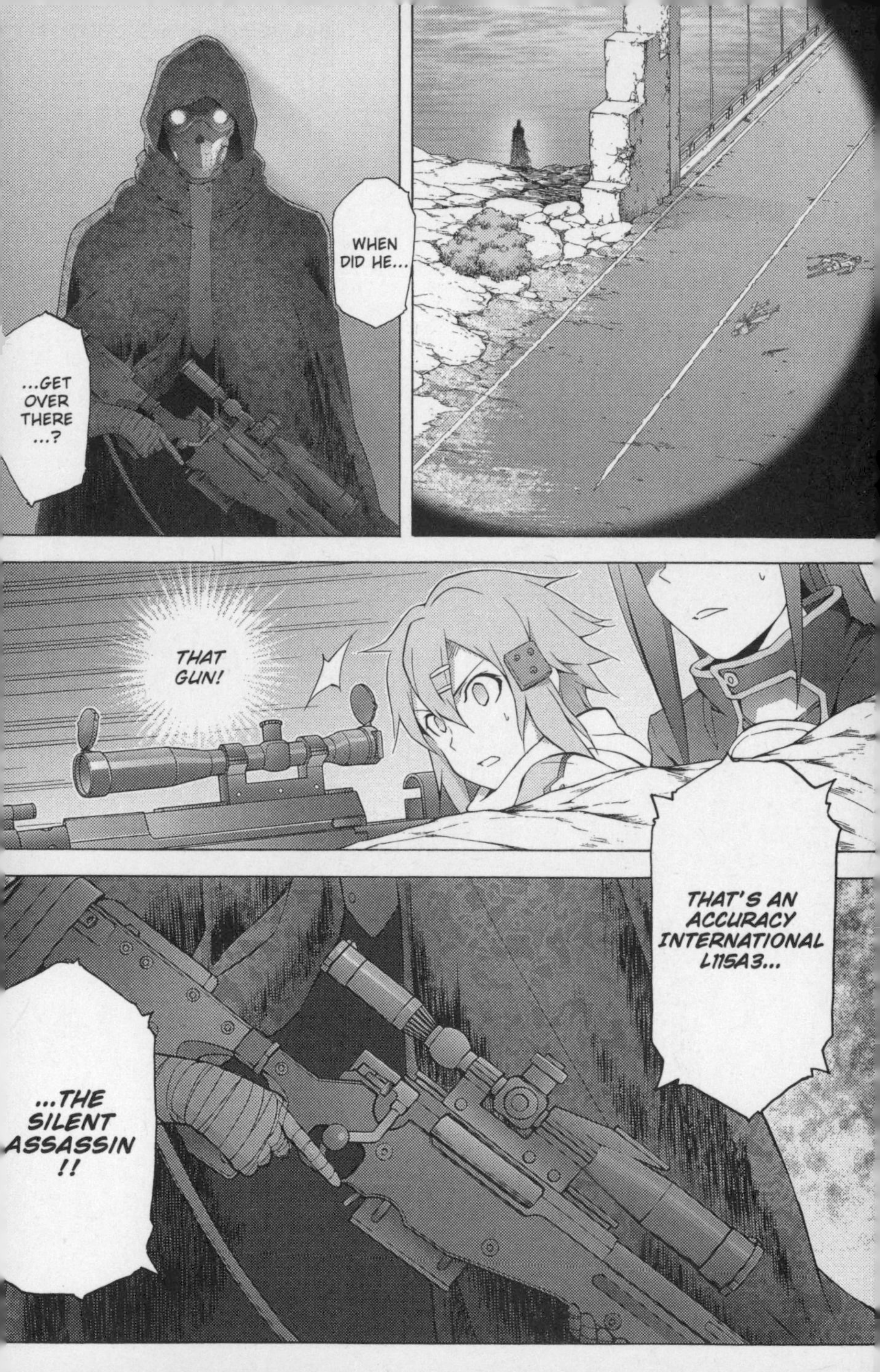
WHEN DID HE...
...GET OVER THERE ...?
THAT GUN!
THAT'S AN ACCURACY INTERNATIONAL L115A3...
...THE SILENT ASSASSIN !!

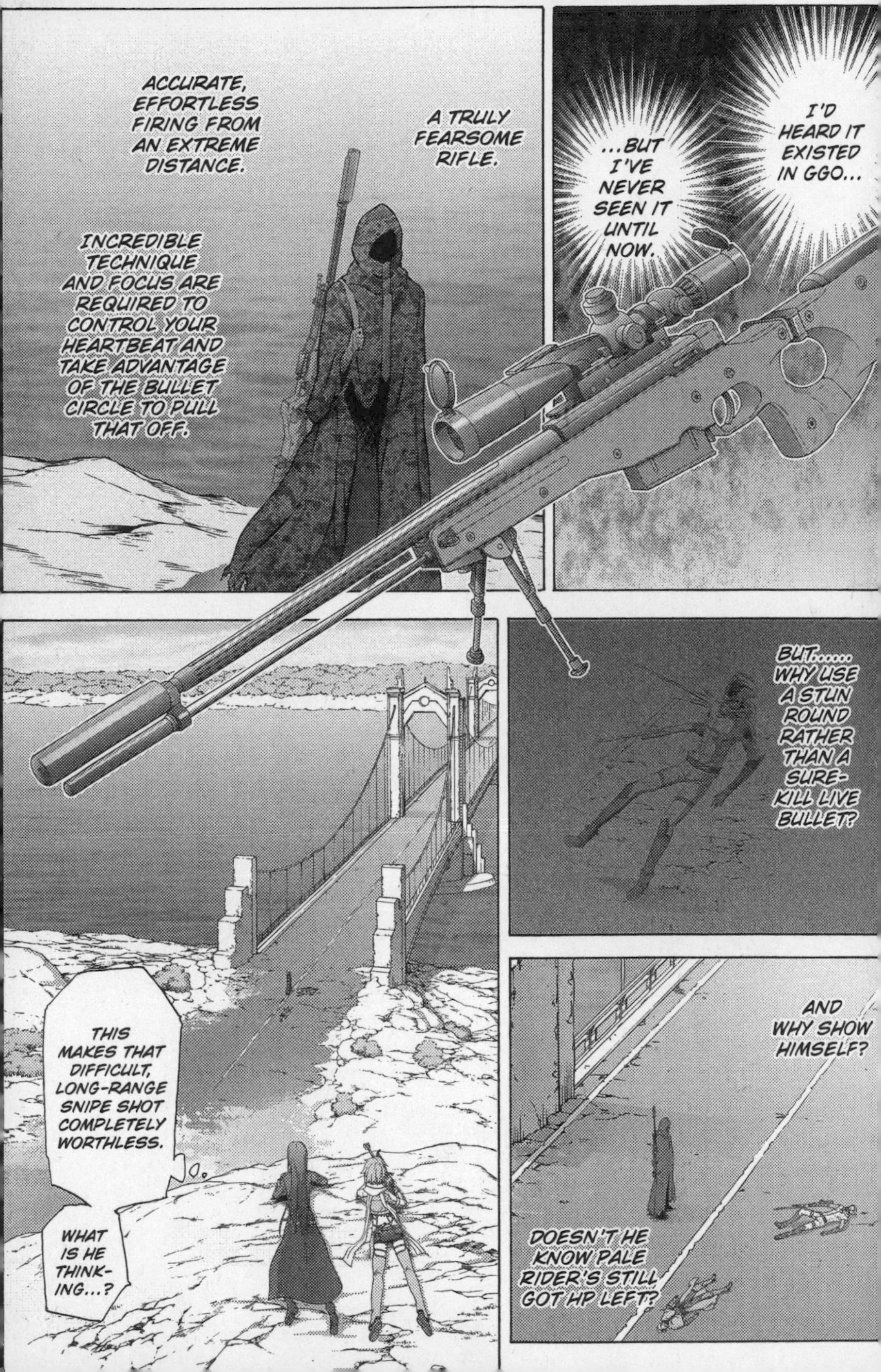
I'D HEARD IT EXISTED IN GGO...
...BUT I'VE NEVER SEEN IT UNTIL NOW.
ACCURATE, EFFORTLESS FIRING FROM AN EXTREME DISTANCE.
A TRULY FEARSOME RIFLE.
INCREDIBLE TECHNIQUE AND FOCUS ARE REQUIRED TO CONTROL YOUR HEARTBEAT AND TAKE ADVANTAGE OF THE BULLET CIRCLE TO PULL THAT OFF.
BUT...... WHY USE A STUN ROUND RATHER THAN A SURE-KILL LIVE BULLET?
AND WHY SHOW HIMSELF?
DOESN'T HE KNOW PALE RIDER'S STILL GOT HP LEFT?
THIS MAKES THAT DIFFICULT, LONG-RANGE SNIPE SHOT COMPLETELY WORTHLESS.
WHAT IS HE THINKING...?

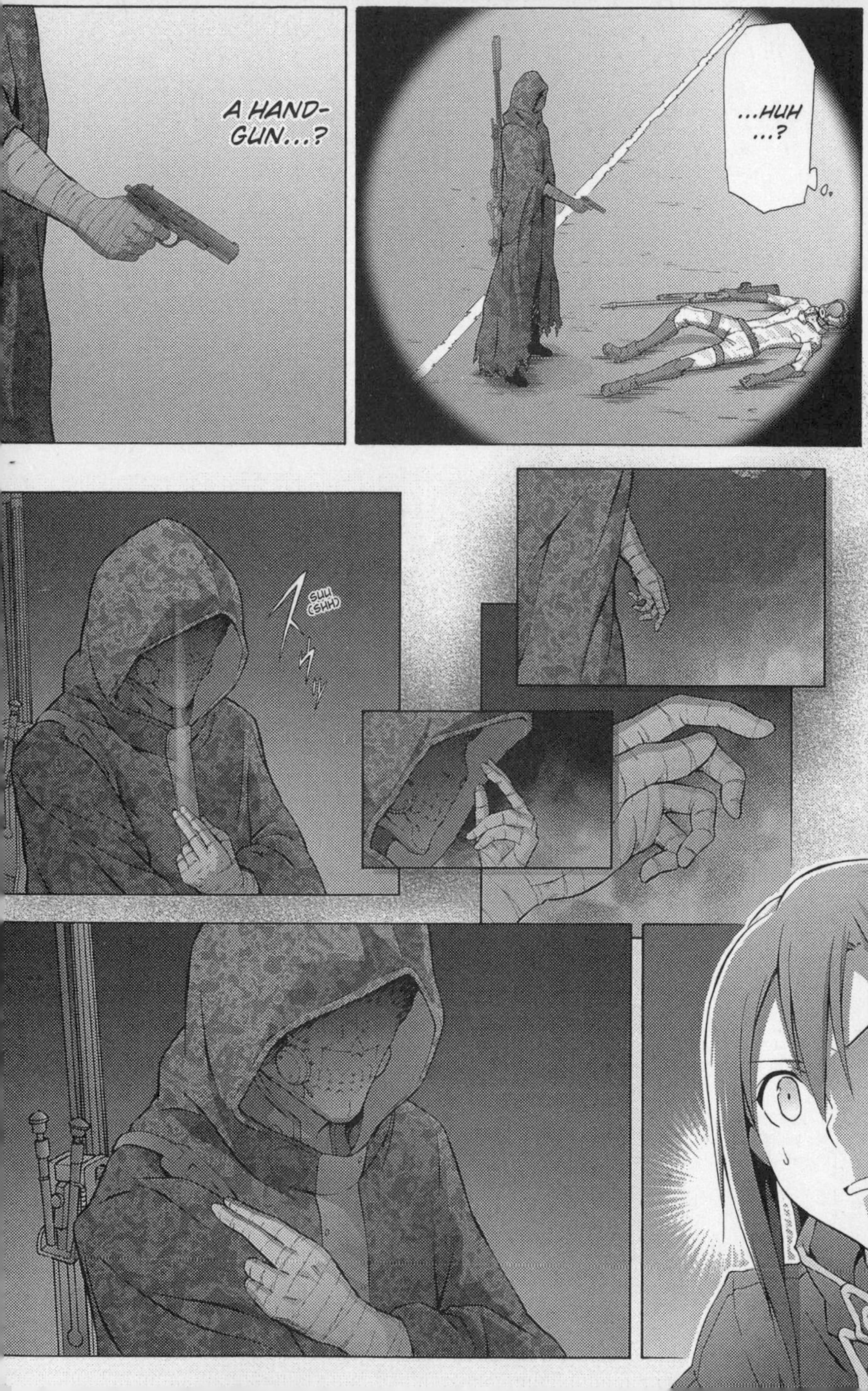
...HUH ...?
A HAND-GUN...?
SUU (SHH)

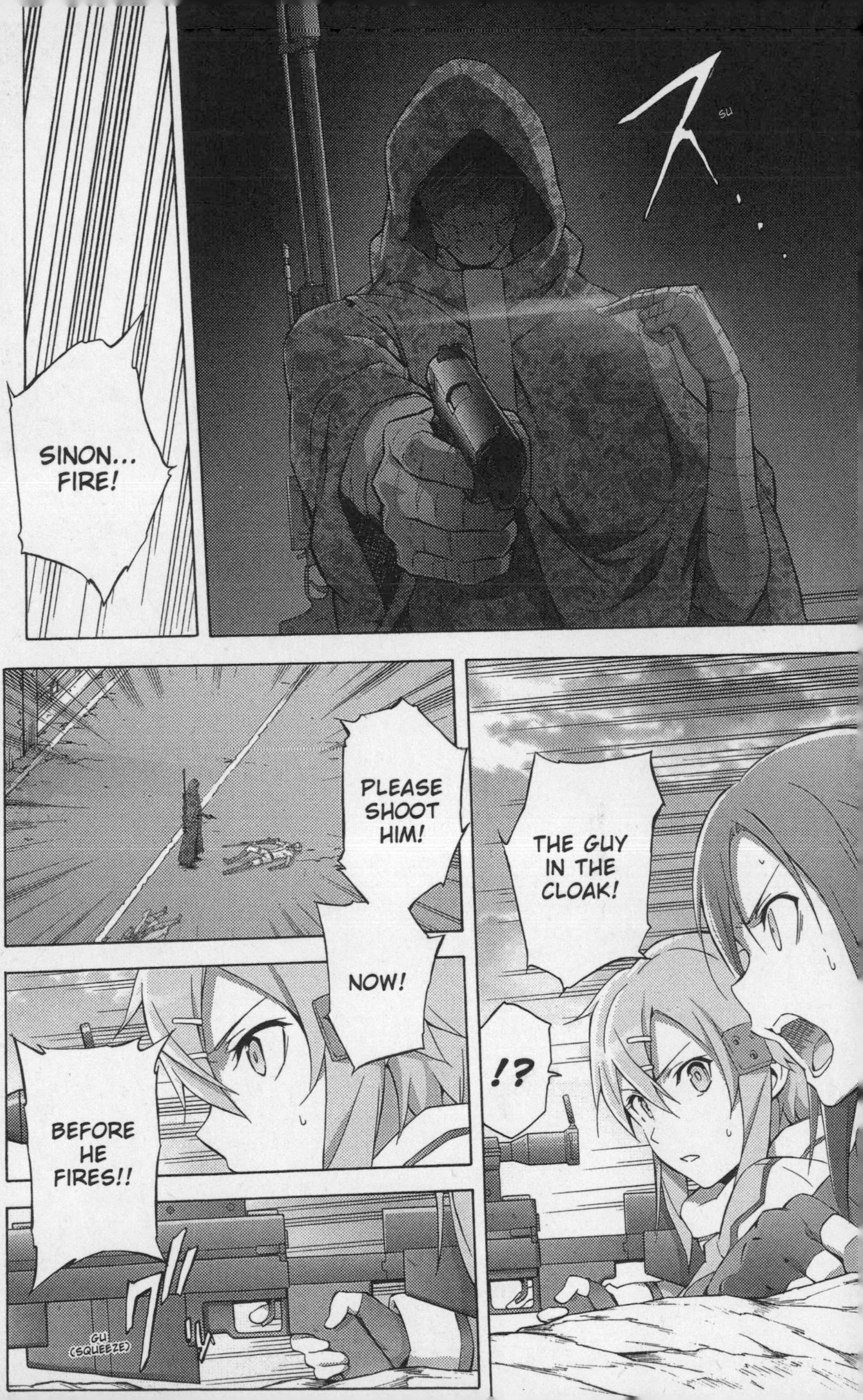
SU
SINON... FIRE!
THE GUY IN THE CLOAK!
!?
PLEASE SHOOT HIM!
NOW!
BEFORE HE FIRES!!
GU (SQUEEZE)

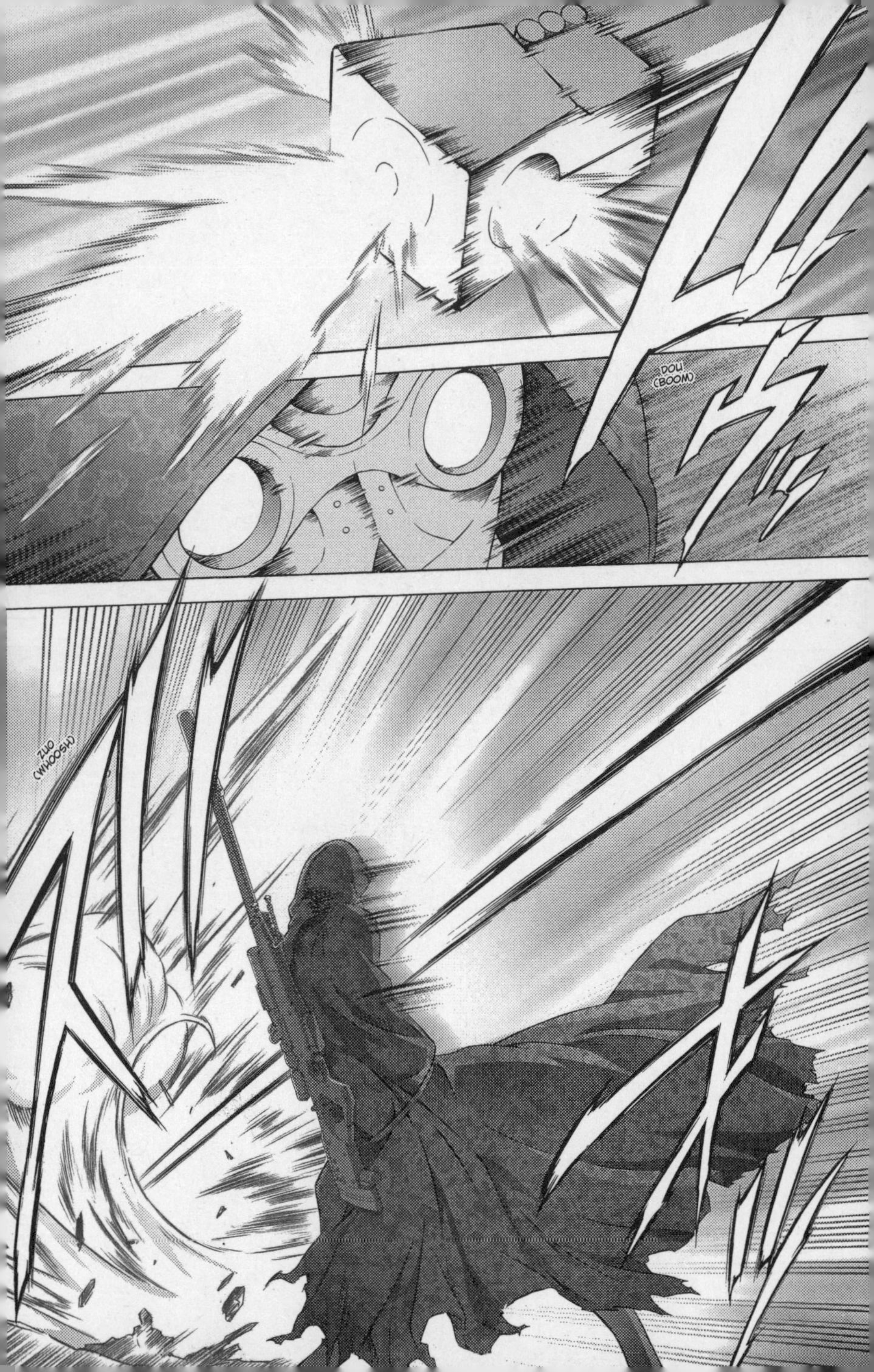
DOU
(BOOM)
ZUO
(WHOOSH)

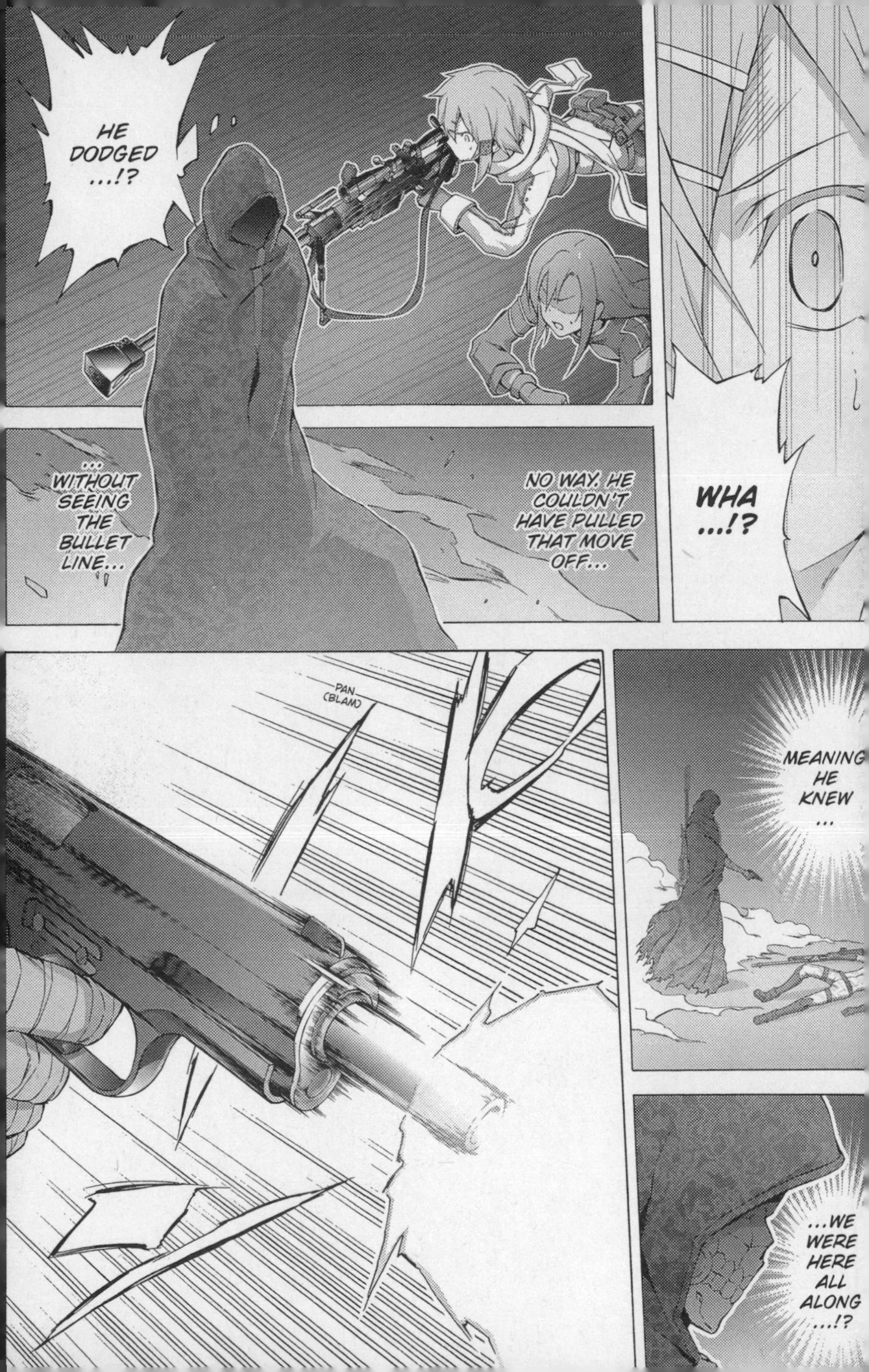
WHA ...!?
HE DODGED ...!?
NO WAY. HE COULDN'T HAVE PULLED THAT MOVE OFF...
...WITHOUT SEEING THE BULLET LINE...
MEANING HE KNEW ...
...WE WERE HERE ALL ALONG ...!?
PAN (BLAM)

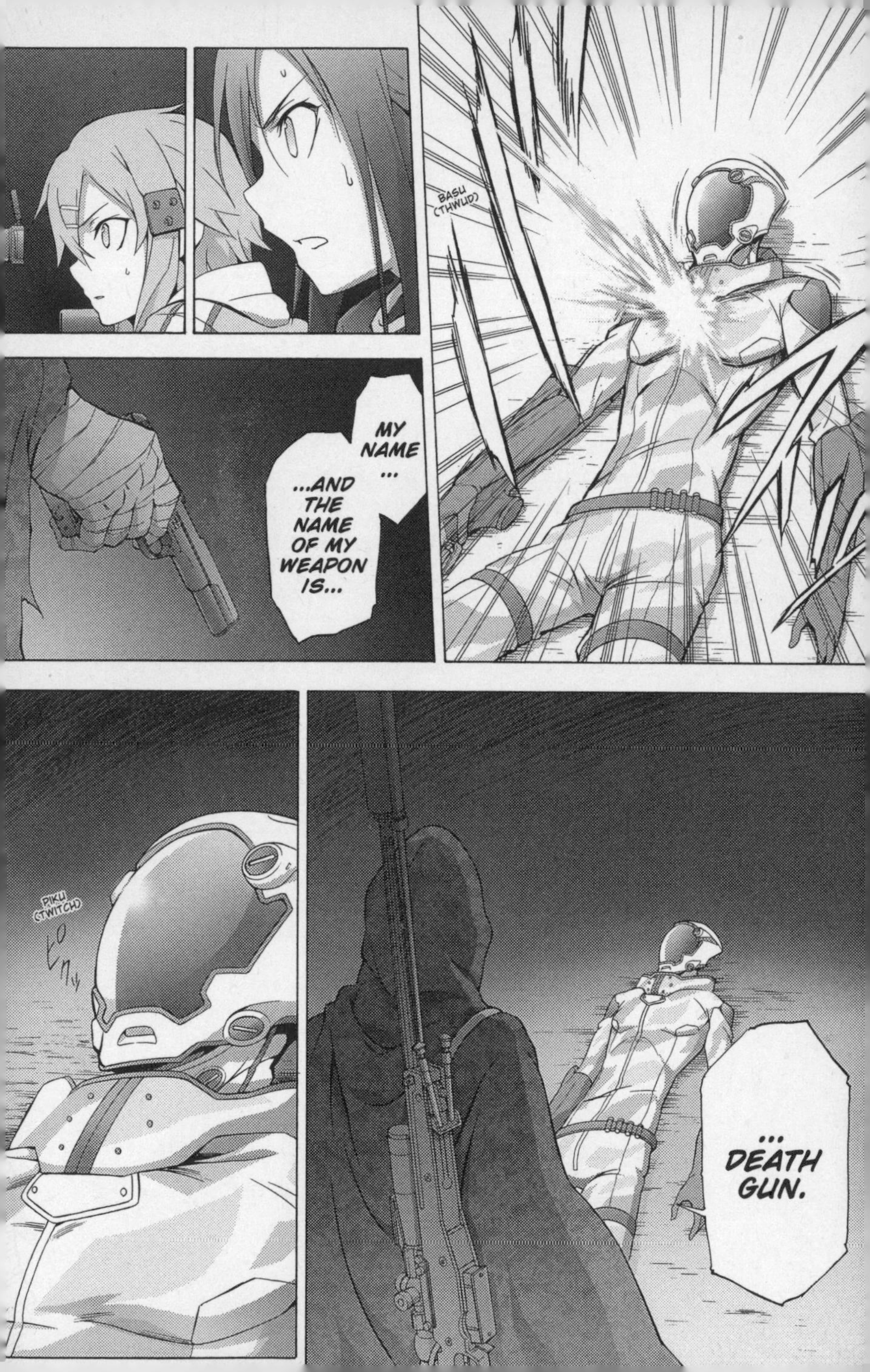
BASU (THWUD)
MY NAME...
...AND THE NAME OF MY WEAPON IS...
...DEATH GUN.
PIKU (TWITCH)
ピクッ

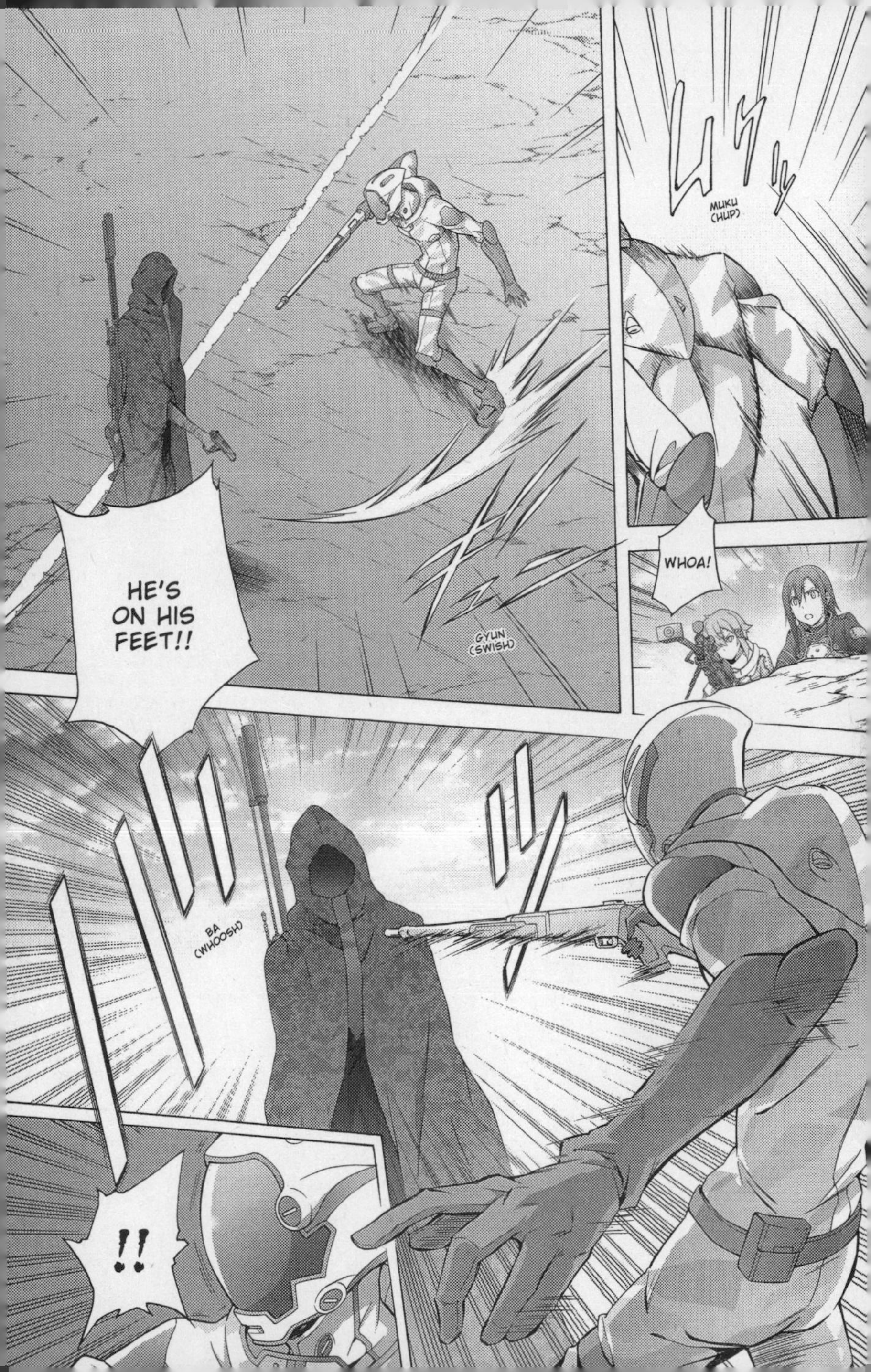
MUKU (HUP)
WHOA!
GYUN (SWISH)
HE'S ON HIS FEET!!
BA (WHOOSH)
!!

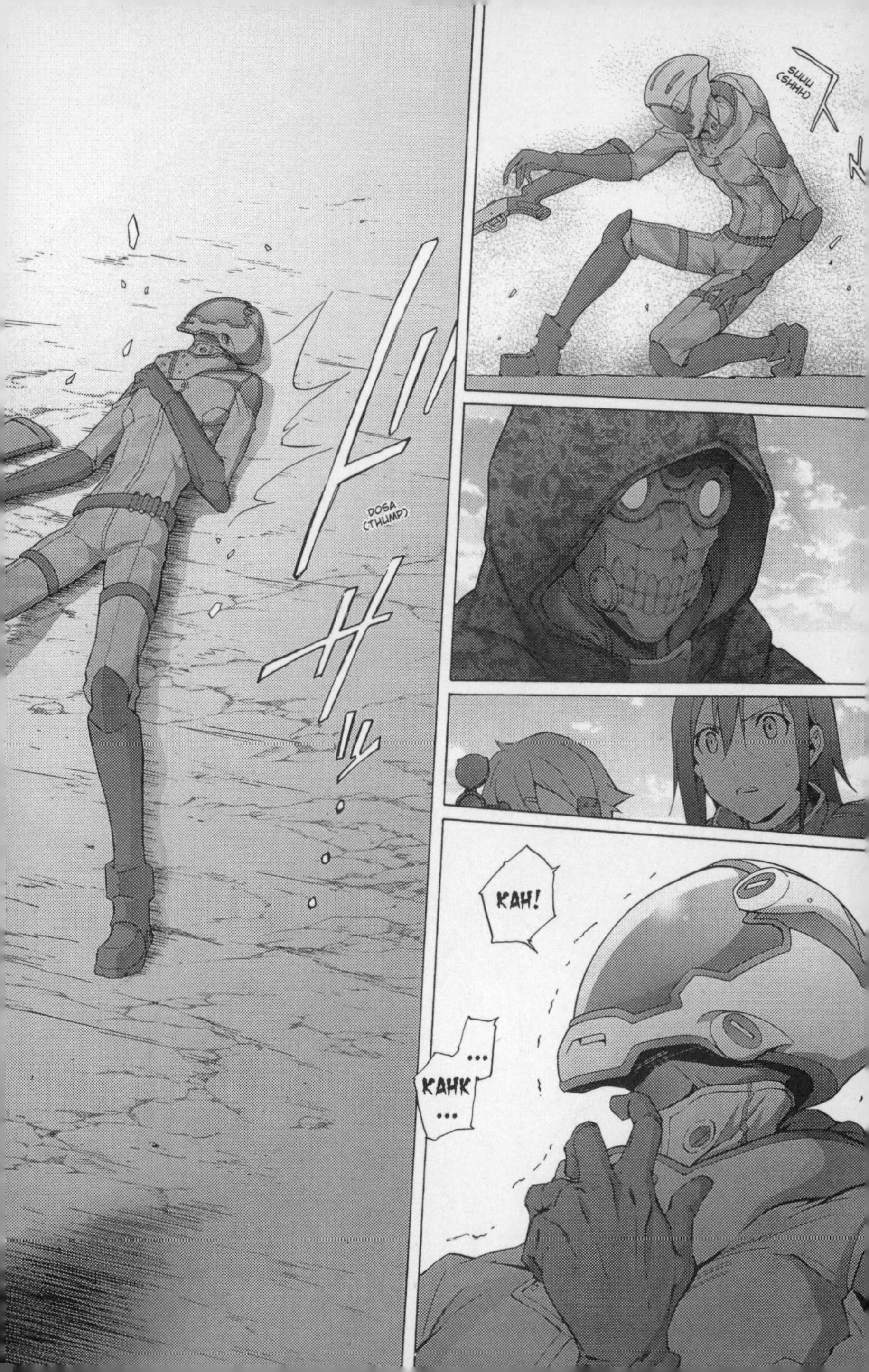
SUUU
(SHHH)
KAH!
...KAHK...
DOSA
(THUMP)

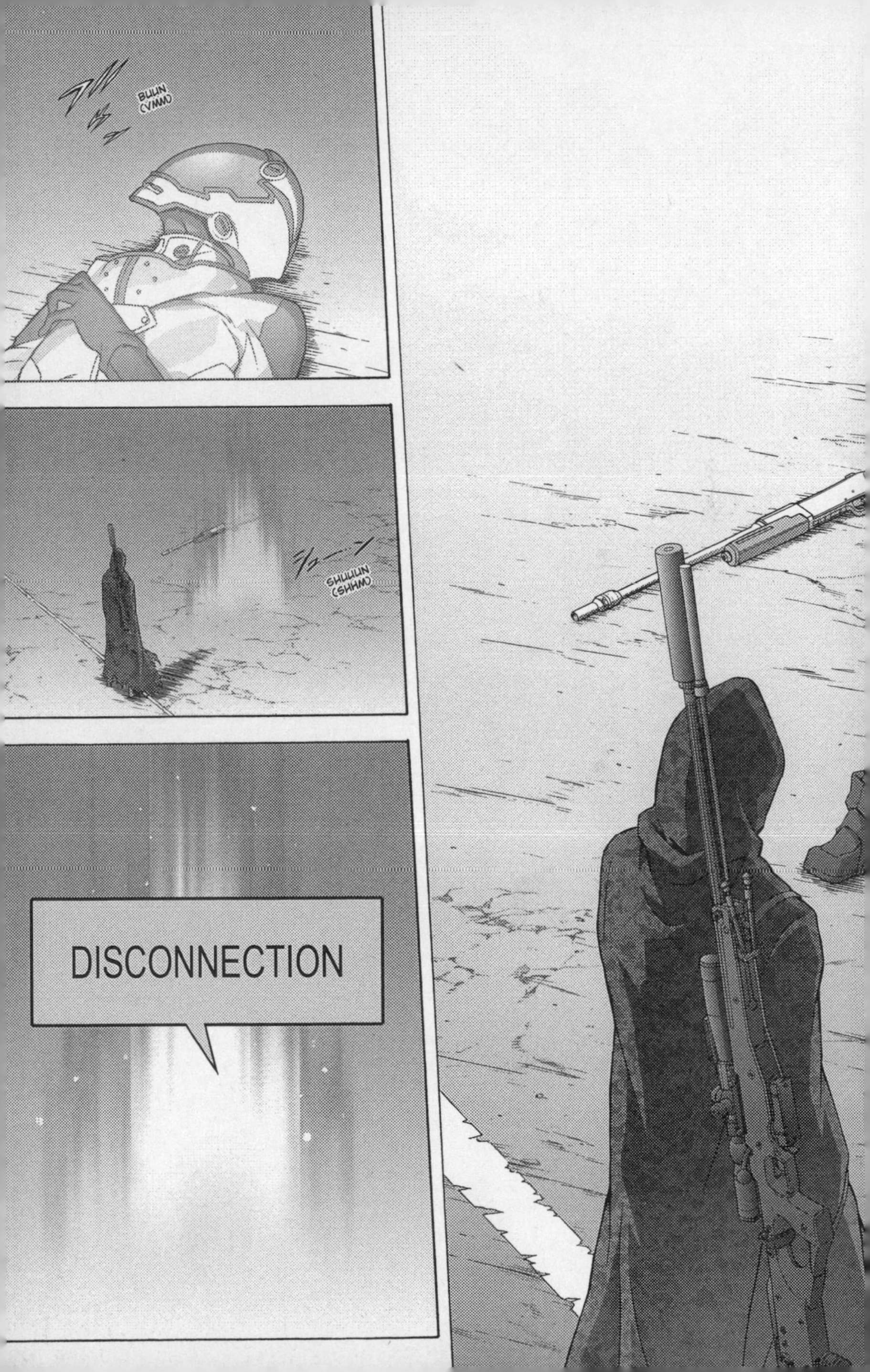
BUUN (VMM)
SHUUUN (SHHM)
DISCONNECTION

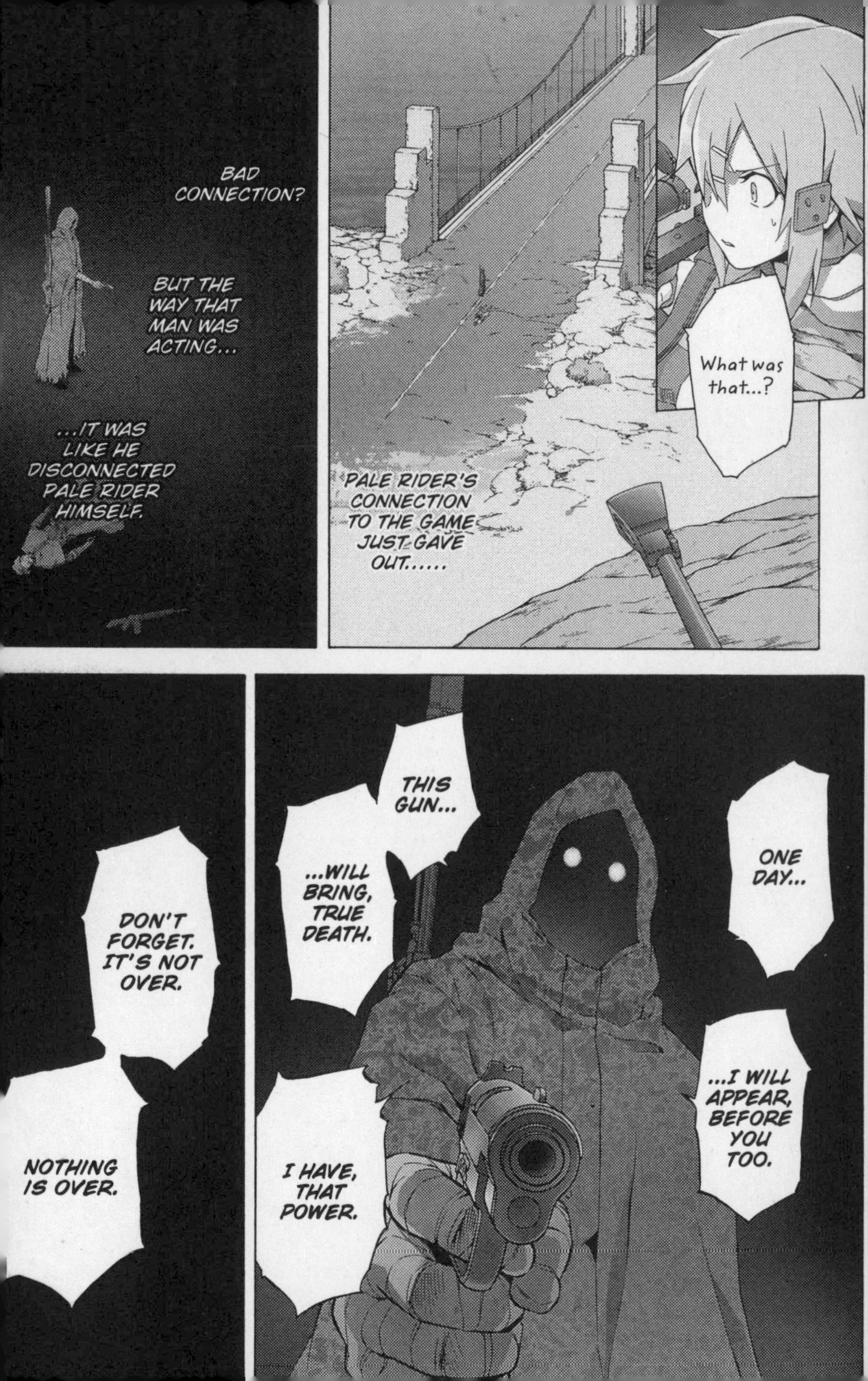
What was that...?
PALE RIDER'S CONNECTION TO THE GAME JUST GAVE OUT......
BAD CONNECTION?
BUT THE WAY THAT MAN WAS ACTING...
...IT WAS LIKE HE DISCONNECTED PALE RIDER HIMSELF.
THIS GUN...
...WILL BRING, TRUE DEATH.
ONE DAY...
...I WILL APPEAR, BEFORE YOU TOO.
I HAVE, THAT POWER.
DON'T FORGET. IT'S NOT OVER.
NOTHING IS OVER.

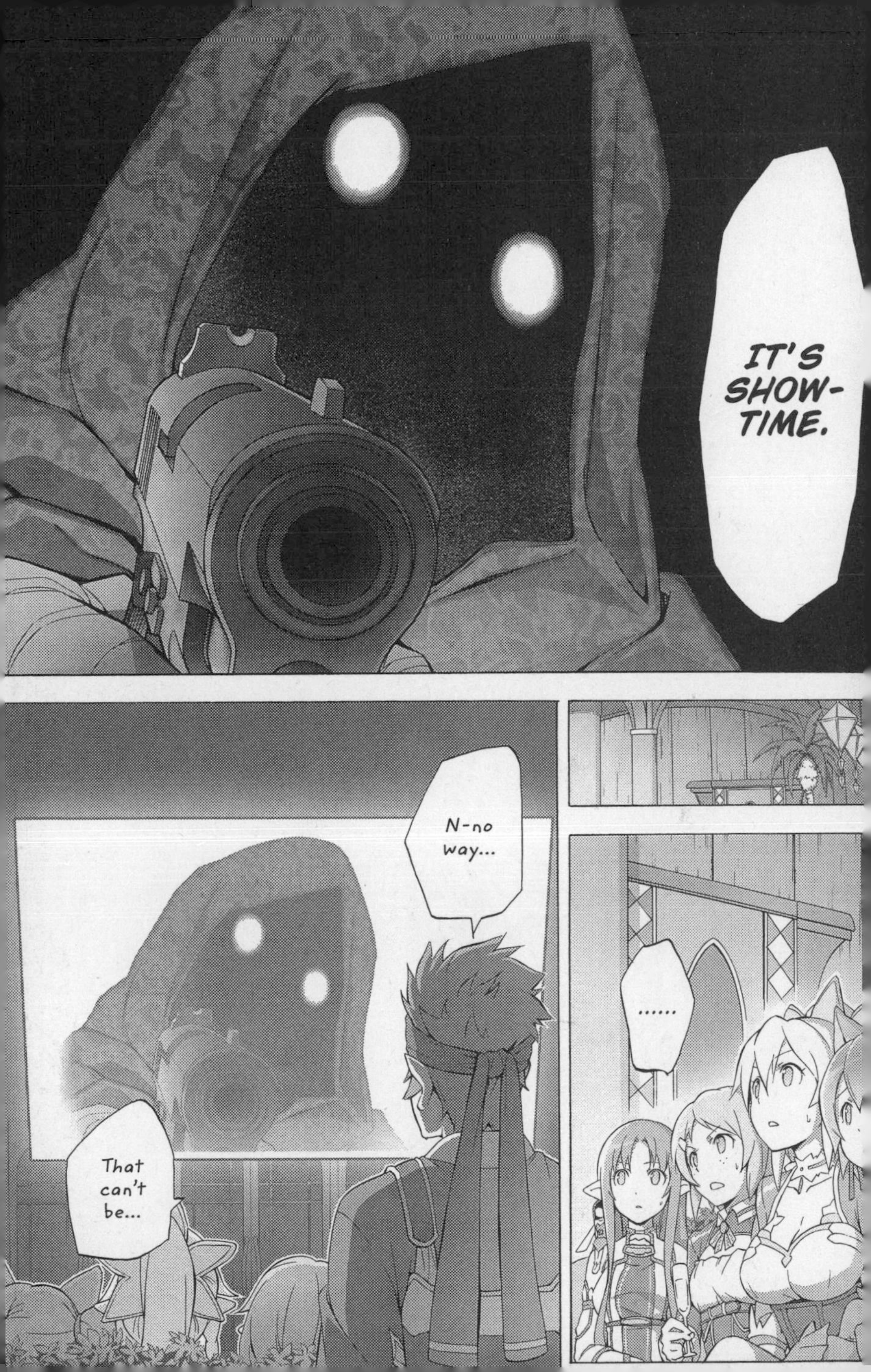
IT'S SHOW-TIME.
......
N-no way...
That can't be...

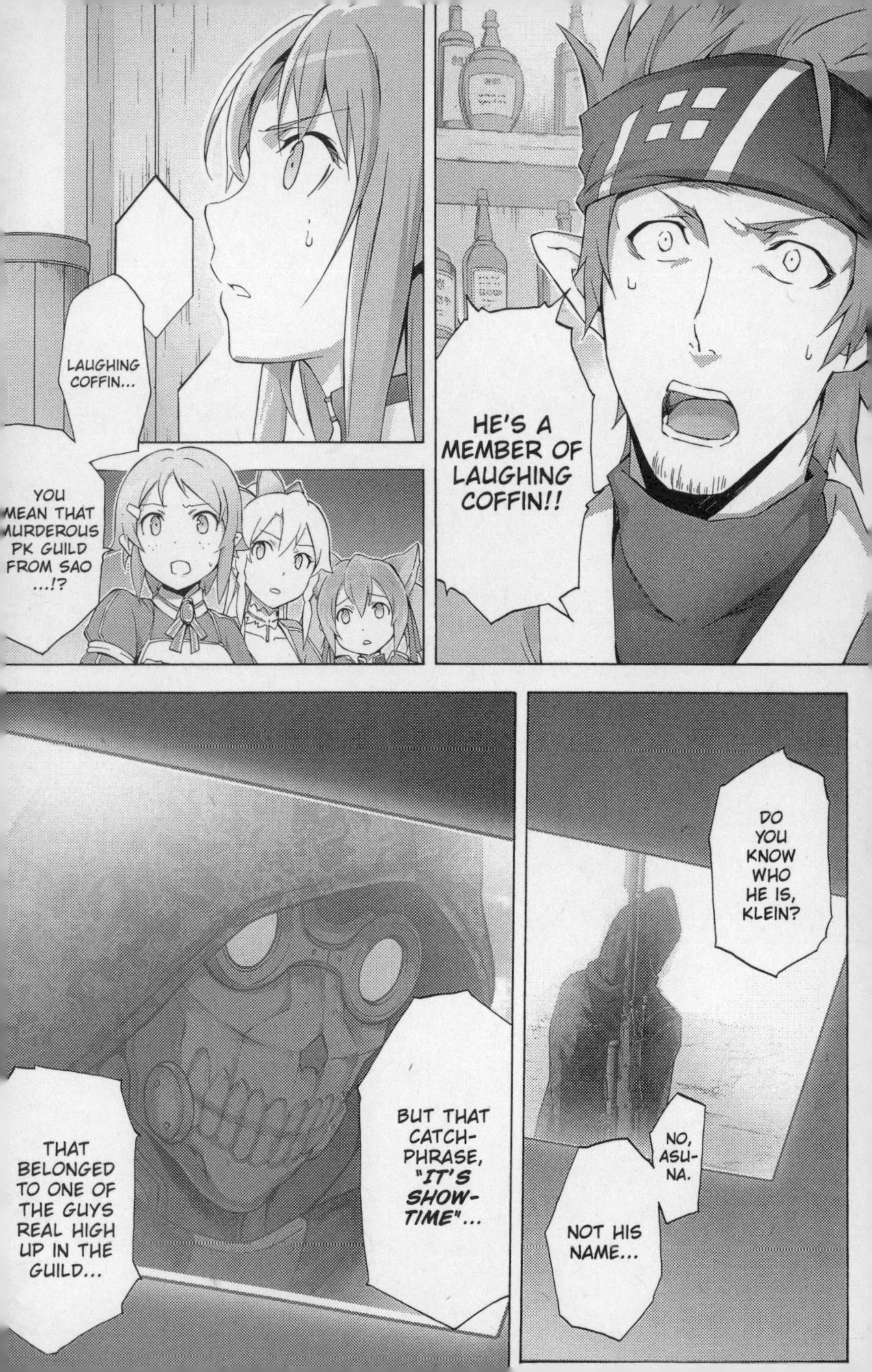
HE'S A MEMBER OF LAUGHING COFFIN!!
LAUGHING COFFIN...
YOU MEAN THAT MURDEROUS PK GUILD FROM SAO ...!?
DO YOU KNOW WHO HE IS, KLEIN?
NO, ASUNA.
NOT HIS NAME...
BUT THAT CATCH-PHRASE, "*IT'S SHOW-TIME*"...
THAT BELONGED TO ONE OF THE GUYS REAL HIGH UP IN THE GUILD...

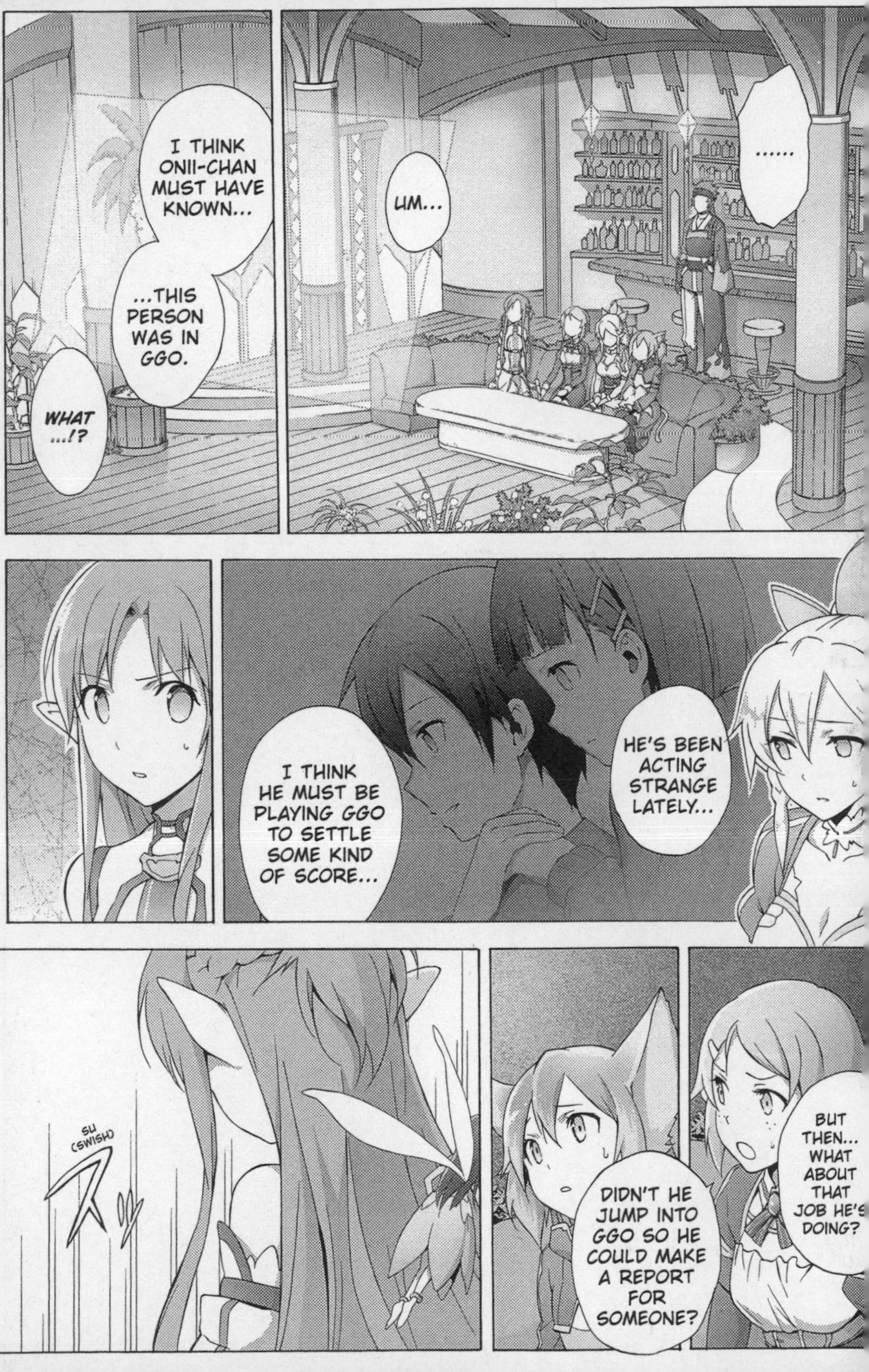

......
UM...
I THINK ONII-CHAN MUST HAVE KNOWN...
...THIS PERSON WAS IN GGO.
WHAT ...!?
HE'S BEEN ACTING STRANGE LATELY...
I THINK HE MUST BE PLAYING GGO TO SETTLE SOME KIND OF SCORE...
BUT THEN... WHAT ABOUT THAT JOB HE'S DOING?
DIDN'T HE JUMP INTO GGO SO HE COULD MAKE A REPORT FOR SOMEONE?
SU (SWISH)

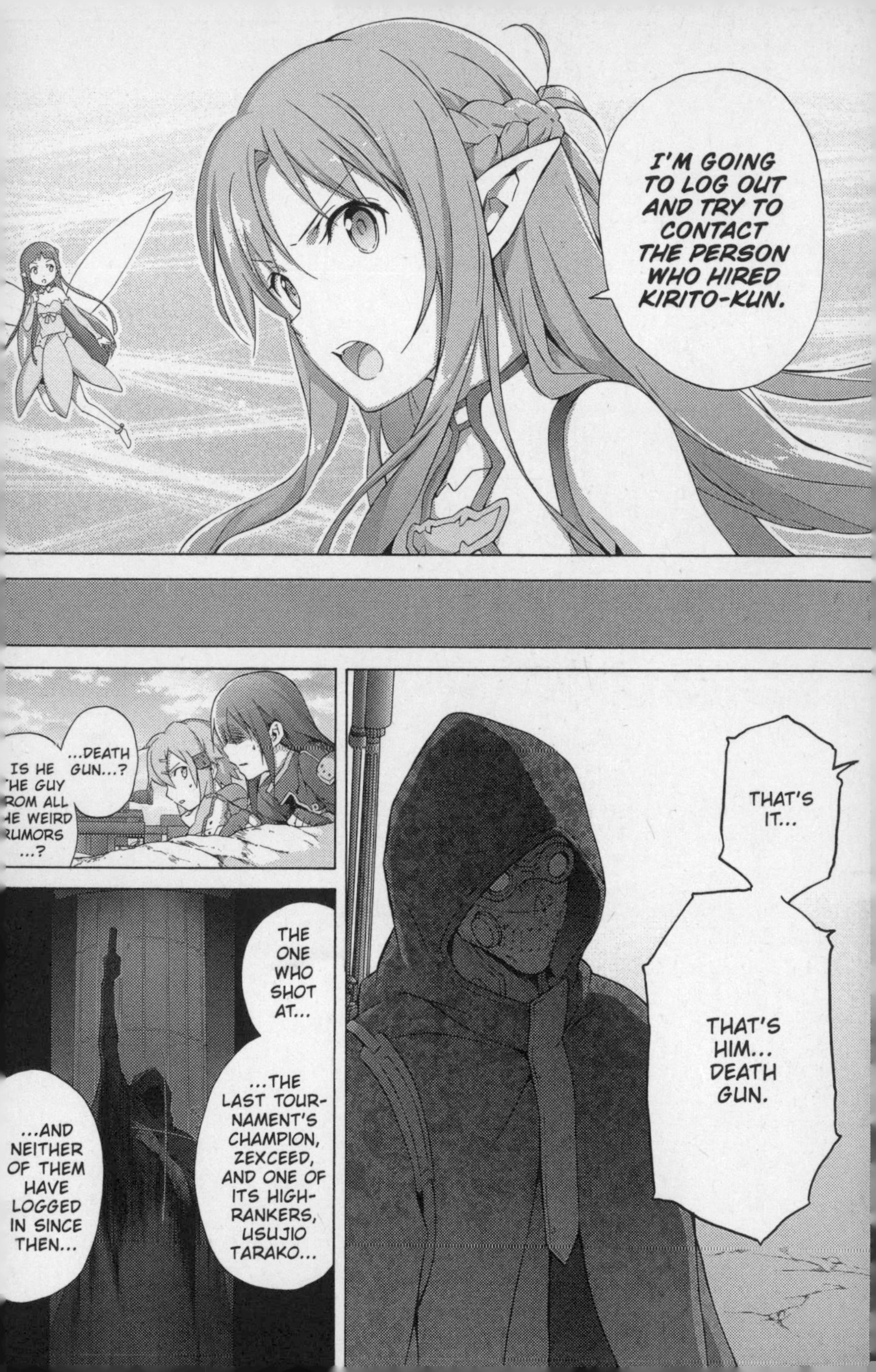
I'M GOING TO LOG OUT AND TRY TO CONTACT THE PERSON WHO HIRED KIRITO-KUN.
THAT'S IT...
THAT'S HIM... DEATH GUN.
...DEATH GUN...?
IS HE THE GUY FROM ALL THE WEIRD RUMORS ...?
THE ONE WHO SHOT AT...
...THE LAST TOURNAMENT'S CHAMPION, ZEXCEED, AND ONE OF ITS HIGH-RANKERS, USUJIO TARAKO...
...AND NEITHER OF THEM HAVE LOGGED IN SINCE THEN...

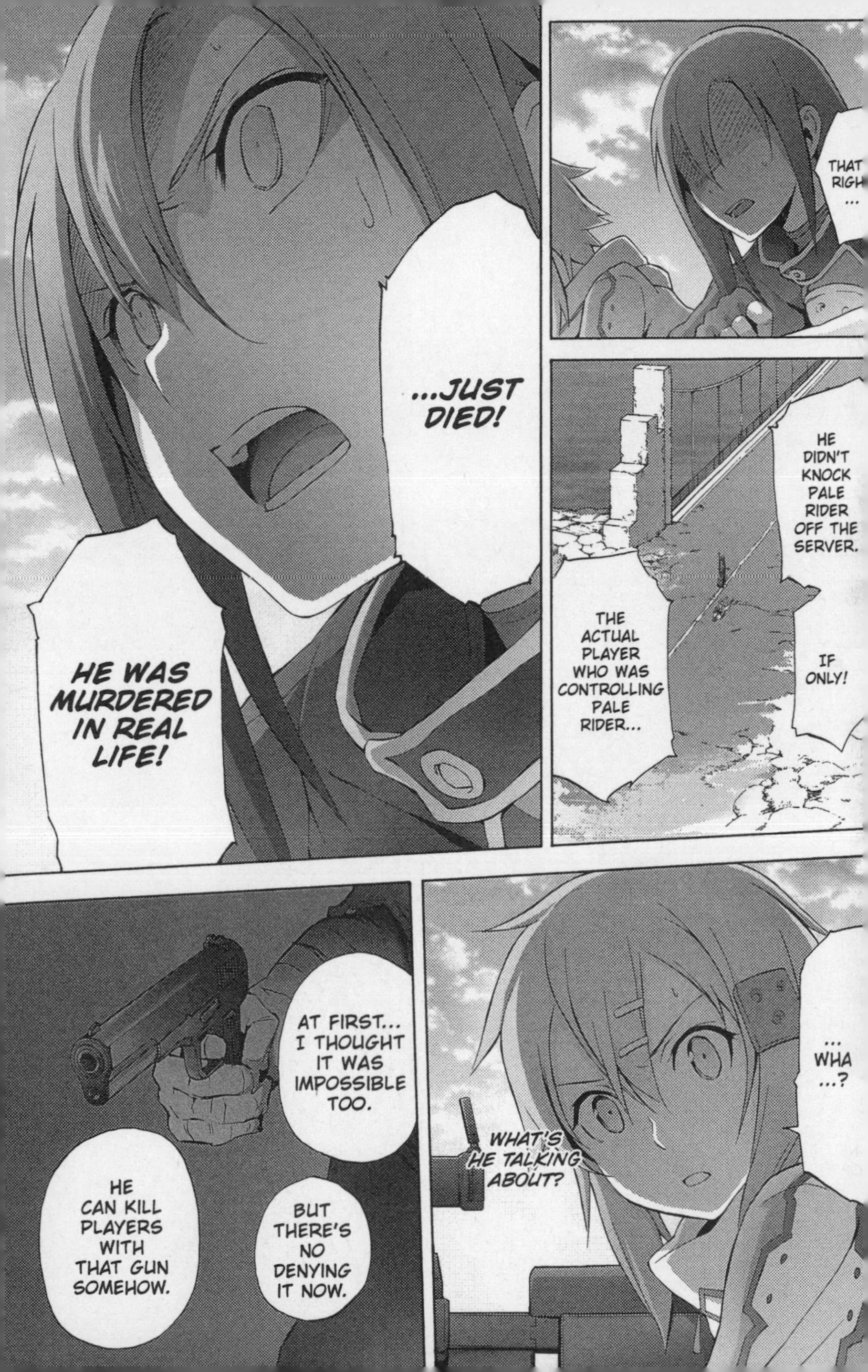
THAT RIGH...
IF ONLY!
HE DIDN'T KNOCK PALE RIDER OFF THE SERVER.
THE ACTUAL PLAYER WHO WAS CONTROLLING PALE RIDER...
...JUST DIED!
HE WAS MURDERED IN REAL LIFE!
...WHA...?
WHAT'S HE TALKING ABOUT?
AT FIRST... I THOUGHT IT WAS IMPOSSIBLE TOO.
BUT THERE'S NO DENYING IT NOW.
HE CAN KILL PLAYERS WITH THAT GUN SOMEHOW.

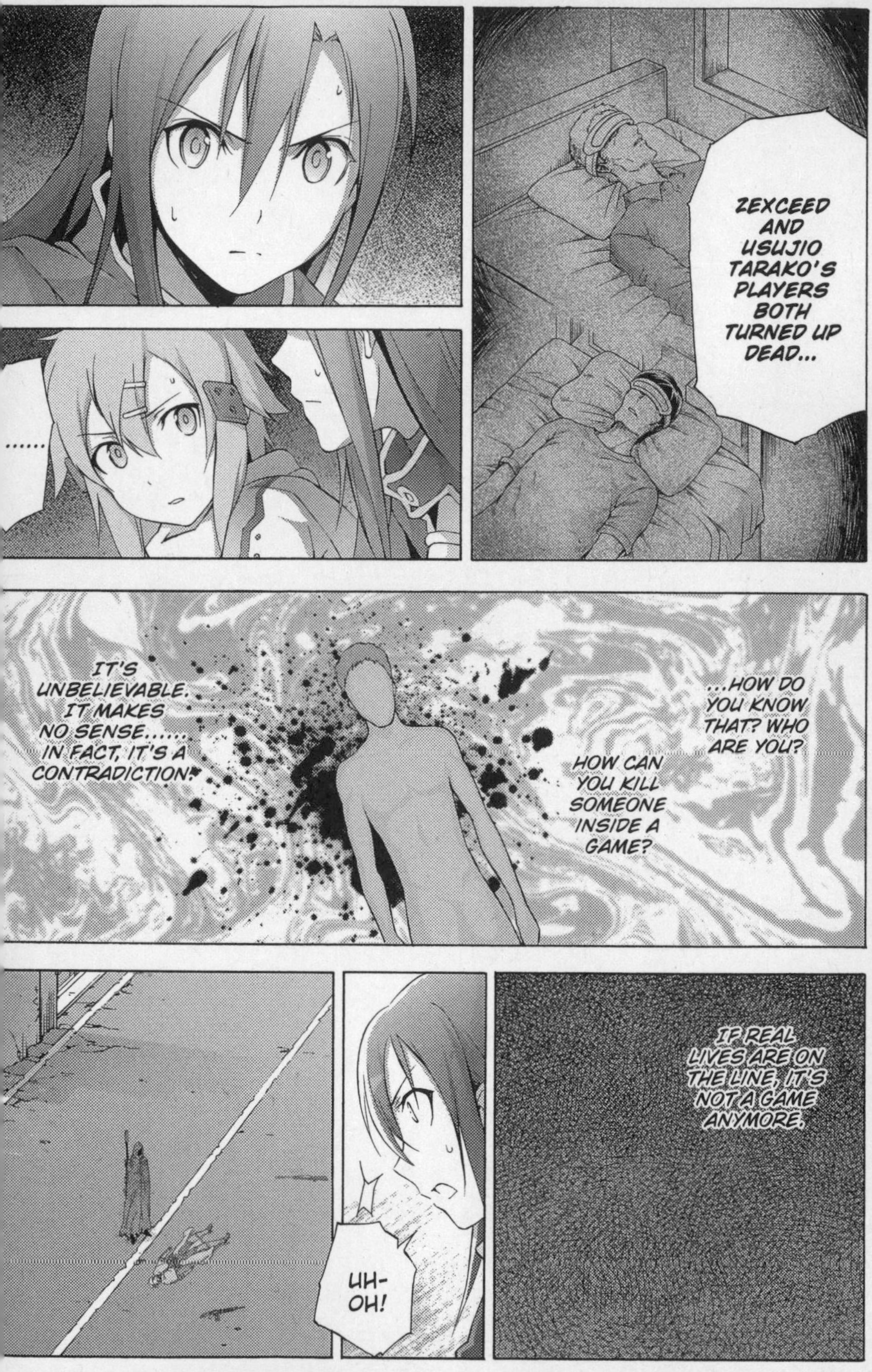
ZEXCEED AND USUJIO TARAKO'S PLAYERS BOTH TURNED UP DEAD...
......
...HOW DO YOU KNOW THAT? WHO ARE YOU?
HOW CAN YOU KILL SOMEONE INSIDE A GAME?
IT'S UNBELIEVABLE. IT MAKES NO SENSE...... IN FACT, IT'S A CONTRADICTION!
IF REAL LIVES ARE ON THE LINE, IT'S NOT A GAME ANYMORE.
UH-OH!

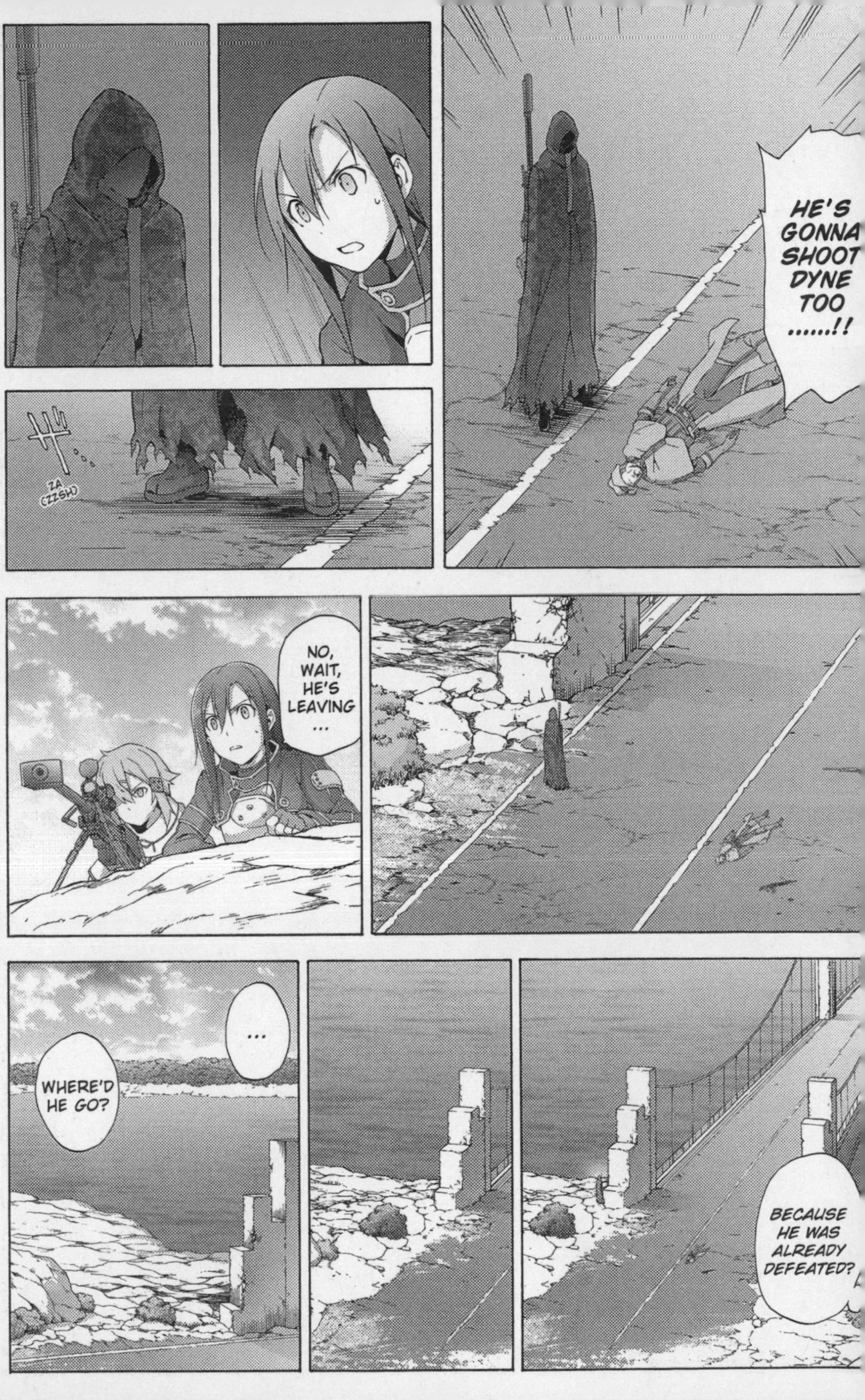
HE'S GONNA SHOOT DYNE TOO ......!!
ZA (ZZISH)
NO, WAIT, HE'S LEAVING ...
BECAUSE HE WAS ALREADY DEFEATED?
...
WHERE'D HE GO?

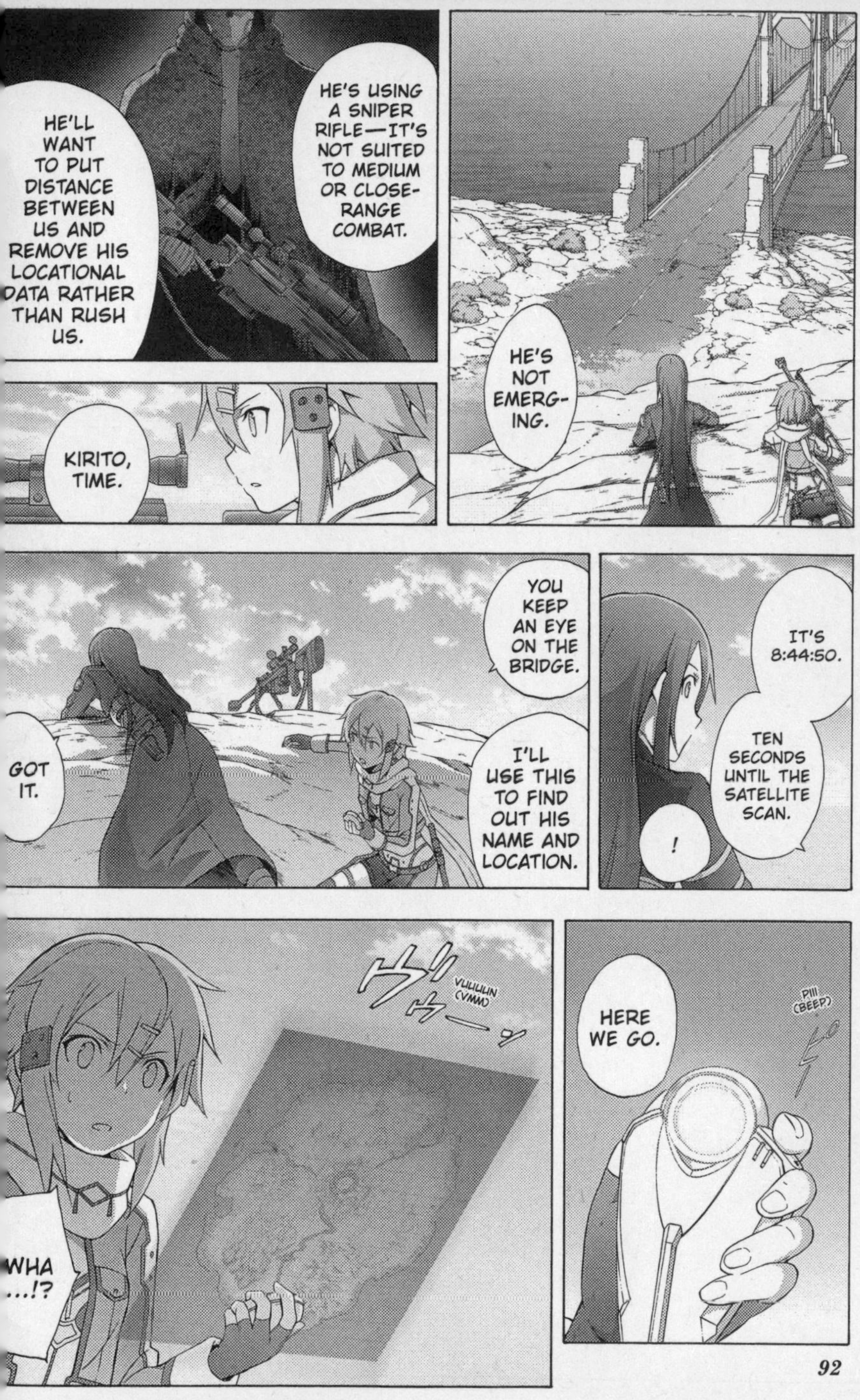
HE'S NOT EMERG-ING.
HE'S USING A SNIPER RIFLE—IT'S NOT SUITED TO MEDIUM OR CLOSE-RANGE COMBAT.
HE'LL WANT TO PUT DISTANCE BETWEEN US AND REMOVE HIS LOCATIONAL DATA RATHER THAN RUSH US.
KIRITO, TIME.
IT'S 8:44:50.
TEN SECONDS UNTIL THE SATELLITE SCAN.
!
YOU KEEP AN EYE ON THE BRIDGE.
I'LL USE THIS TO FIND OUT HIS NAME AND LOCATION.
GOT IT.
HERE WE GO.
PIII (BEEP)
VUUUUN (VMM)
WHA ...!?

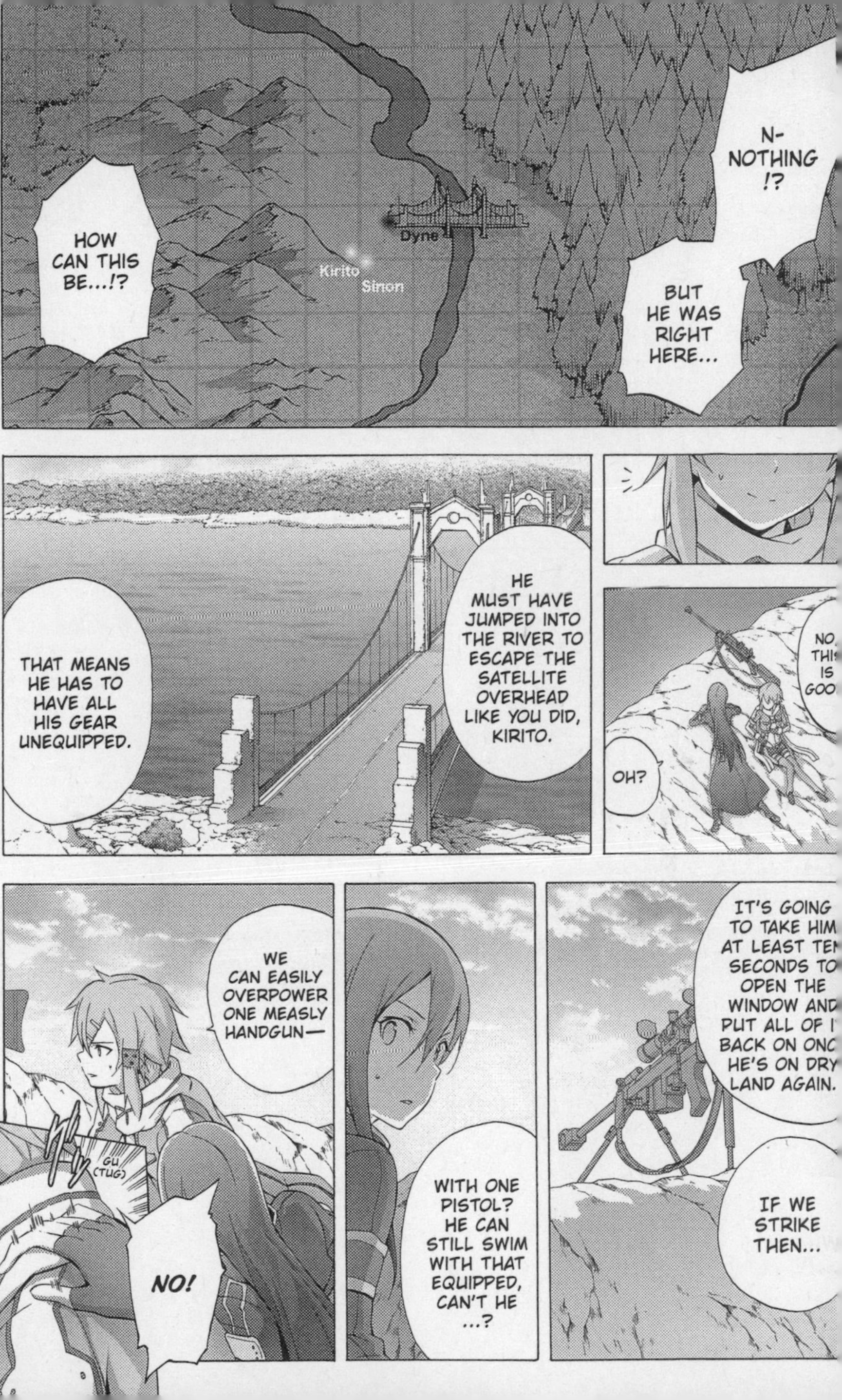

N- NOTHING !?
BUT HE WAS RIGHT HERE...
Dyne
Kirito
Sinon
HOW CAN THIS BE...!?
NO, THIS IS GOO
OH?
HE MUST HAVE JUMPED INTO THE RIVER TO ESCAPE THE SATELLITE OVERHEAD LIKE YOU DID, KIRITO.
THAT MEANS HE HAS TO HAVE ALL HIS GEAR UNEQUIPPED.
IT'S GOING TO TAKE HIM AT LEAST TEN SECONDS TO OPEN THE WINDOW AND PUT ALL OF IT BACK ON ONCE HE'S ON DRY LAND AGAIN.
IF WE STRIKE THEN...
WITH ONE PISTOL? HE CAN STILL SWIM WITH THAT EQUIPPED, CAN'T HE ...?
WE CAN EASILY OVERPOWER ONE MEASLY HANDGUN—
GU (TUG)
NO!

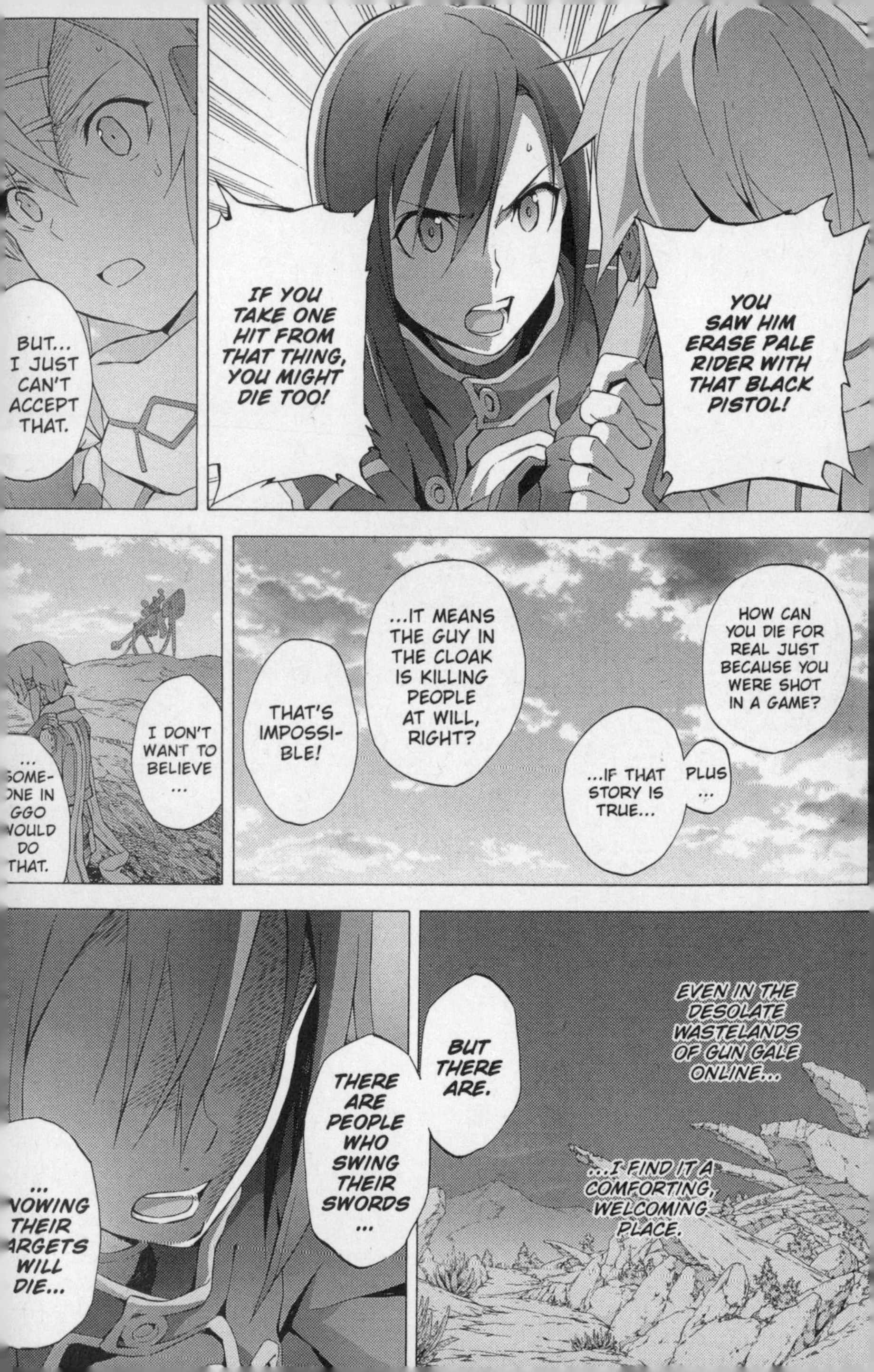
YOU SAW HIM ERASE PALE RIDER WITH THAT BLACK PISTOL!
IF YOU TAKE ONE HIT FROM THAT THING, YOU MIGHT DIE TOO!
BUT... I JUST CAN'T ACCEPT THAT.
HOW CAN YOU DIE FOR REAL JUST BECAUSE YOU WERE SHOT IN A GAME?
PLUS...
...IF THAT STORY IS TRUE...
...IT MEANS THE GUY IN THE CLOAK IS KILLING PEOPLE AT WILL, RIGHT?
THAT'S IMPOSSI-BLE!
I DON'T WANT TO BELIEVE...
...SOME-ONE IN GGO WOULD DO THAT.
EVEN IN THE DESOLATE WASTELANDS OF GUN GALE ONLINE...
...I FIND IT A COMFORTING, WELCOMING PLACE.
BUT THERE ARE.
THERE ARE PEOPLE WHO SWING THEIR SWORDS...
...NOWING THEIR ARGETS WILL DIE...

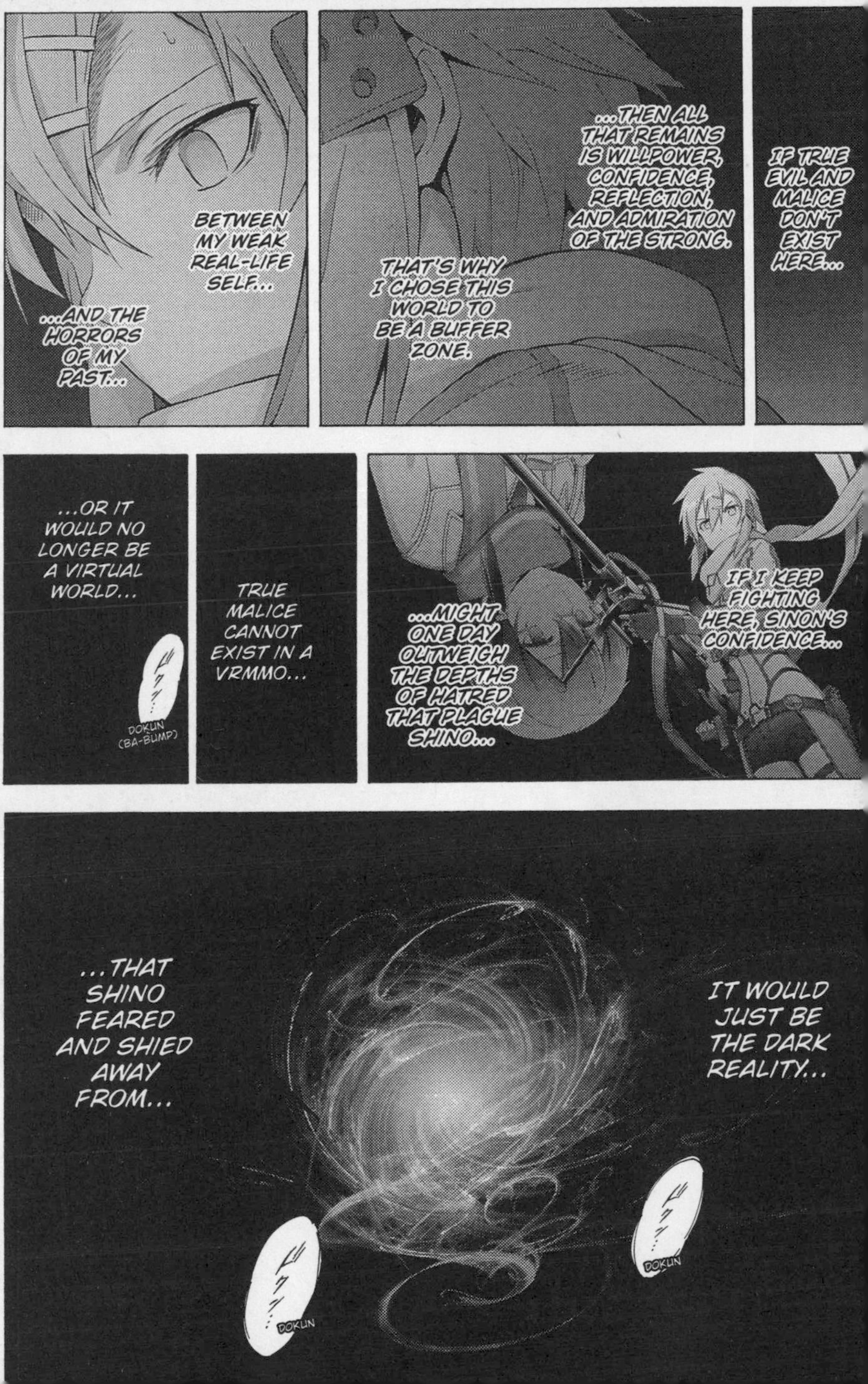
IF TRUE EVIL AND MALICE DON'T EXIST HERE...
...THEN ALL THAT REMAINS IS WILLPOWER, CONFIDENCE, REFLECTION, AND ADMIRATION OF THE STRONG.
THAT'S WHY I CHOSE THIS WORLD TO BE A BUFFER ZONE.
BETWEEN MY WEAK REAL-LIFE SELF...
...AND THE HORRORS OF MY PAST...
IF I KEEP FIGHTING HERE, SINON'S CONFIDENCE...
...MIGHT ONE DAY OUTWEIGH THE DEPTHS OF HATRED THAT PLAGUE SHINO...
TRUE MALICE CANNOT EXIST IN A VRMMO...
...OR IT WOULD NO LONGER BE A VIRTUAL WORLD...
DOKUN (BA-BUMP)
IT WOULD JUST BE THE DARK REALITY...
...THAT SHINO FEARED AND SHIED AWAY FROM...
DOKUN
DOKUN

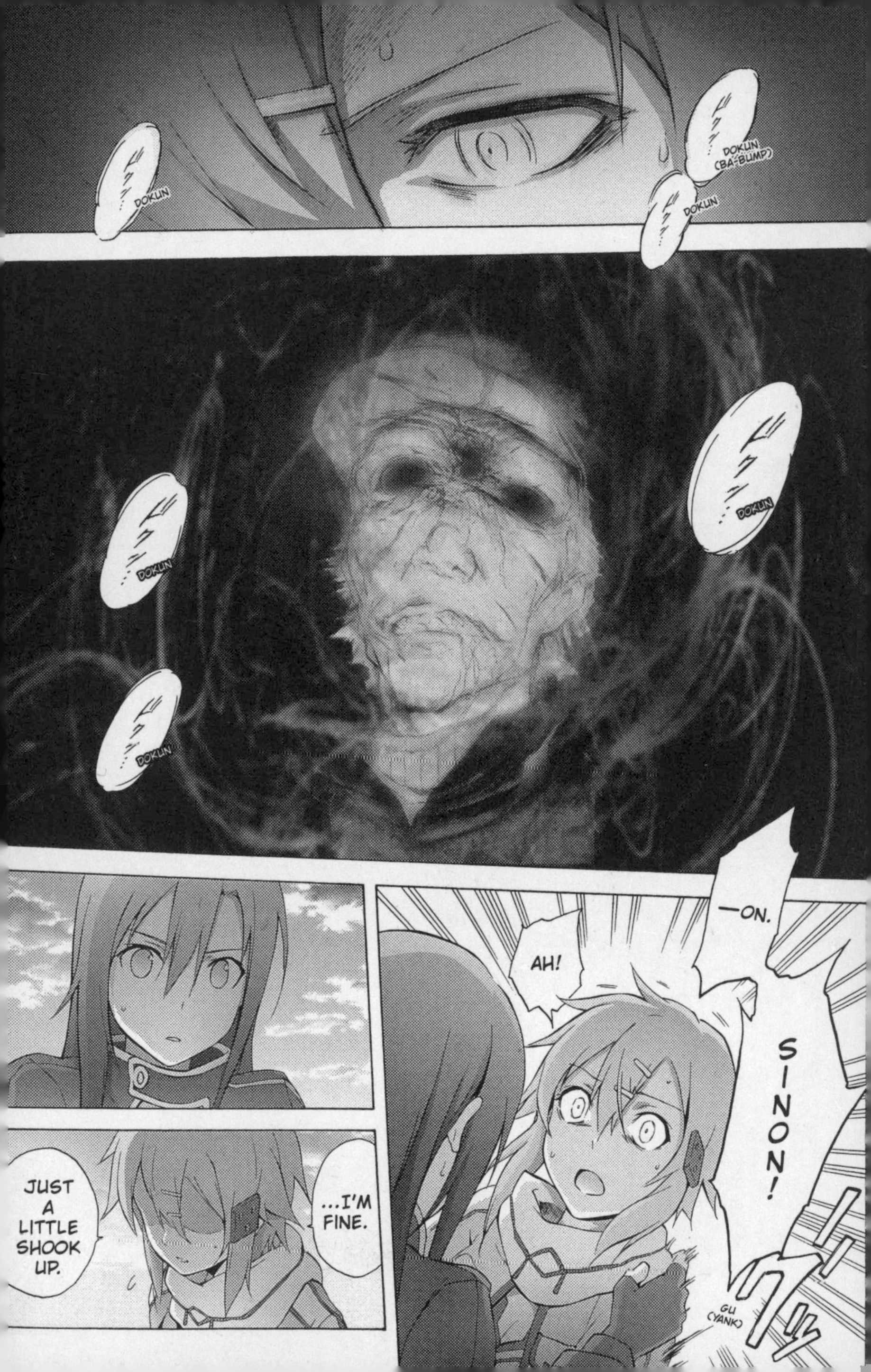
DOKUN (BA-BUMP)
DOKUN
DOKUN
DOKUN
DOKUN
DOKUN
—ON.
SINON!
AH!
GU (YANK)
...I'M FINE.
JUST A LITTLE SHOOK UP.

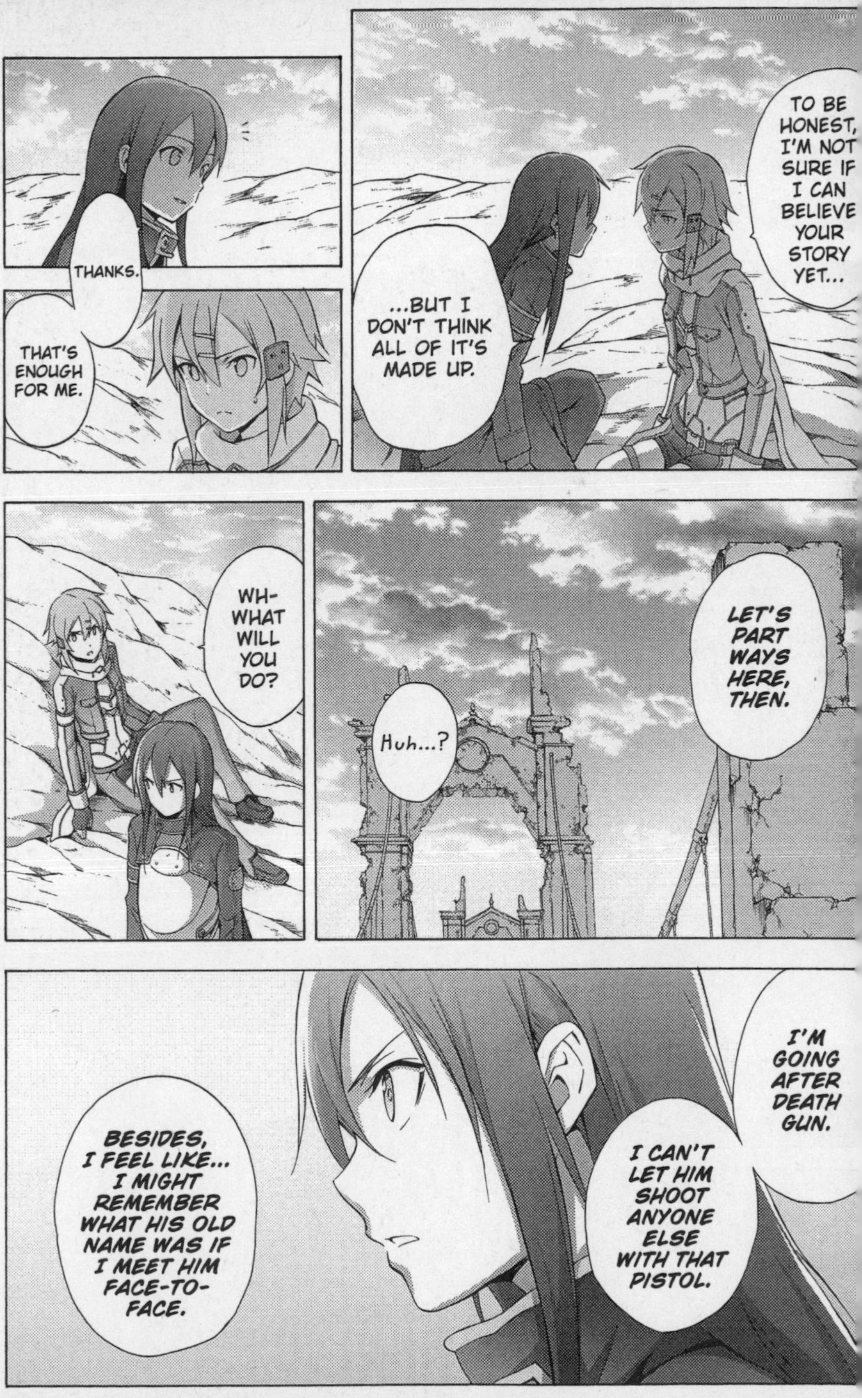
TO BE HONEST, I'M NOT SURE IF I CAN BELIEVE YOUR STORY YET...
...BUT I DON'T THINK ALL OF IT'S MADE UP.
THANKS.
THAT'S ENOUGH FOR ME.
LET'S PART WAYS HERE, THEN.
Huh...?
WH-WHAT WILL YOU DO?
I'M GOING AFTER DEATH GUN.
I CAN'T LET HIM SHOOT ANYONE ELSE WITH THAT PISTOL.
BESIDES, I FEEL LIKE... I MIGHT REMEMBER WHAT HIS OLD NAME WAS IF I MEET HIM FACE-TO-FACE.

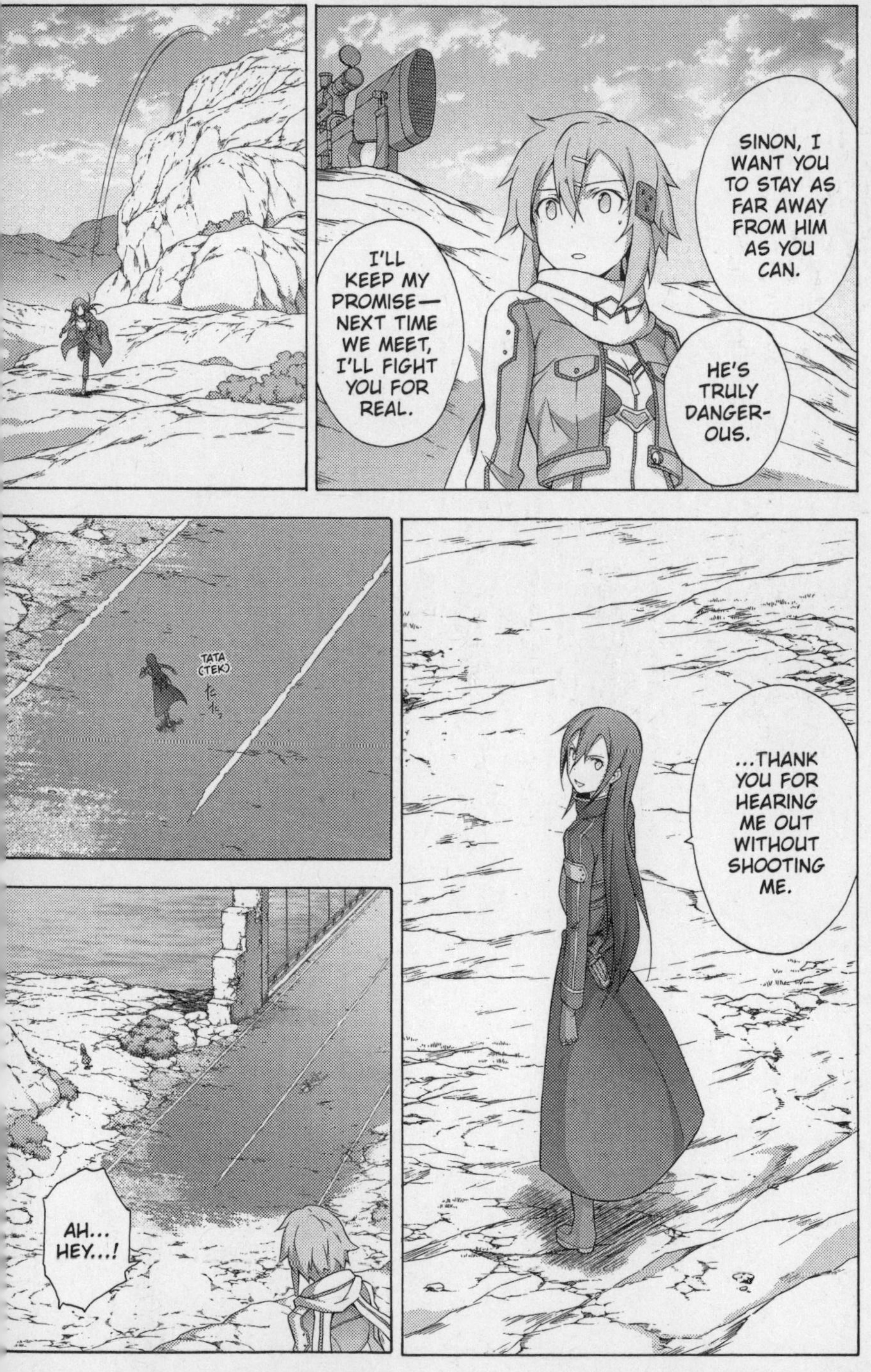
SINON, I WANT YOU TO STAY AS FAR AWAY FROM HIM AS YOU CAN.
HE'S TRULY DANGER-OUS.
I'LL KEEP MY PROMISE—NEXT TIME WE MEET, I'LL FIGHT YOU FOR REAL.
...THANK YOU FOR HEARING ME OUT WITHOUT SHOOTING ME.
TATA (TEK)
AH... HEY...!

GRR...

HOW WILL WE HAVE A REMATCH IF YOU LOSE TO HIM FIRST!?

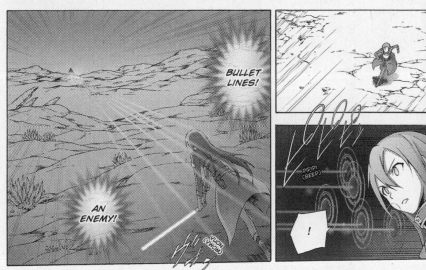

BULLET LINES!

AN ENEMY!

PIPIPI (BEEP)

!

YOU FOOL!

WHAT KIND OF IDIOT RUNS OUT IN THE OPEN!?

BABABABA (RAT-A-TAT)

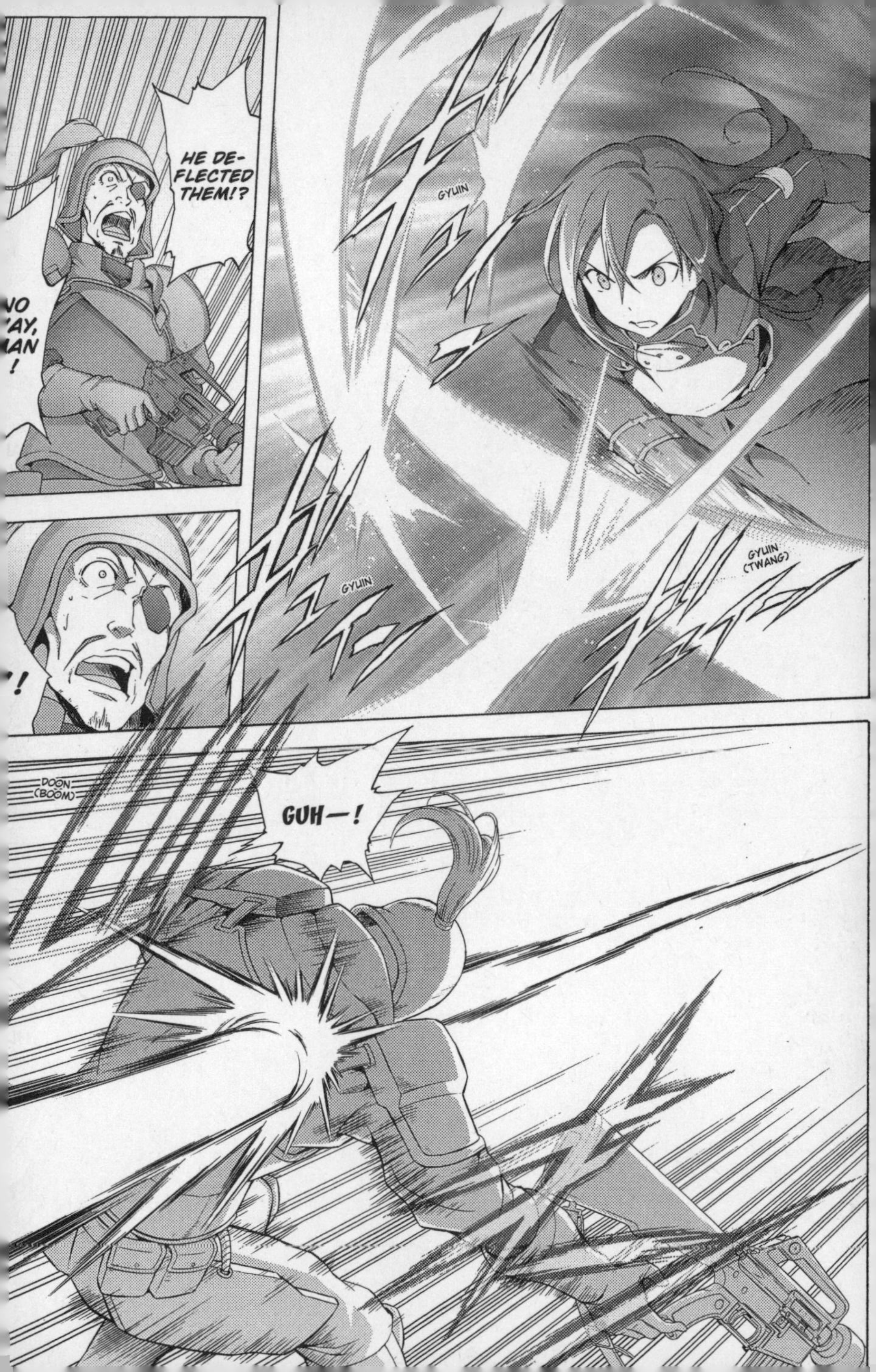
GYUIN
GYUIN
(TWANG)
GYUIN
HE DE-
FLECTED
THEM!?
GUH—!
DOON
(BOOM)

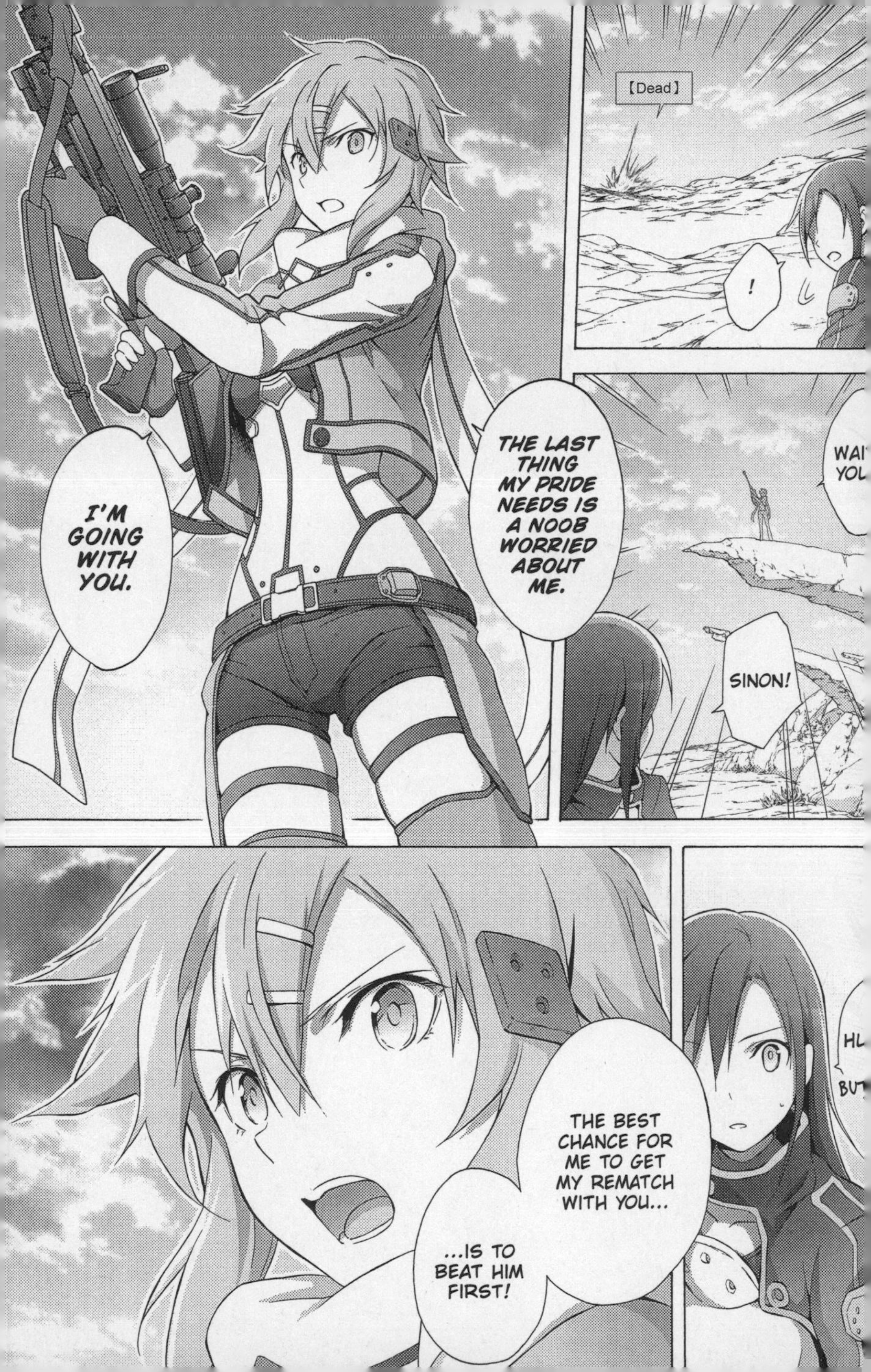
【Dead】
!
WAI YOU
SINON!
THE LAST THING MY PRIDE NEEDS IS A NOOB WORRIED ABOUT ME.
I'M GOING WITH YOU.
HU BU
THE BEST CHANCE FOR ME TO GET MY REMATCH WITH YOU...
...IS TO BEAT HIM FIRST!

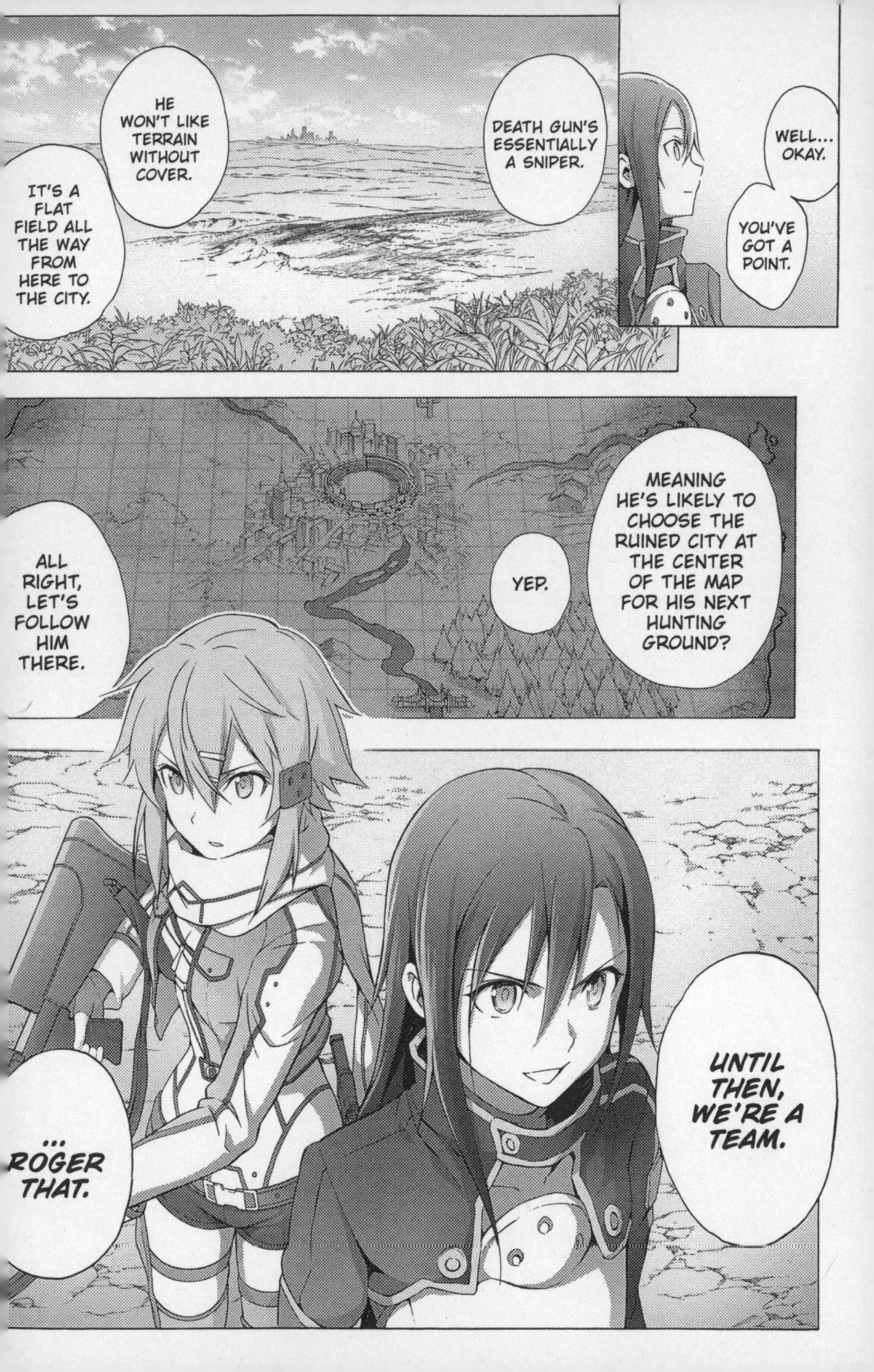

WELL... OKAY.
YOU'VE GOT A POINT.
DEATH GUN'S ESSENTIALLY A SNIPER.
HE WON'T LIKE TERRAIN WITHOUT COVER.
IT'S A FLAT FIELD ALL THE WAY FROM HERE TO THE CITY.
MEANING HE'S LIKELY TO CHOOSE THE RUINED CITY AT THE CENTER OF THE MAP FOR HIS NEXT HUNTING GROUND?
YEP.
ALL RIGHT, LET'S FOLLOW HIM THERE.
UNTIL THEN, WE'RE A TEAM.
...ROGER THAT.

SWORD ART ONLINE
phantom bullet

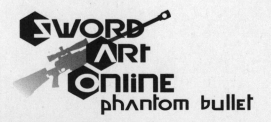

SWORD ART ONLINE
phantom bullet

check point! 003

PALE RIDER'S ARMALITE AR-17: ITEM

PALE RIDER DEFEATED DYNE AND HIS FANCY RIFLE SKILLS WITH THIS AR-17 SHOTGUN. (A SHOTGUN SHOOTS A HIGHLY LETHAL SPRAY OF PROJECTILES IN ONE BLAST.) THIS IS A PARTICULARLY LIGHT SHOTGUN, BUT IT ONLY HOLDS TWO SHELLS AT ONCE, AND BECAUSE SHOTGUNS SPRAY THEIR BULLETS, THEY ARE TYPICALLY ONLY EFFECTIVE AT CLOSE RANGE. THEREFORE, IT'S PROBABLY NOT HIGHLY VALUED IN GGO. PALE RIDER WAS ABLE TO USE IT EFFECTIVELY THANKS TO HIS EXCELLENT ACROBATICS AND AGILITY.

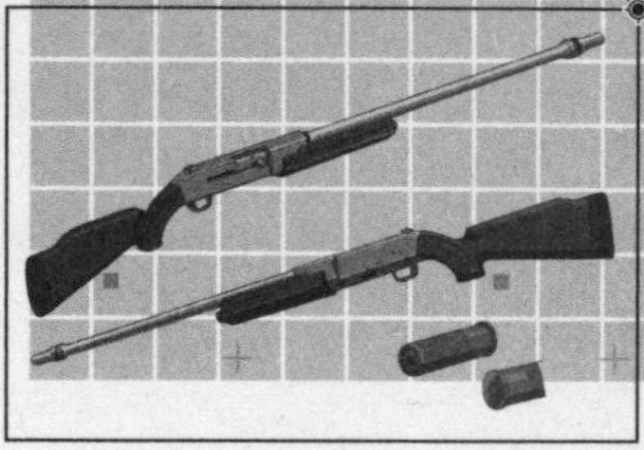

DEATH GUN'S SILENT ASSASSIN (L115A3): ITEM

A SNIPER RIFLE DEVELOPED AND MANUFACTURED BY ACCURACY INTERNATIONAL IN ENGLAND. IN THE STORY, IT'S USED TO FIRE STUN ROUNDS, BUT IN REALITY, THEY FIRE MASSIVE .338 LAPUA MAGNUM CARTRIDGES AND CAN ACCURATELY HIT TARGETS OVER A KILOMETER AWAY. AS THE "SILENT" NAME SUGGESTS, THEY CAN BE FITTED WITH A LARGE SILENCER TO PREVENT THE GUNSHOT BEING HEARD PAST A CERTAIN DISTANCE. THIS GUN IS TRULY WORTHY OF ITS NAME.

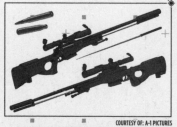

COURTESY OF: A-1 PICTURES
©2014 REKI KAWAHARA/KADOKAWA ASCII MEDIA WORKS/SAO II PROJECT

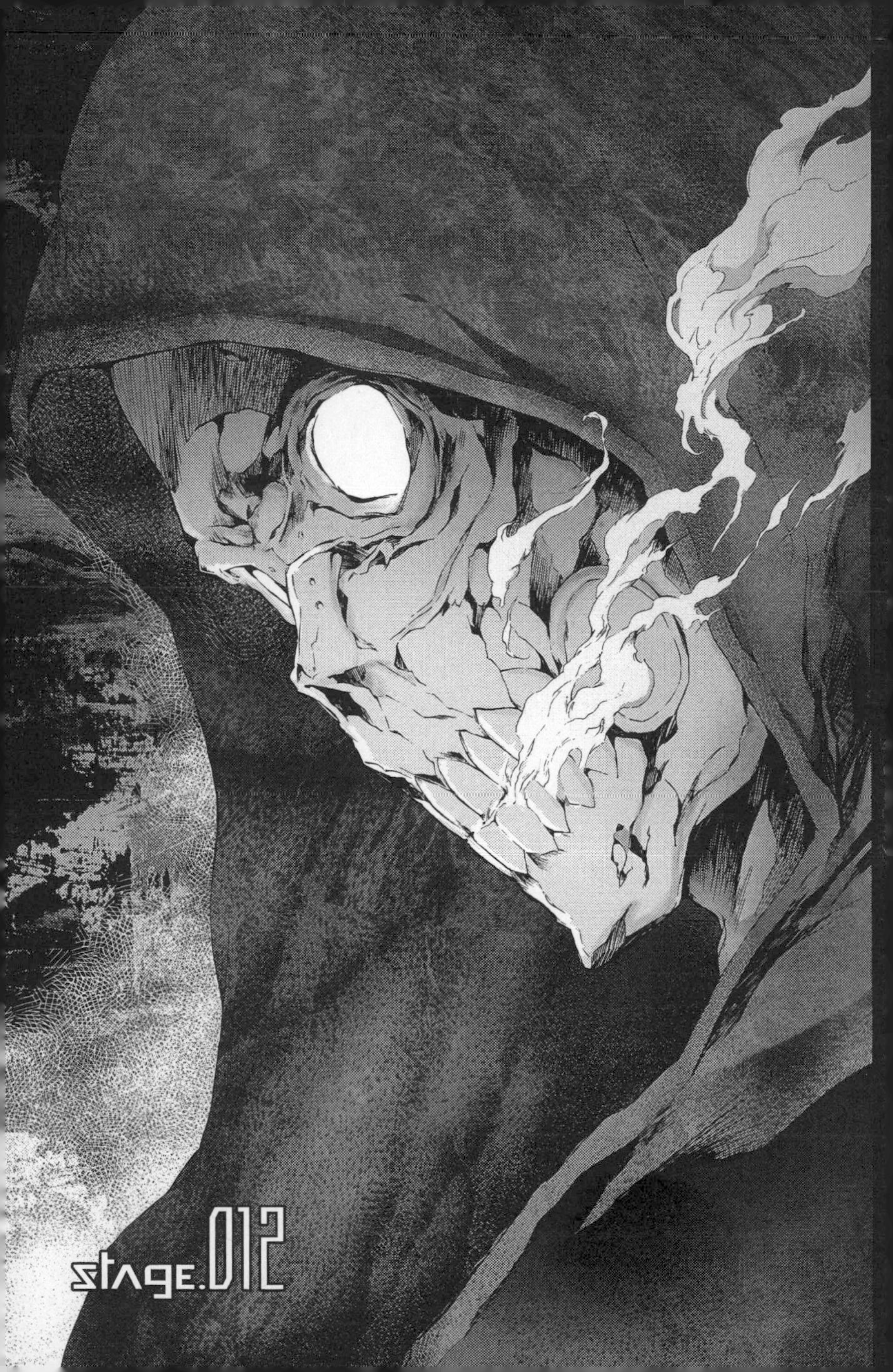
stage.012

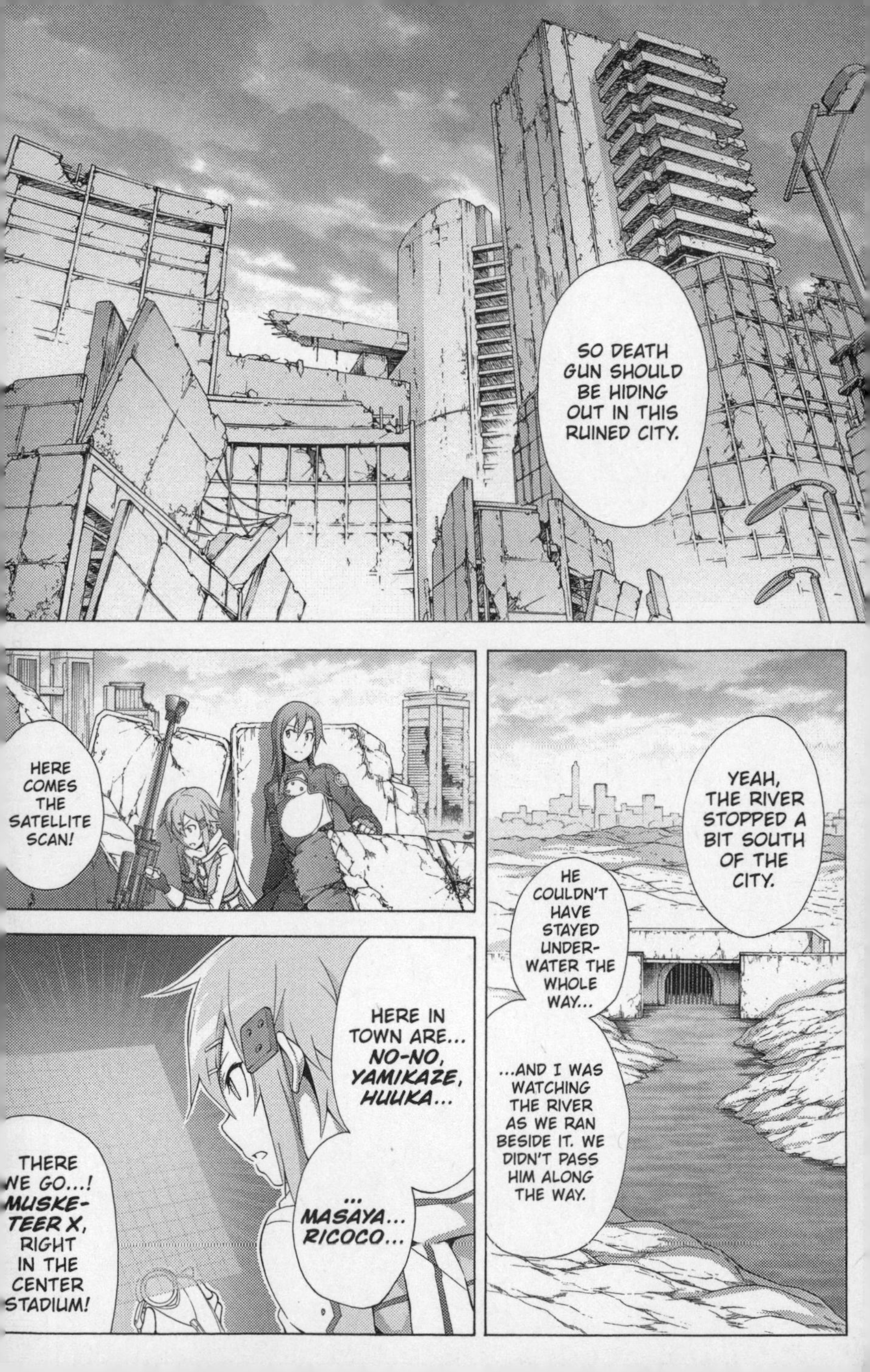
SO DEATH GUN SHOULD BE HIDING OUT IN THIS RUINED CITY.
YEAH, THE RIVER STOPPED A BIT SOUTH OF THE CITY.
HE COULDN'T HAVE STAYED UNDER-WATER THE WHOLE WAY...
...AND I WAS WATCHING THE RIVER AS WE RAN BESIDE IT. WE DIDN'T PASS HIM ALONG THE WAY.
HERE COMES THE SATELLITE SCAN!
HERE IN TOWN ARE... ***NO-NO, YAMIKAZE, HUUKA...***
...MASAYA... RICOCO...
THERE WE GO...! ***MUSKETEER X,*** RIGHT IN THE CENTER STADIUM!

OF THE NEW FACES, PALE RIDER'S ALREADY DOWN, AND I DON'T SEE "STEVEN" HERE.

...THAT WOULD MEAN MUSKETEER X HAS TO BE DEATH GUN!

WELL...A MUSKET IS A TYPE OF GUN. AND IF YOU TURN THE X DIAGONALLY...

...IT BECOMES A CROSS, LIKE THE SIGN HE MADE...

OR IS THAT TOO CONVENIENT?

...SAME.

...

I DUNNO, I THINK MOST MMO CHARACTER NAMES ARE CLICHÉ.

MINE'S JUST A PLAY ON MY REAL NAME. WHAT ABOUT YOU?

LET'S GET TO THE STADIUM.

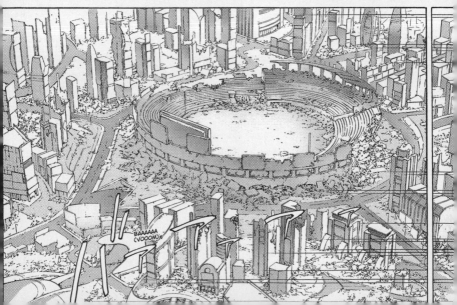

BAAAAAA
(VOOOM)

ACTIVATE HAWKEYE SKILL!

BUN
(VMM)

FOUND
HIM.

PI
(BEEP)

PI
(BEEP)

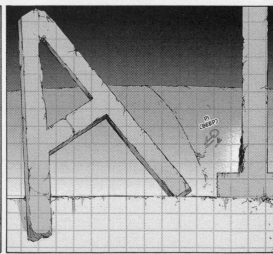

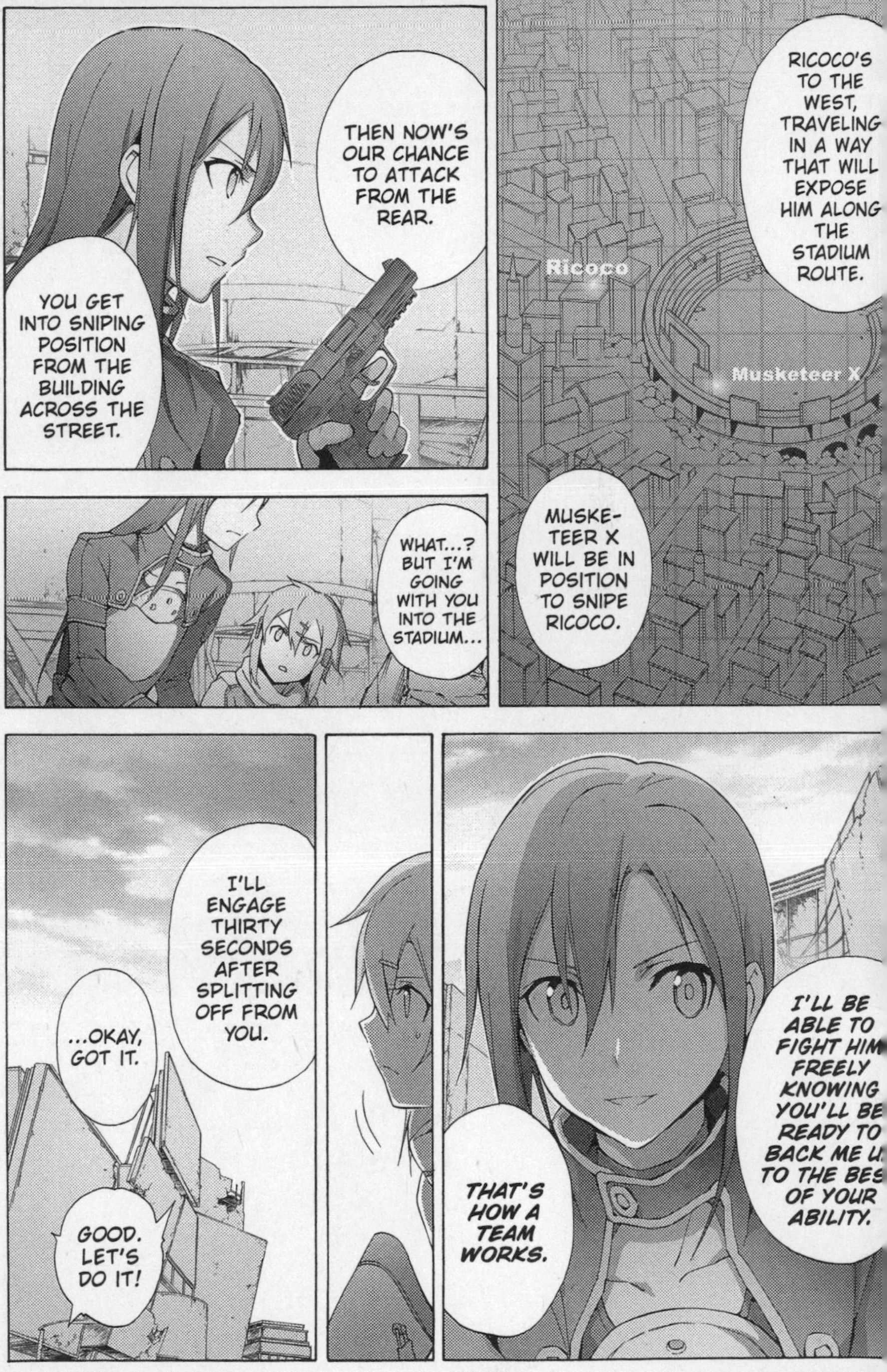
RICOCO'S TO THE WEST, TRAVELING IN A WAY THAT WILL EXPOSE HIM ALONG THE STADIUM ROUTE.
Ricoco
Musketeer X
MUSKE-TEER X WILL BE IN POSITION TO SNIPE RICOCO.
THEN NOW'S OUR CHANCE TO ATTACK FROM THE REAR.
YOU GET INTO SNIPING POSITION FROM THE BUILDING ACROSS THE STREET.
WHAT...? BUT I'M GOING WITH YOU INTO THE STADIUM...
I'LL BE ABLE TO FIGHT HIM FREELY KNOWING YOU'LL BE READY TO BACK ME U TO THE BES OF YOUR ABILITY.
THAT'S HOW A TEAM WORKS.
I'LL ENGAGE THIRTY SECONDS AFTER SPLITTING OFF FROM YOU.
...OKAY, GOT IT.
GOOD. LET'S DO IT!

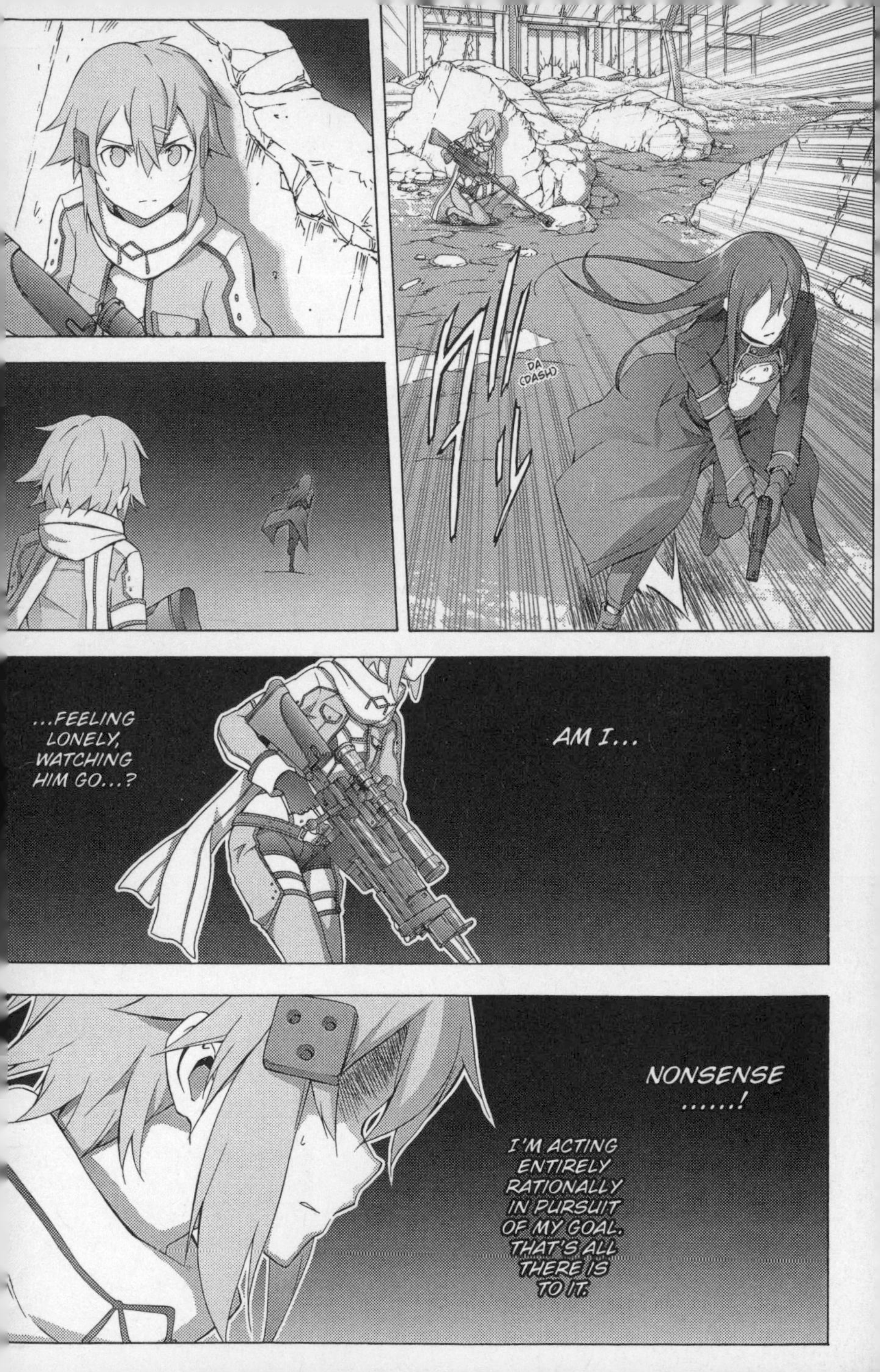
DA (DASH)
AM I...
...FEELING LONELY, WATCHING HIM GO...?
NONSENSE ......!
I'M ACTING ENTIRELY RATIONALLY IN PURSUIT OF MY GOAL. THAT'S ALL THERE IS TO IT.

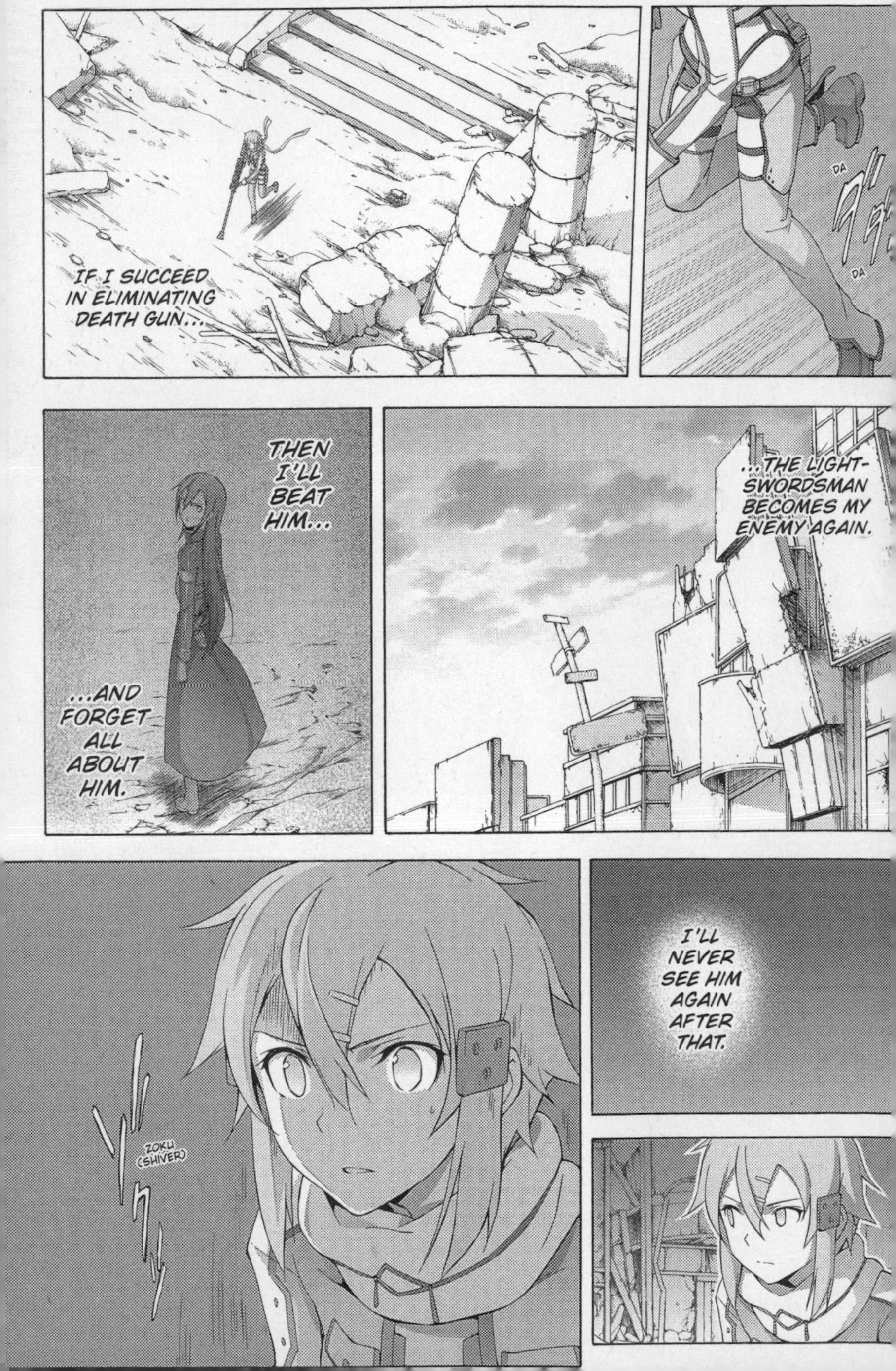
DA
DA
IF I SUCCEED IN ELIMINATING DEATH GUN...
...THE LIGHT-SWORDSMAN BECOMES MY ENEMY AGAIN.
THEN I'LL BEAT HIM...
...AND FORGET ALL ABOUT HIM.
I'LL NEVER SEE HIM AGAIN AFTER THAT.
ZOKU (SHIVER)

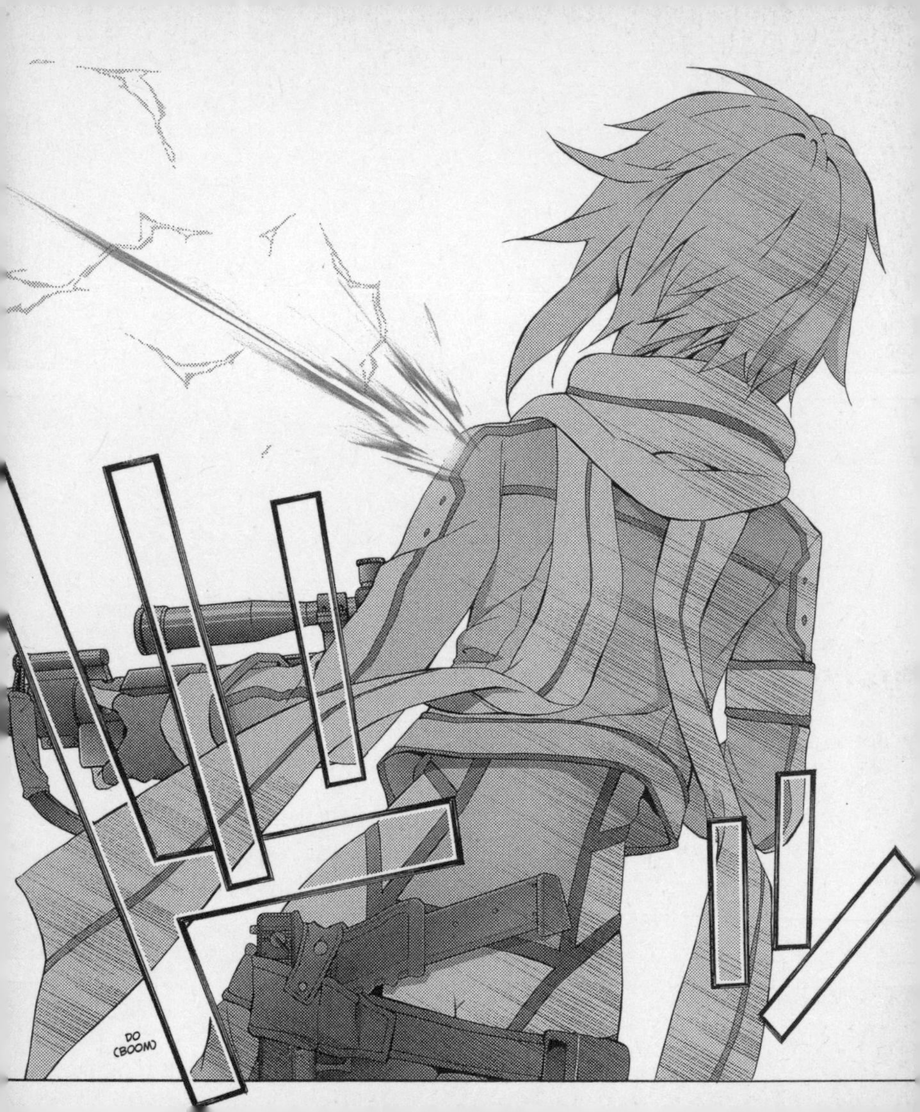
DO
(BOOM)

HUH?

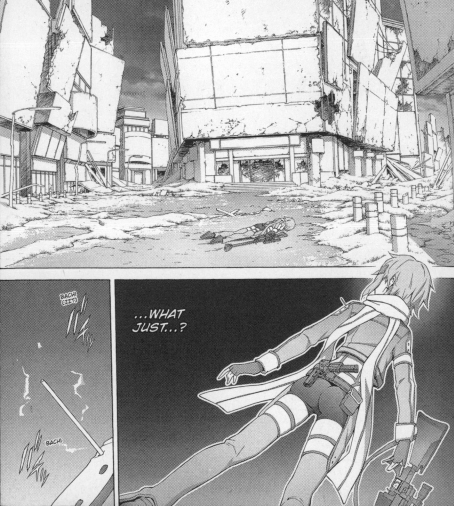

BACHI
(ZZT)

...WHAT
JUST...?

BACHI!

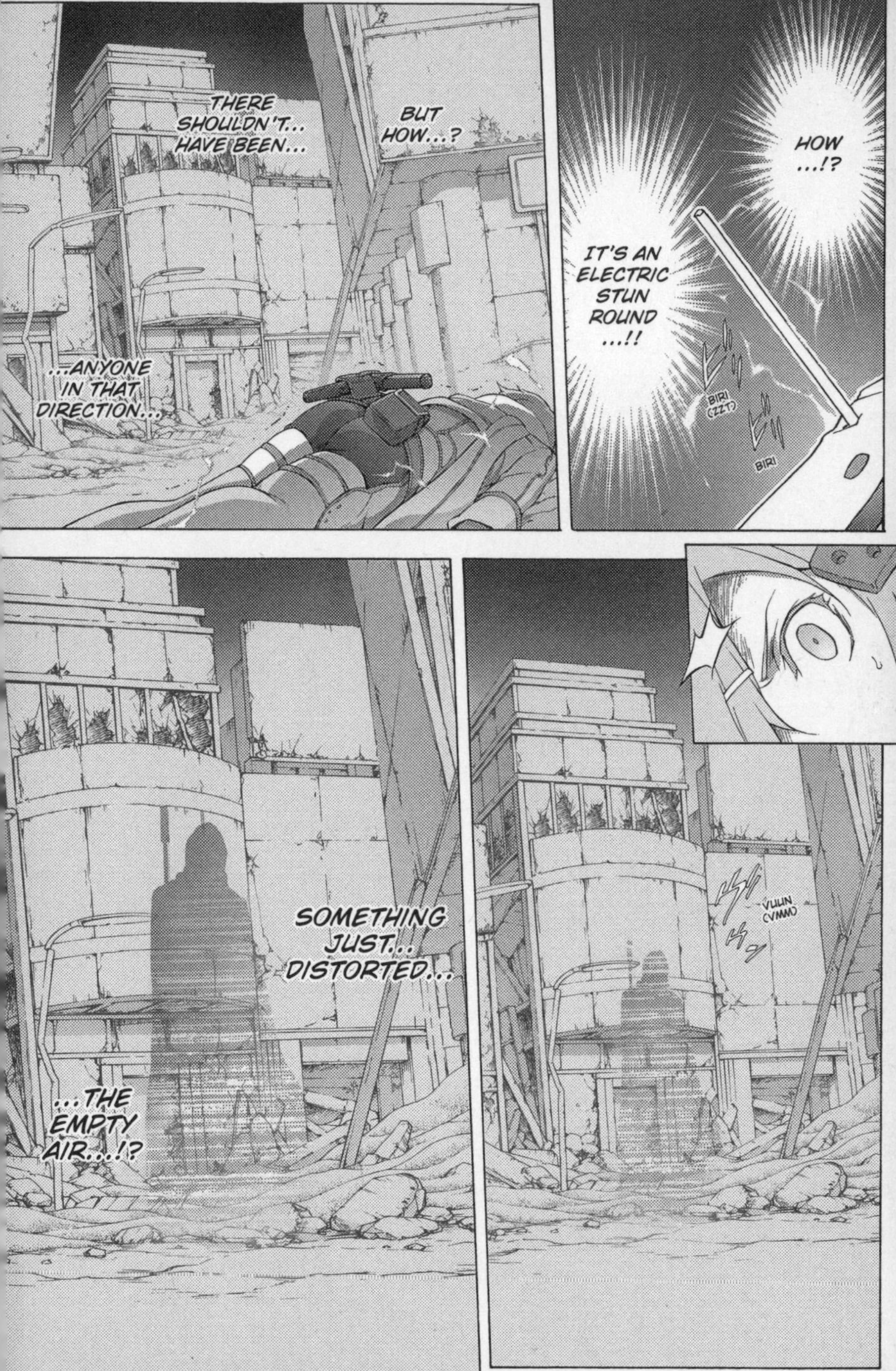
HOW ...!?
IT'S AN ELECTRIC STUN ROUND ...!!
BIRI (ZZT)
BIRI
BUT HOW...?
THERE SHOULDN'T... HAVE BEEN...
...ANYONE IN THAT DIRECTION...
VUUN (VMM)
SOMETHING JUST... DISTORTED...
...THE EMPTY AIR...!?

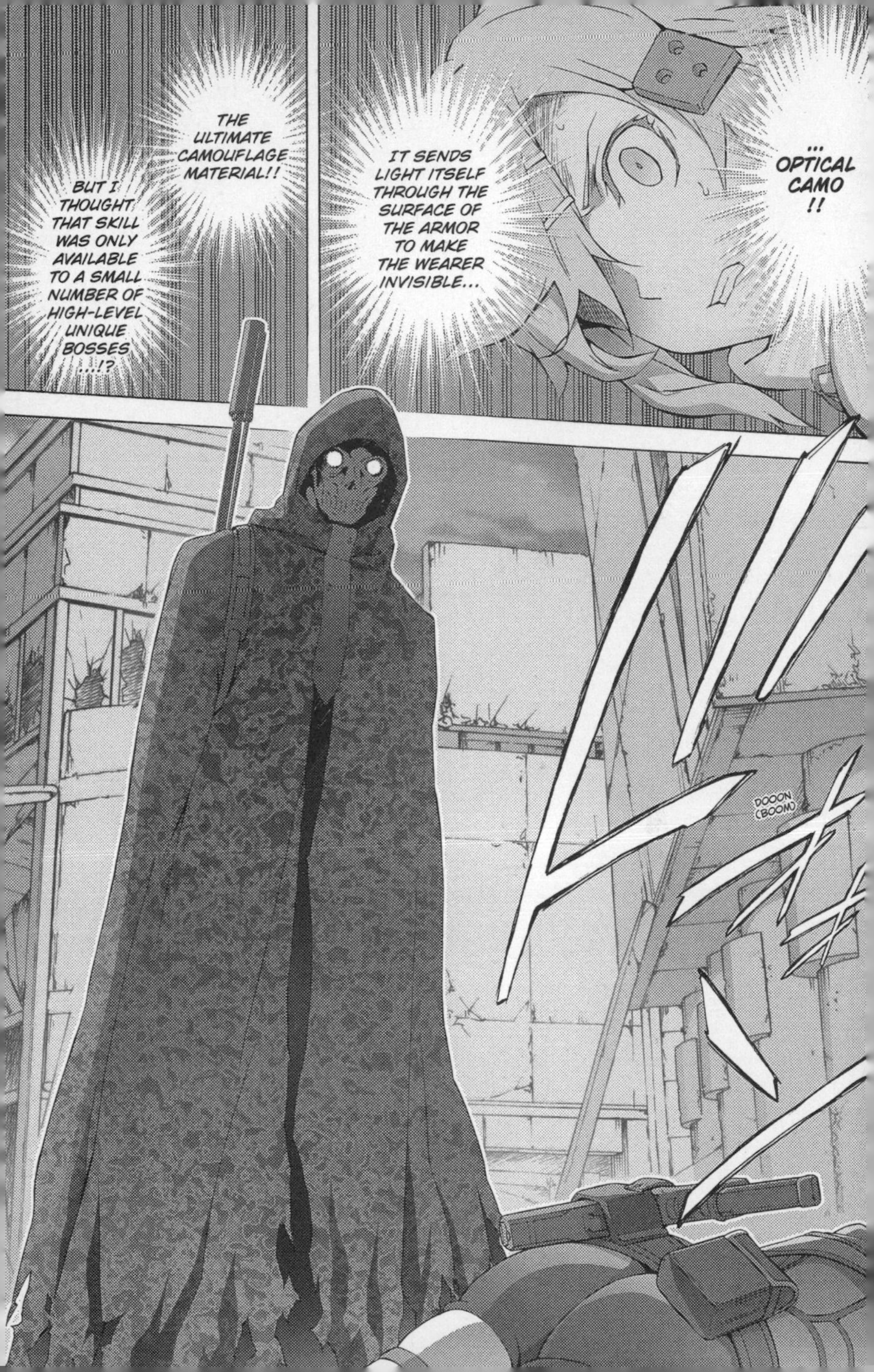
...OPTICAL CAMO!!
IT SENDS LIGHT ITSELF THROUGH THE SURFACE OF THE ARMOR TO MAKE THE WEARER INVISIBLE...
THE ULTIMATE CAMOUFLAGE MATERIAL!!
BUT I THOUGHT THAT SKILL WAS ONLY AVAILABLE TO A SMALL NUMBER OF HIGH-LEVEL UNIQUE BOSSES...!?
DOOON (BOOM)

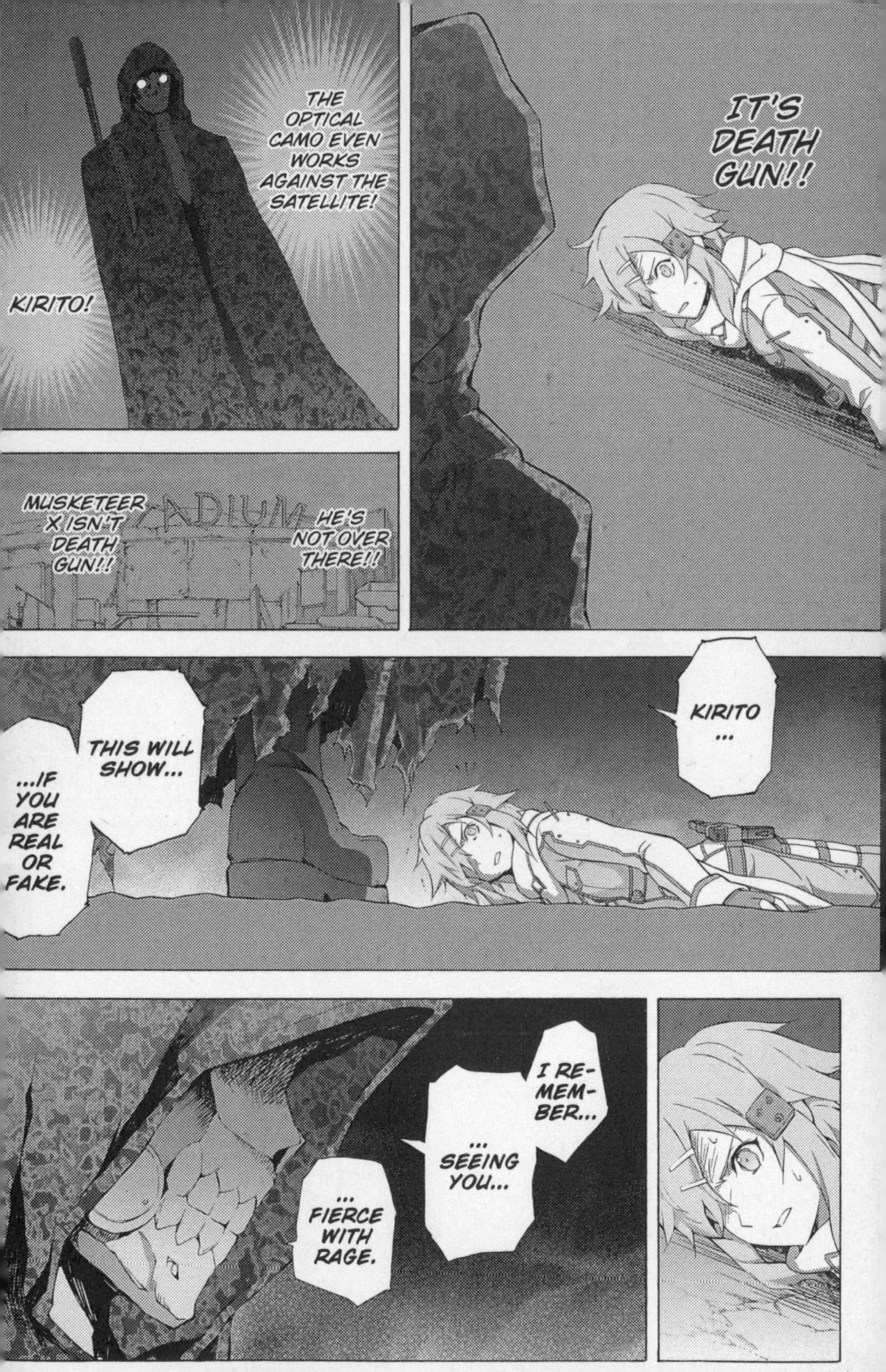
IT'S DEATH GUN!!
THE OPTICAL CAMO EVEN WORKS AGAINST THE SATELLITE!
KIRITO!
MUSKETEER X ISN'T DEATH GUN!!
HE'S NOT OVER THERE!!
KIRITO ...
THIS WILL SHOW...
...IF YOU ARE REAL OR FAKE.
I RE-MEM-BER...
...SEEING YOU...
...FIERCE WITH RAGE.

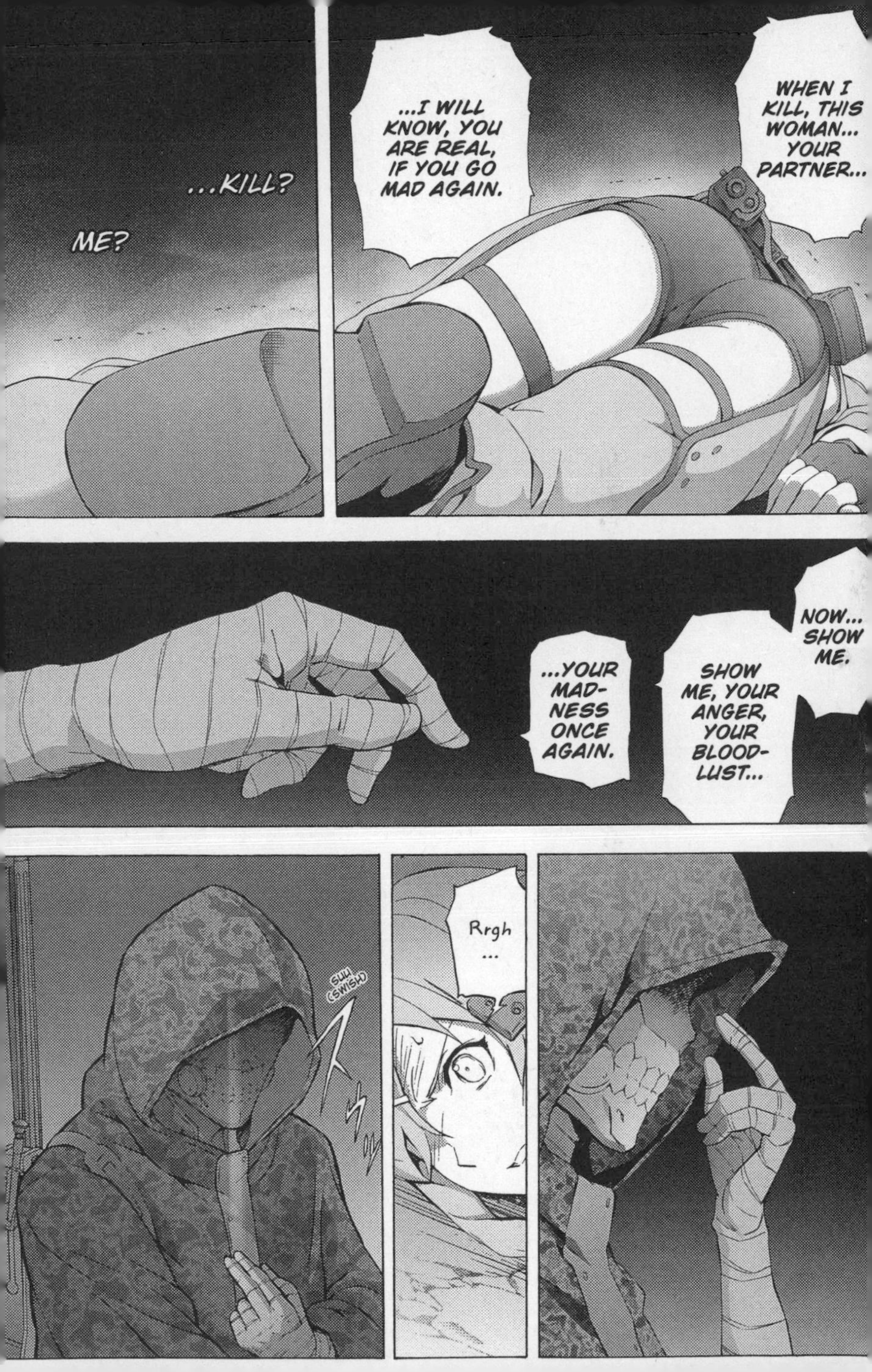
WHEN I KILL, THIS WOMAN... YOUR PARTNER...
...I WILL KNOW, YOU ARE REAL, IF YOU GO MAD AGAIN.
...KILL?
ME?
NOW... SHOW ME.
SHOW ME, YOUR ANGER, YOUR BLOOD-LUST...
...YOUR MAD-NESS ONCE AGAIN.
Rrgh ...
SHU (SWISH)

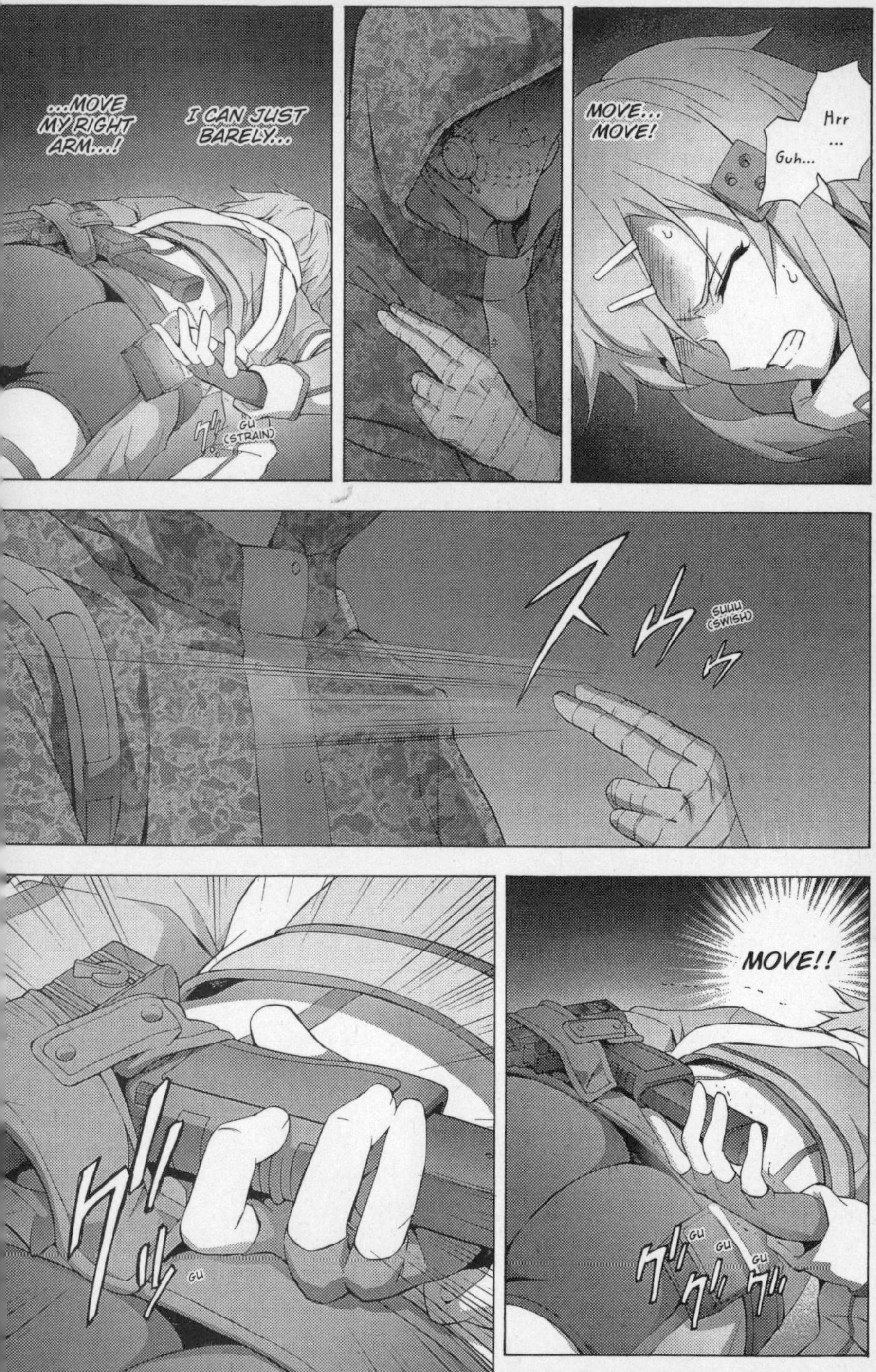
MOVE... MOVE!
Hrr ... Guh...
I CAN JUST BARELY...
...MOVE MY RIGHT ARM...!
GU (STRAIN)
SUUU (SWISH)
MOVE!!
GU
GU
GU
GU

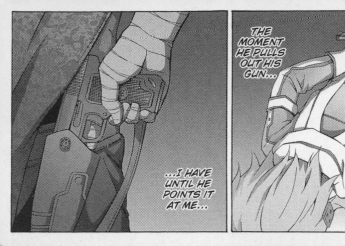

THE MOMENT HE PULLS OUT HIS GUN...

...I HAVE UNTIL HE POINTS IT AT ME...

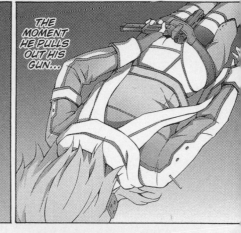

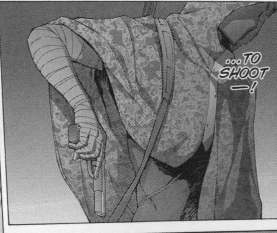

...TO SHOOT —!

!!!

BA (WHOOSH)

NOW!!

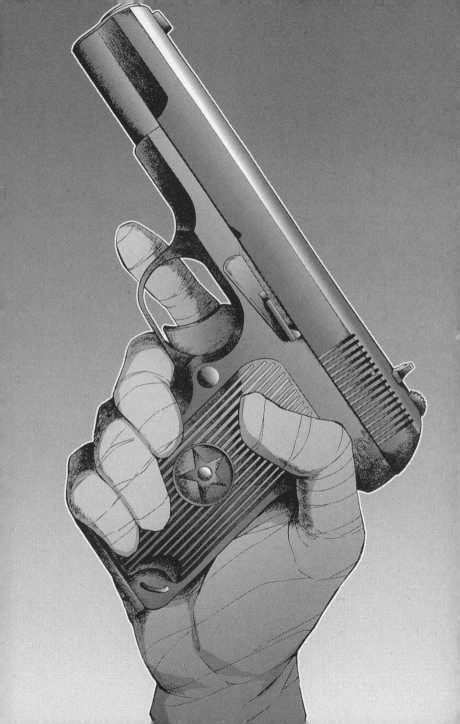

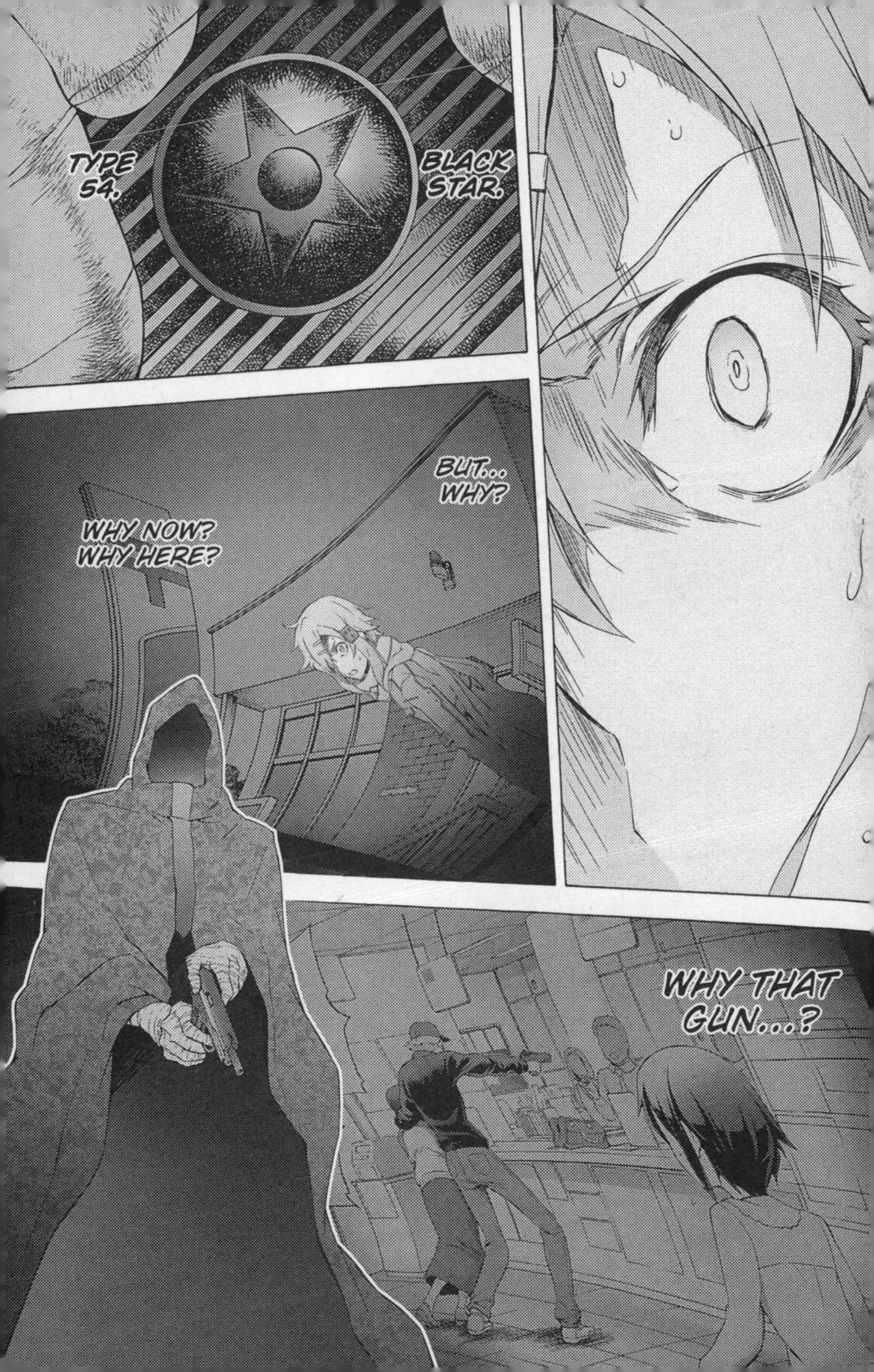
BLACK STAR.
TYPE 54.
BUT... WHY?
WHY NOW? WHY HERE?
WHY THAT GUN...?

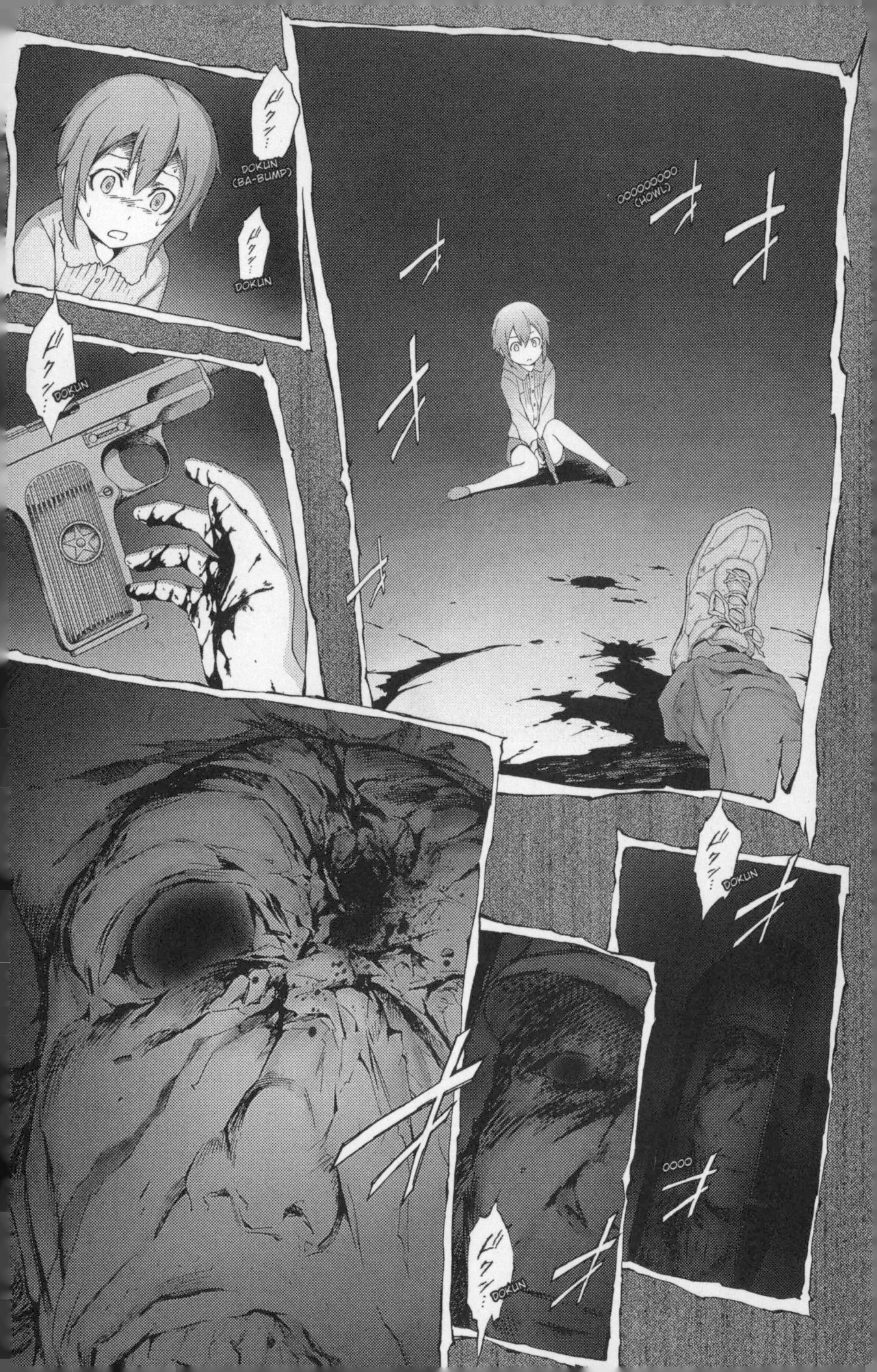
OOOOOOOOO (HOWL)
DOKUN (BA-BUMP)
DOKUN
DOKUN
DOKUN
OOOO
DOKUN

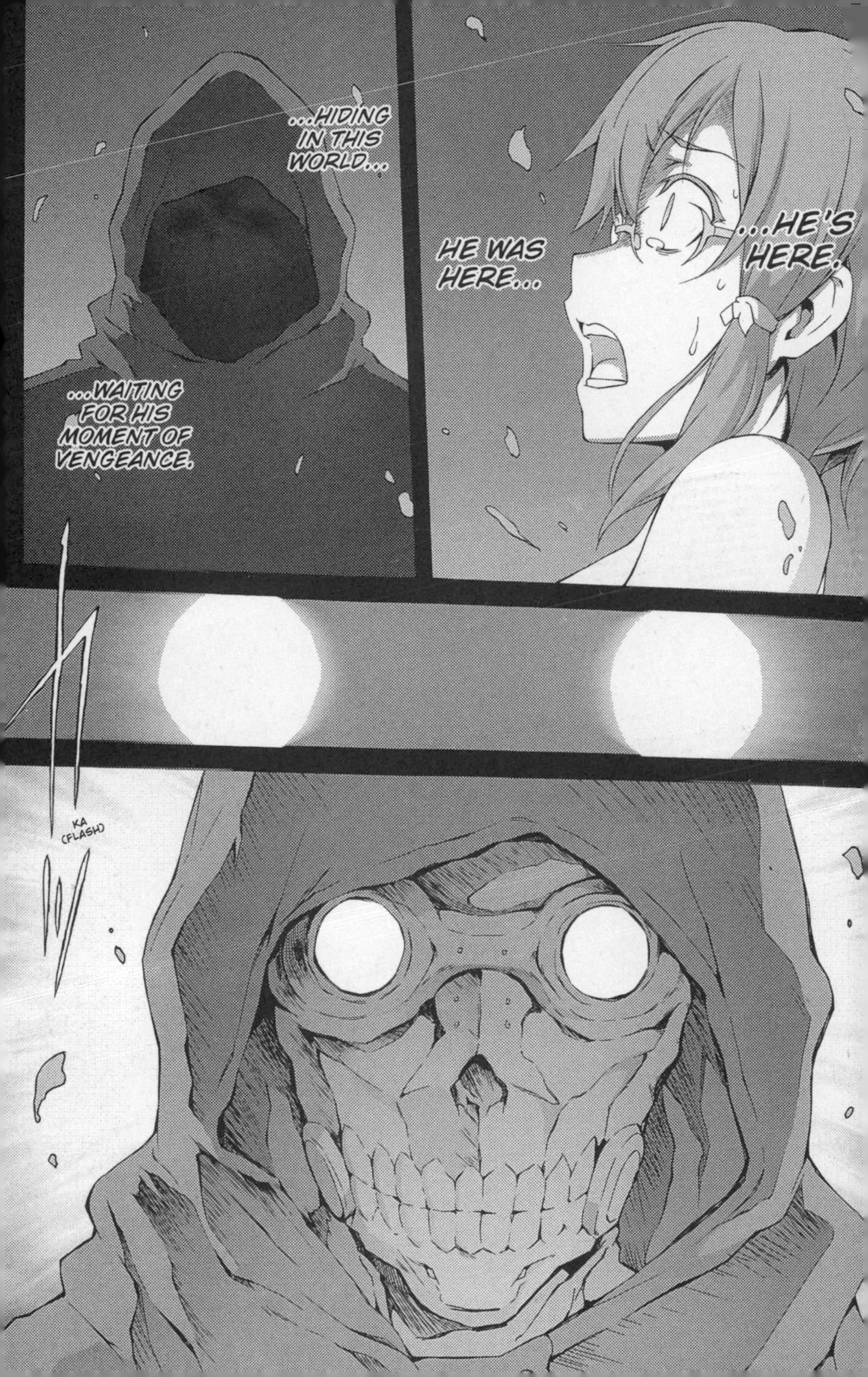
...HE'S HERE.
HE WAS HERE...
...HIDING IN THIS WORLD...
...WAITING FOR HIS MOMENT OF VENGEANCE.
KA (FLASH)

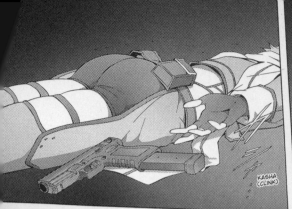

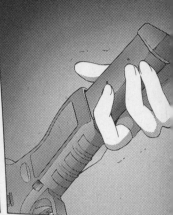

KASHA
(CLINK)

THERE
IS NO
ESCAPE.

THIS IS
FATE.

IT'S
POINTLESS.

EVERYTHING
WAS
POINTLESS.

IT WAS
FUTILE
TRYING TO
SEVER
MYSELF
FROM MY
PAST.

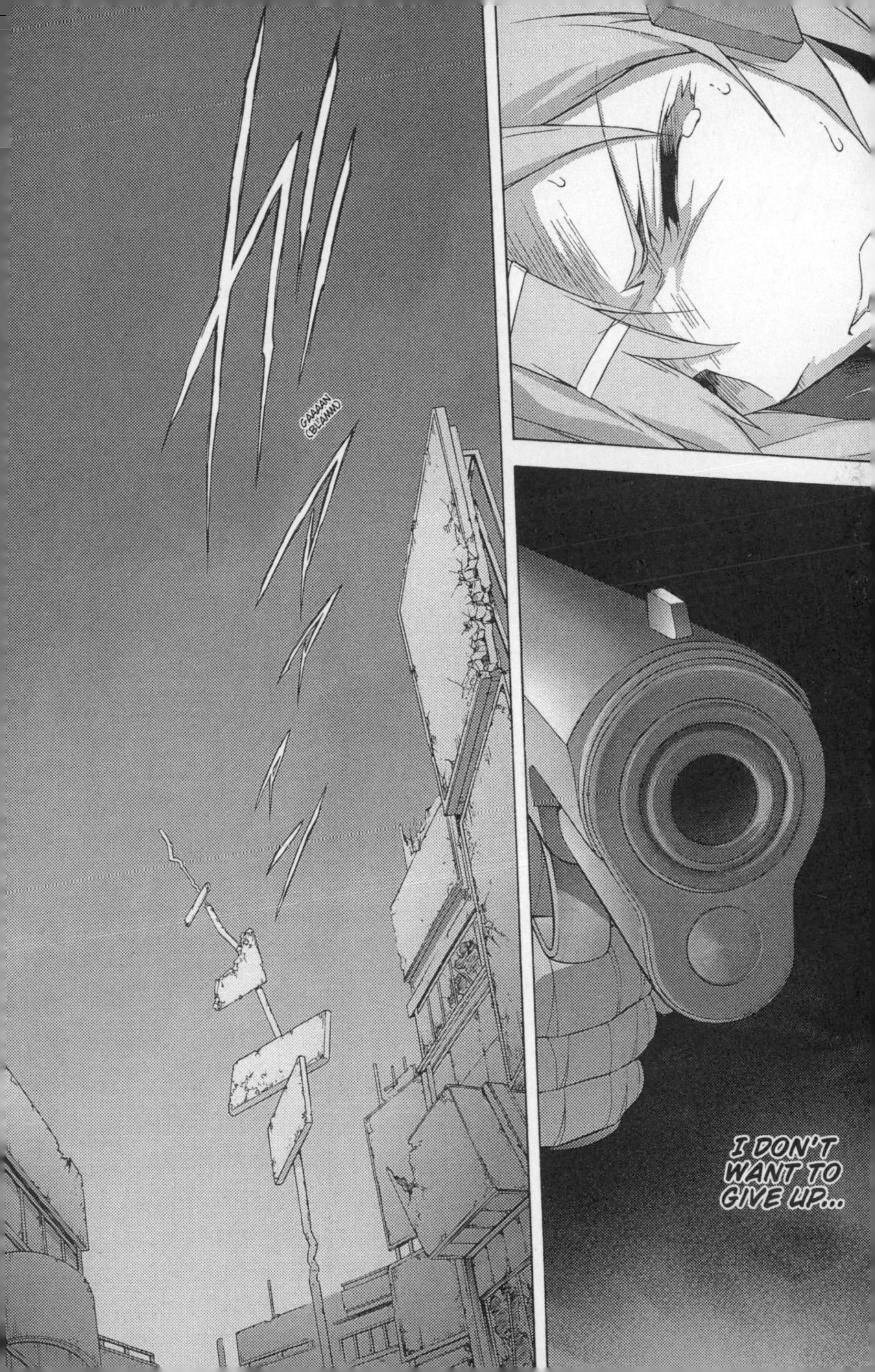
I DON'T WANT TO GIVE UP...
GAAAAN (BLAMM)

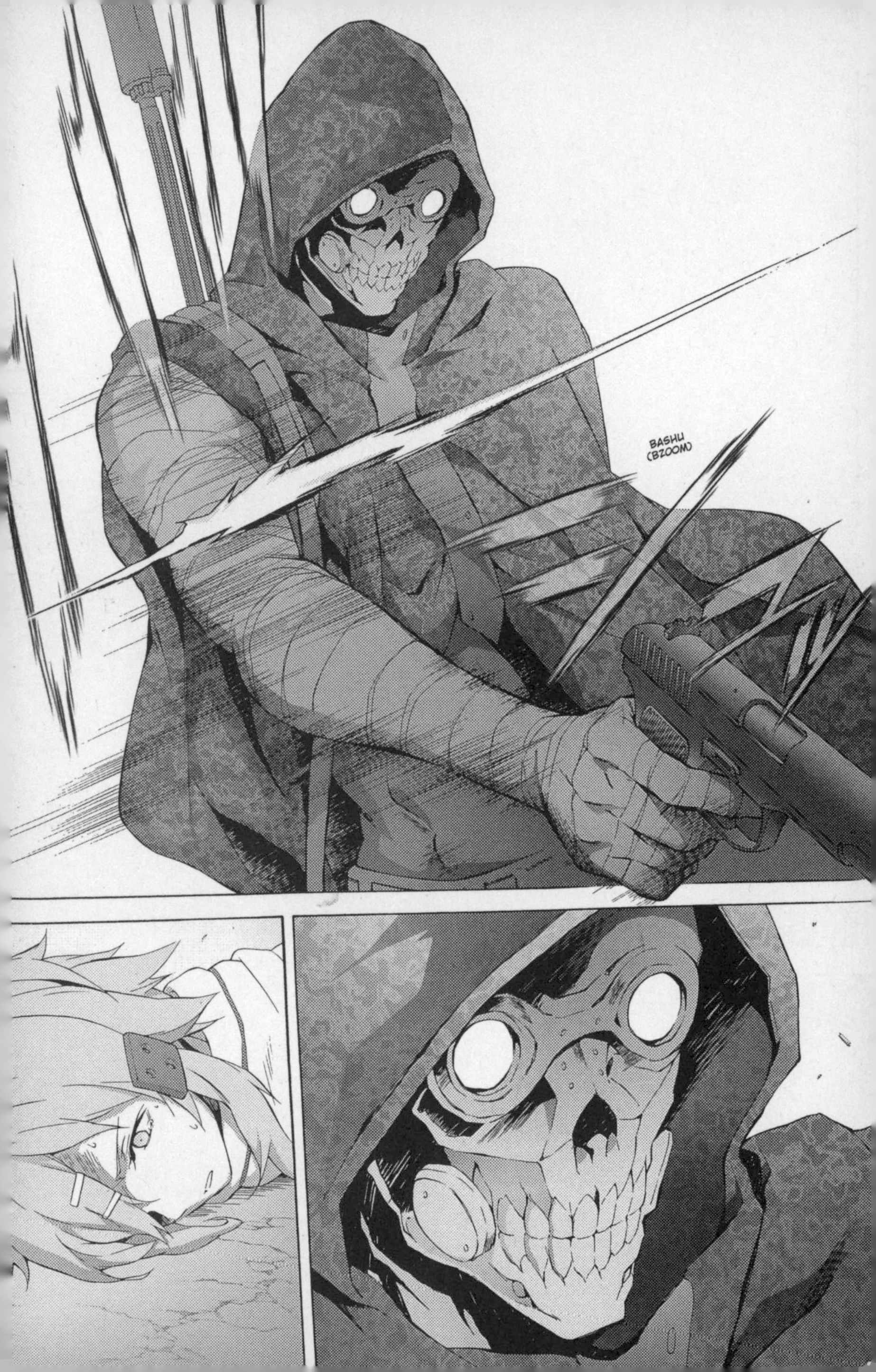
BASHU
(BZOOM)

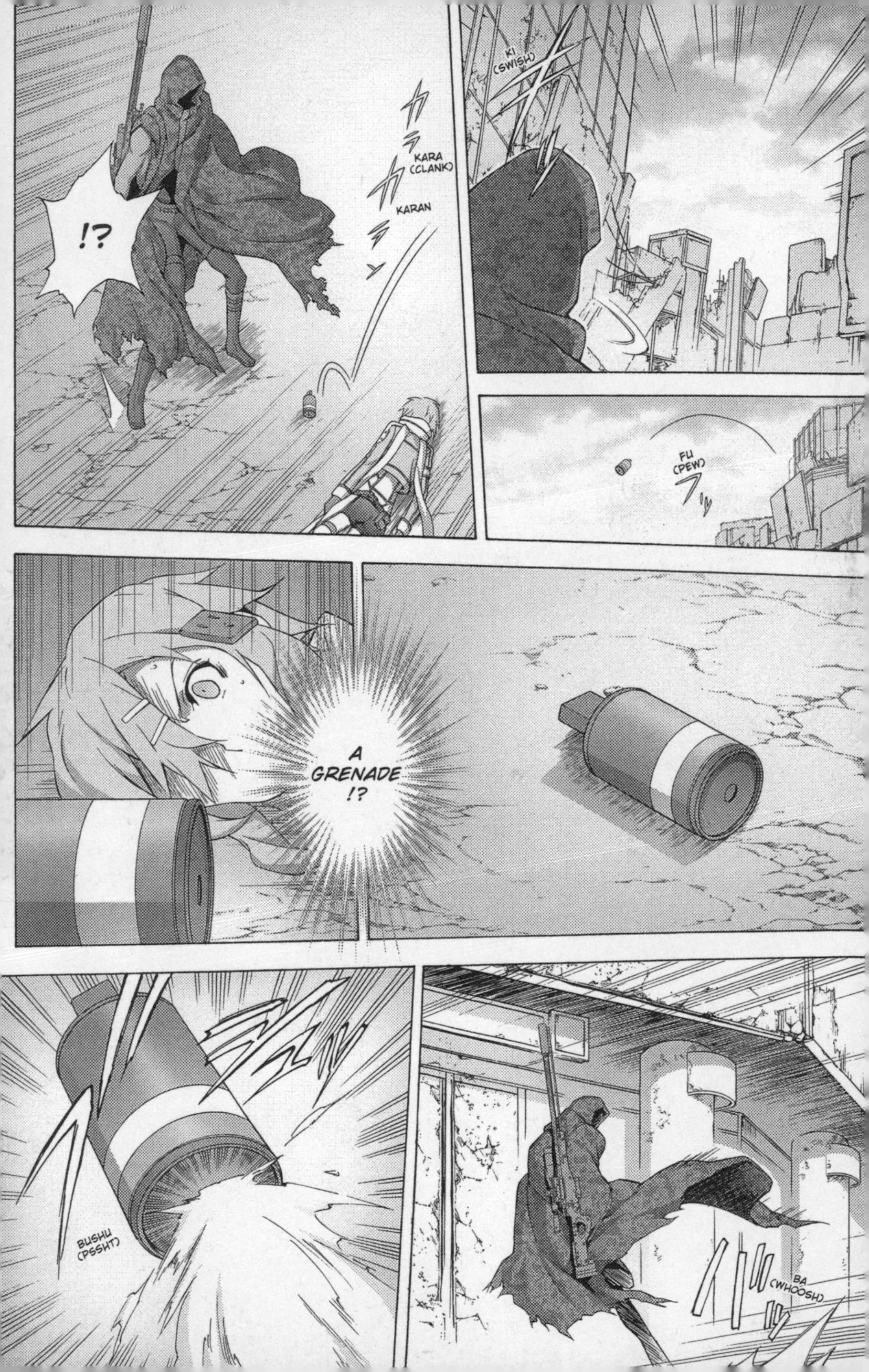
KI (SWISH)
FU (PEW)
KARA (CLANK)
KARAN
!?
A GRENADE !?
BA (WHOOSH)
BUSHU (PSSHT)

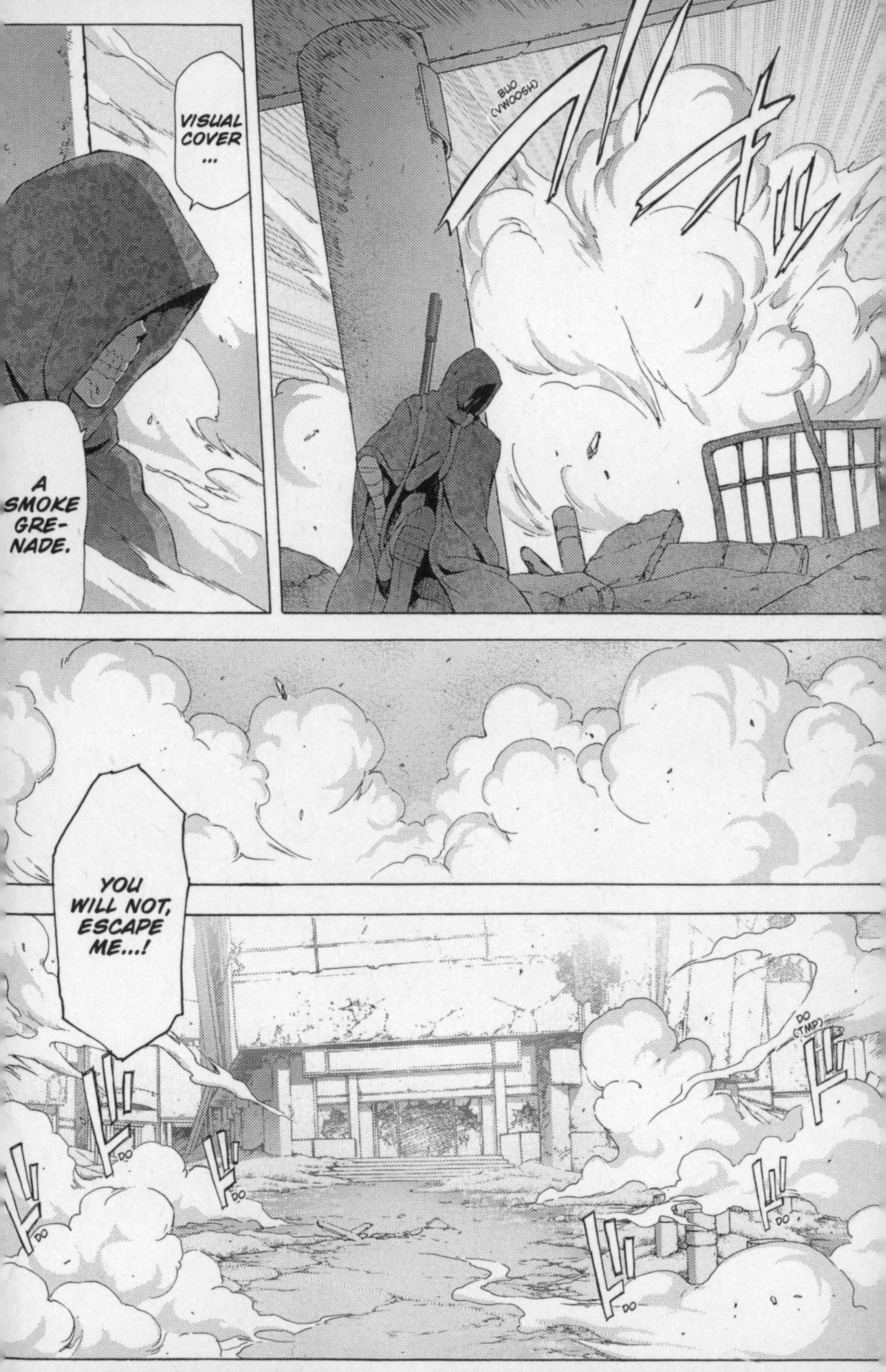
BUO (VWOOSH)
VISUAL COVER ...
A SMOKE GRE-NADE.
YOU WILL NOT, ESCAPE ME...!
DO (TMP)
DO
DO
DO
DO
DO

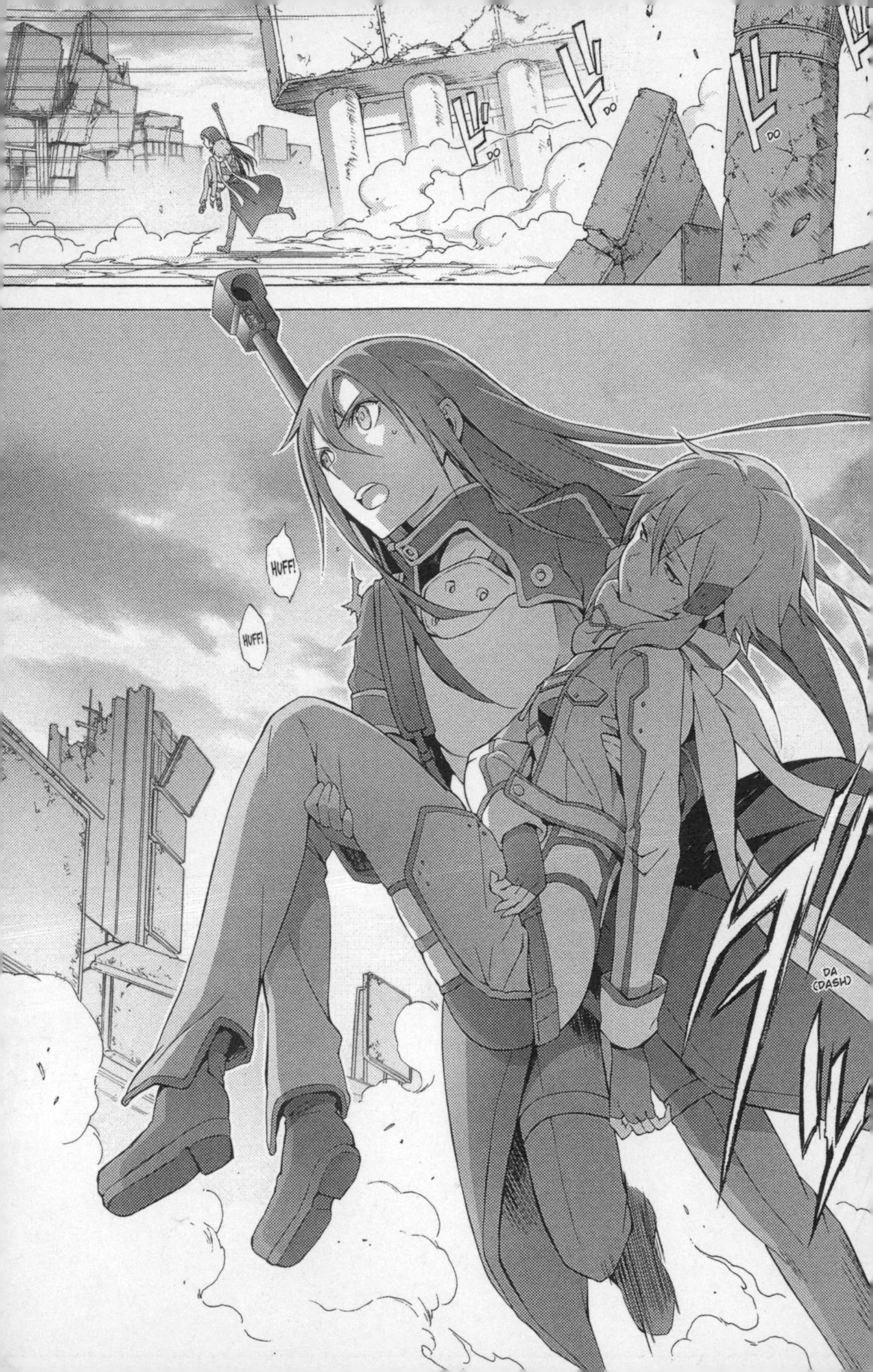
DO
DO
DO
DA (DASH)
HUFF!
HUFF!

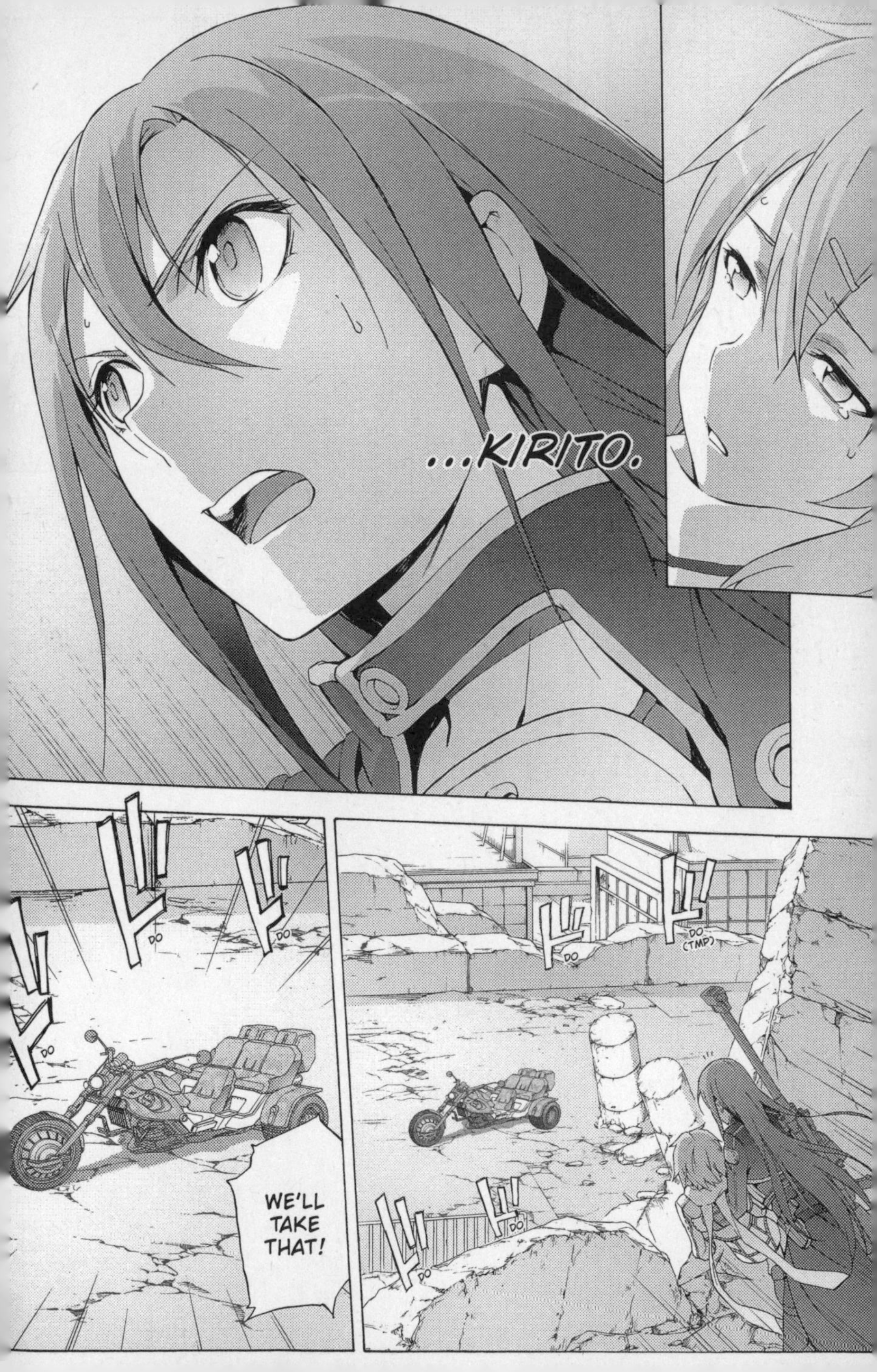
...KIRITO.
DO (TMP)
DO
DO
DO
DO
DO
DO
WE'LL TAKE THAT!

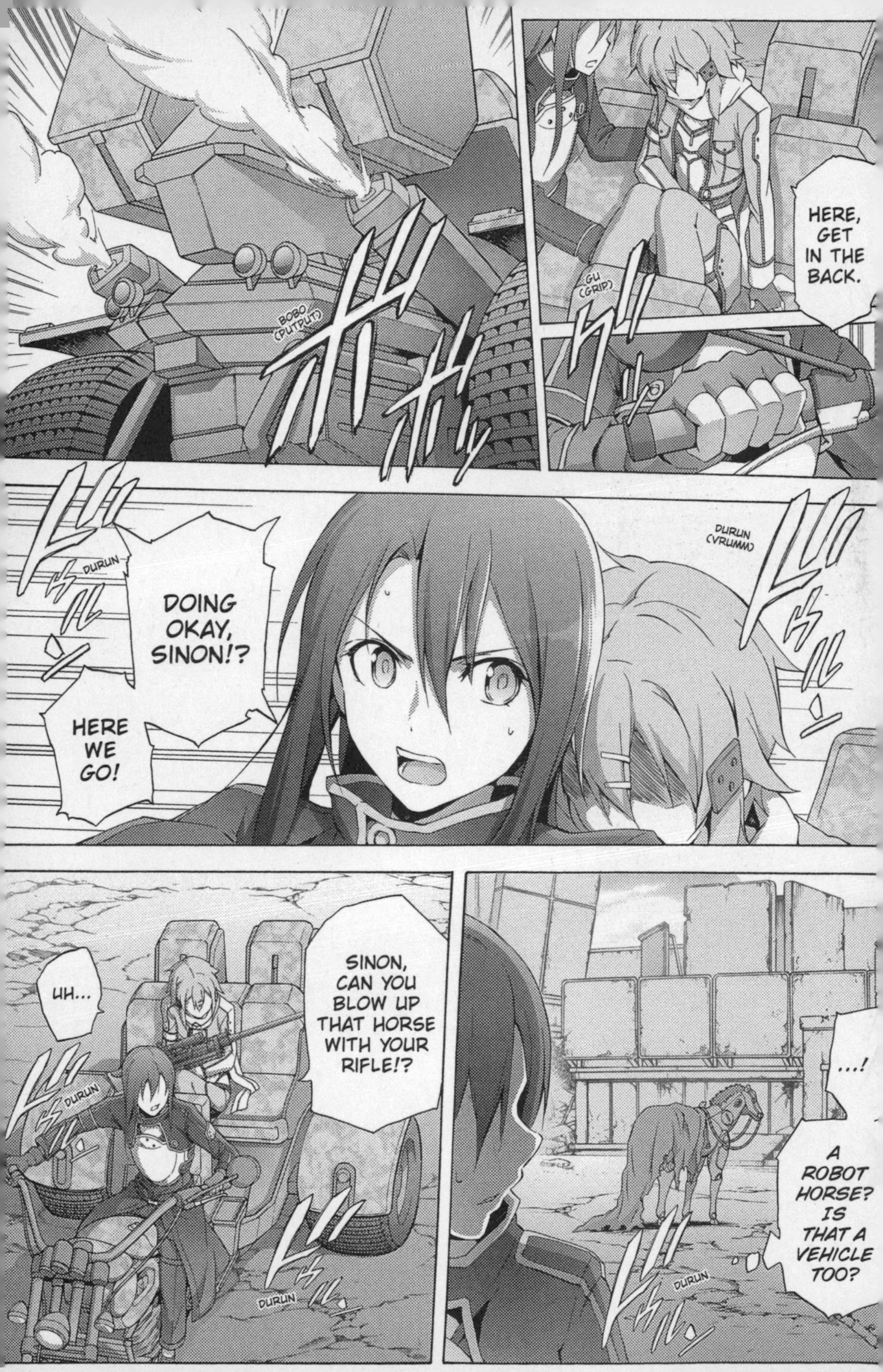
HERE, GET IN THE BACK.
GU (GRIP)
BOBO (PUTPUT)
DURUN (VRUMM)
DOING OKAY, SINON!?
DURUN
HERE WE GO!
...!
A ROBOT HORSE? IS THAT A VEHICLE TOO?
DURUN
SINON, CAN YOU BLOW UP THAT HORSE WITH YOUR RIFLE!?
UH...
DURUN
DURUN

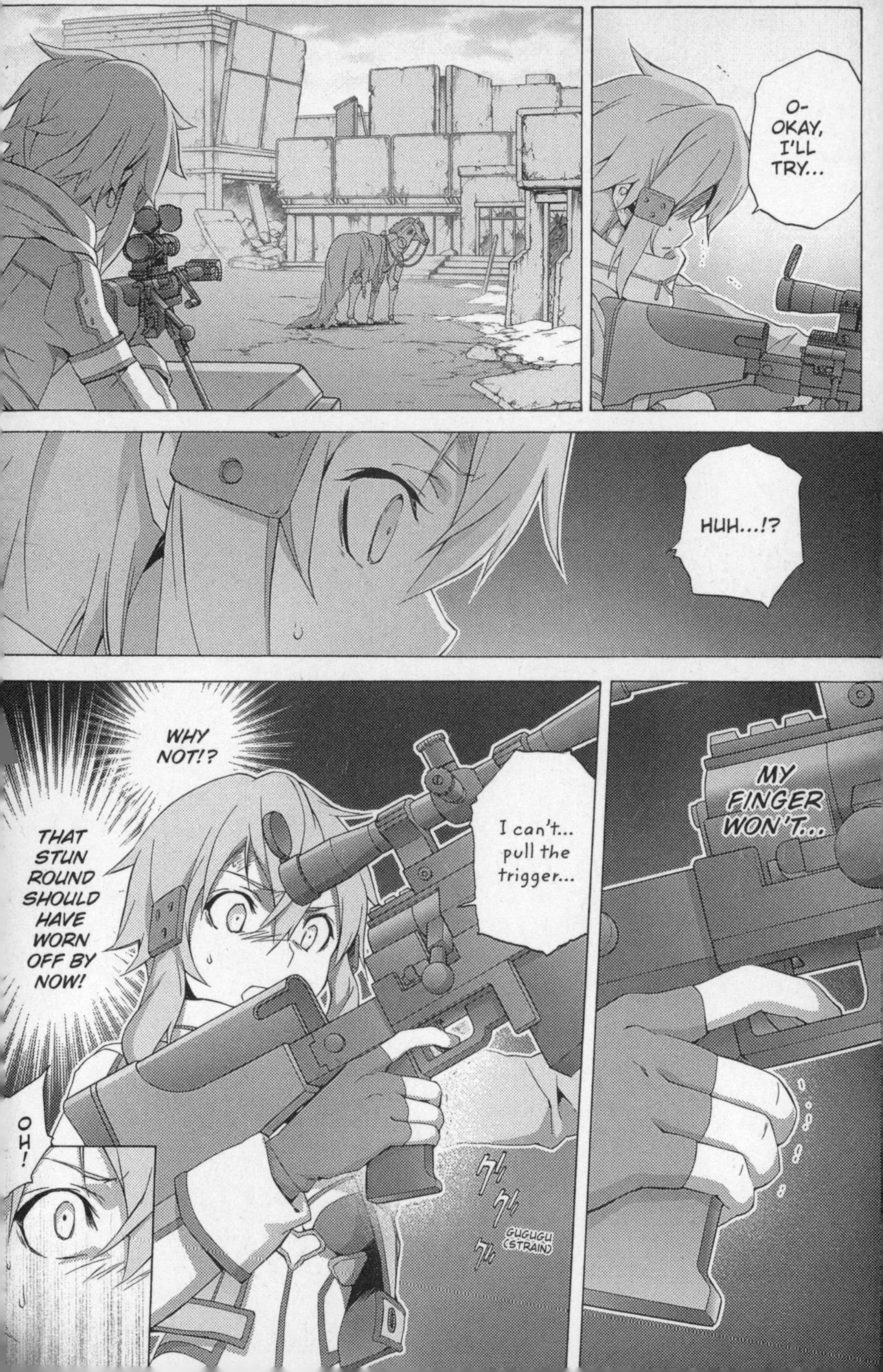
O-OKAY, I'LL TRY...
HUH...!?
MY FINGER WON'T...
I can't... pull the trigger...
WHY NOT!?
THAT STUN ROUND SHOULD HAVE WORN OFF BY NOW!
GUGUGU (STRAIN)
OH!

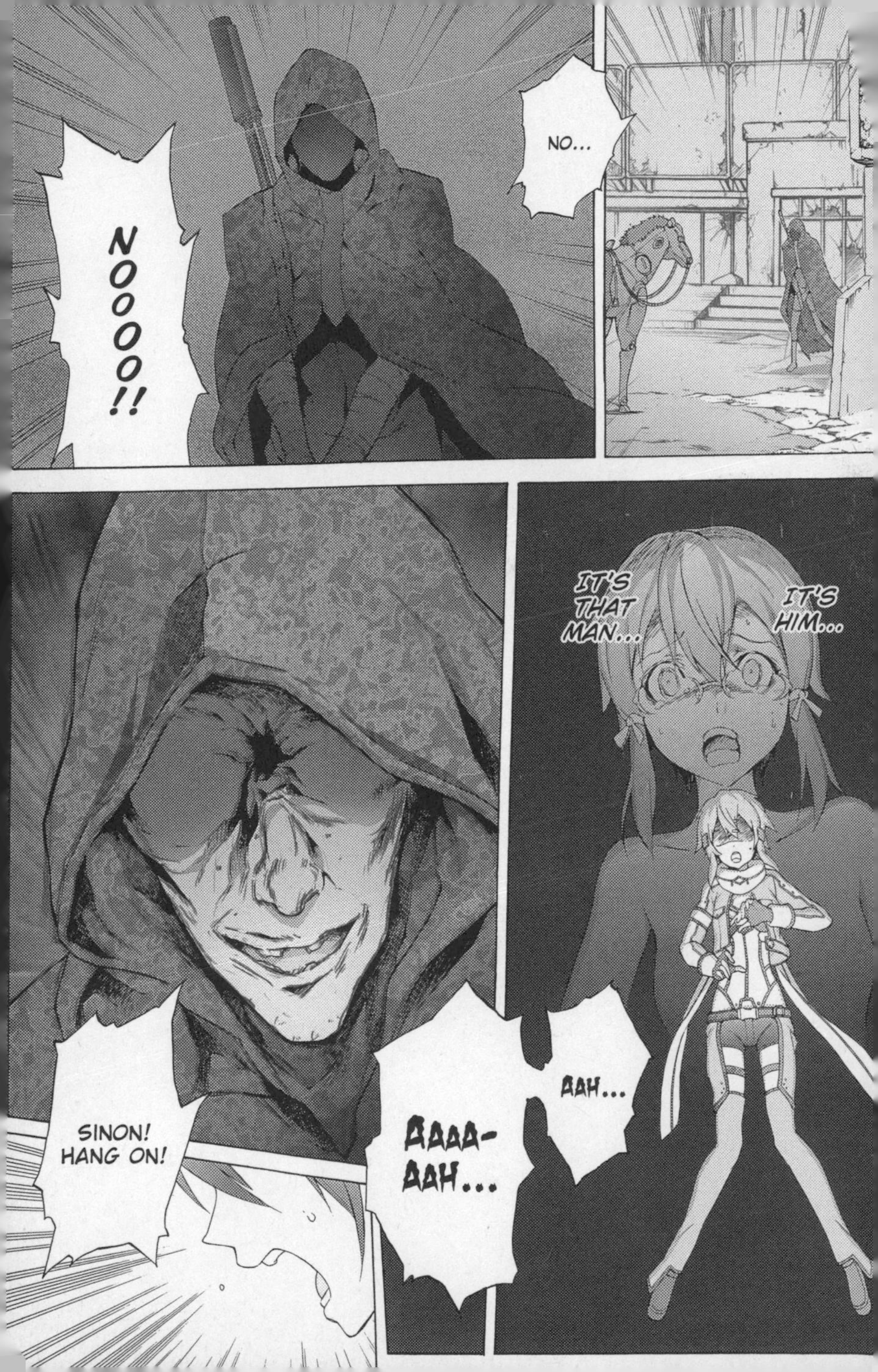
NO...
NOOOOO!!
IT'S HIM...
IT'S THAT MAN...
AAH...
AAAA-AAH...
SINON! HANG ON!

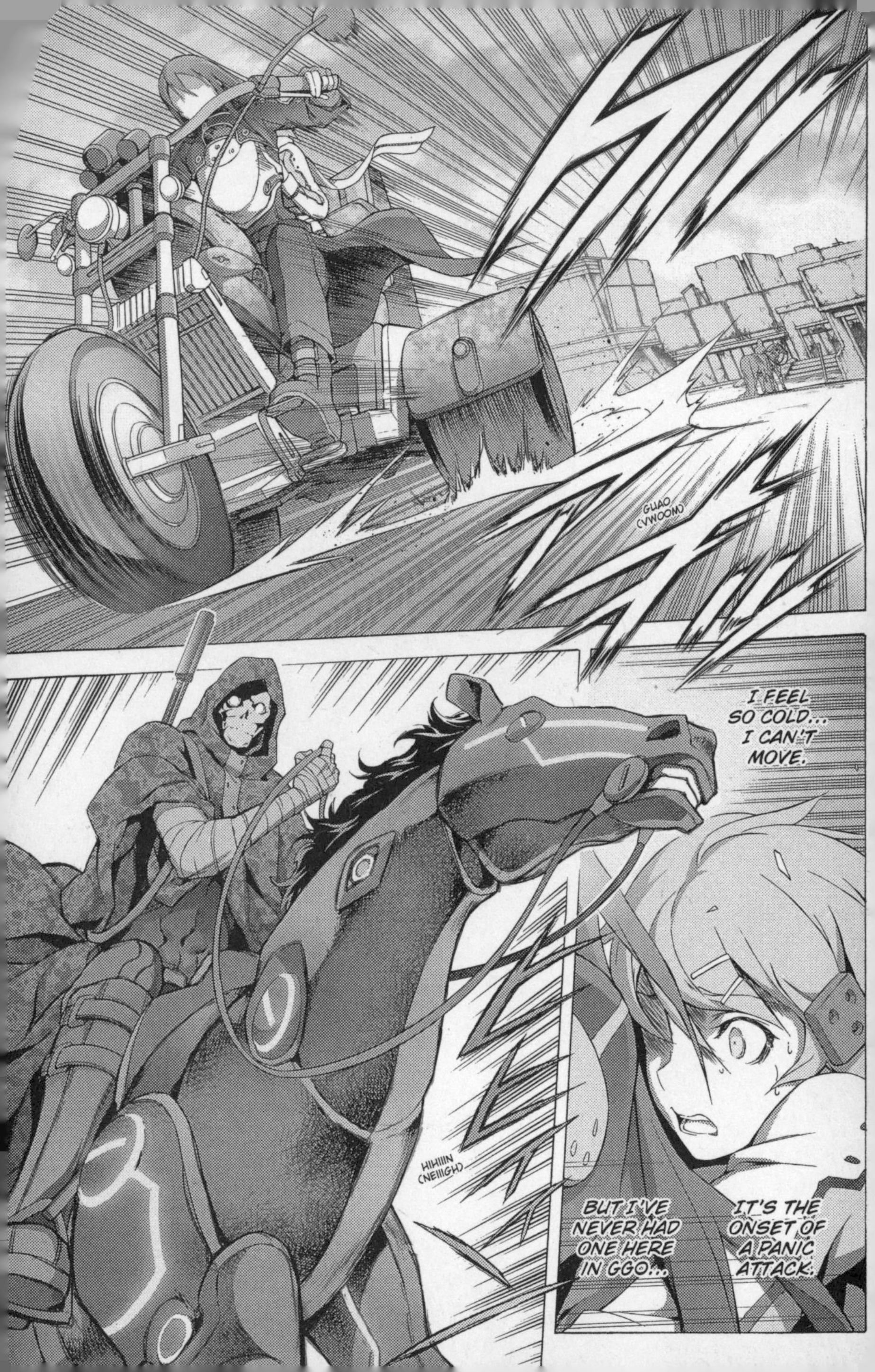
GUAO (VWOOM)
I FEEL SO COLD... I CAN'T MOVE.
IT'S THE ONSET OF A PANIC ATTACK.
BUT I'VE NEVER HAD ONE HERE IN GGO...
HIHIIIN (NEIIIGH)

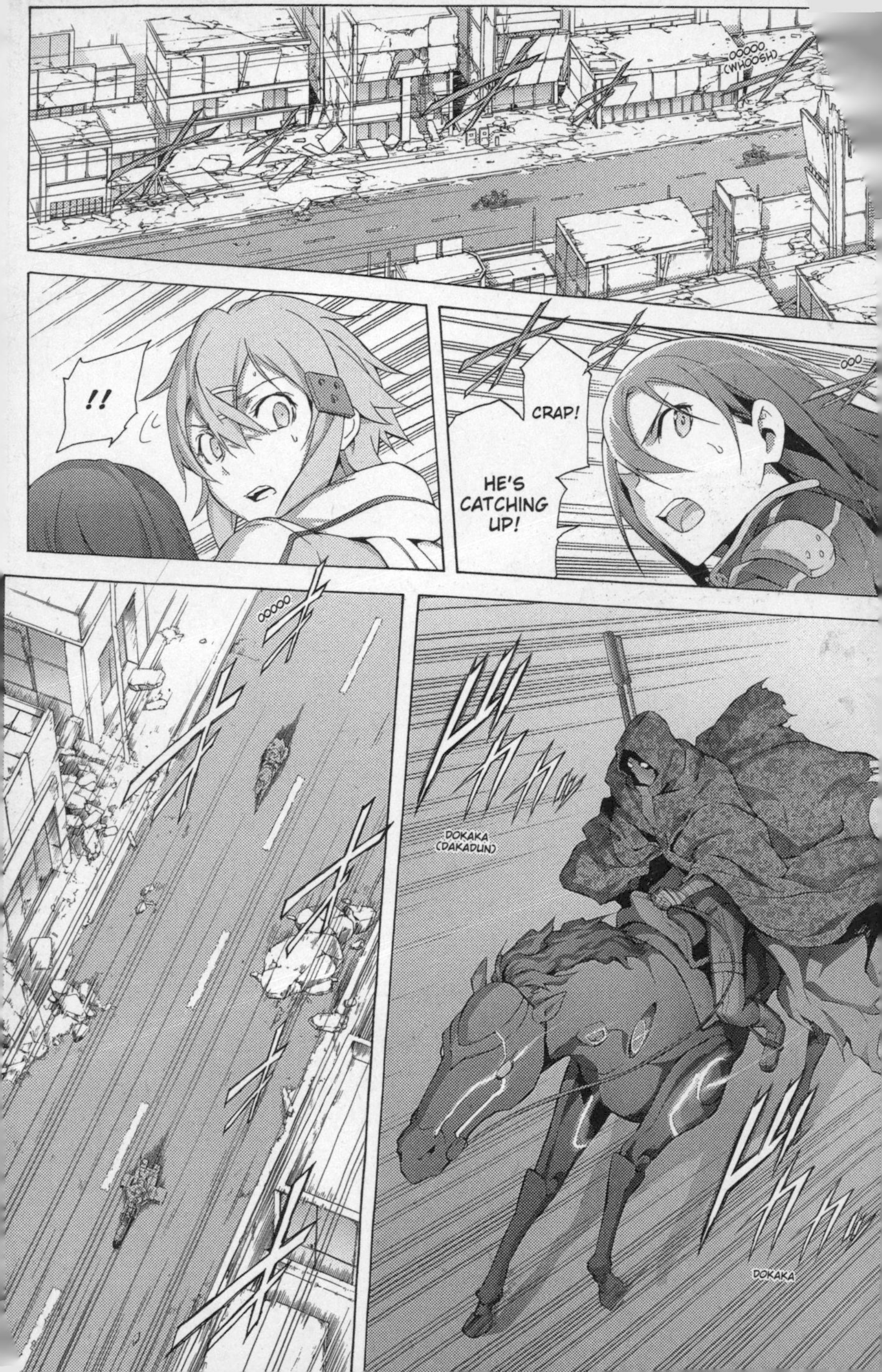
OOOOO (WHOOSH)
OOO
CRAP!
HE'S CATCHING UP!
!!
DOKAKA (DAKADUN)
DOKAKA
OOOOO

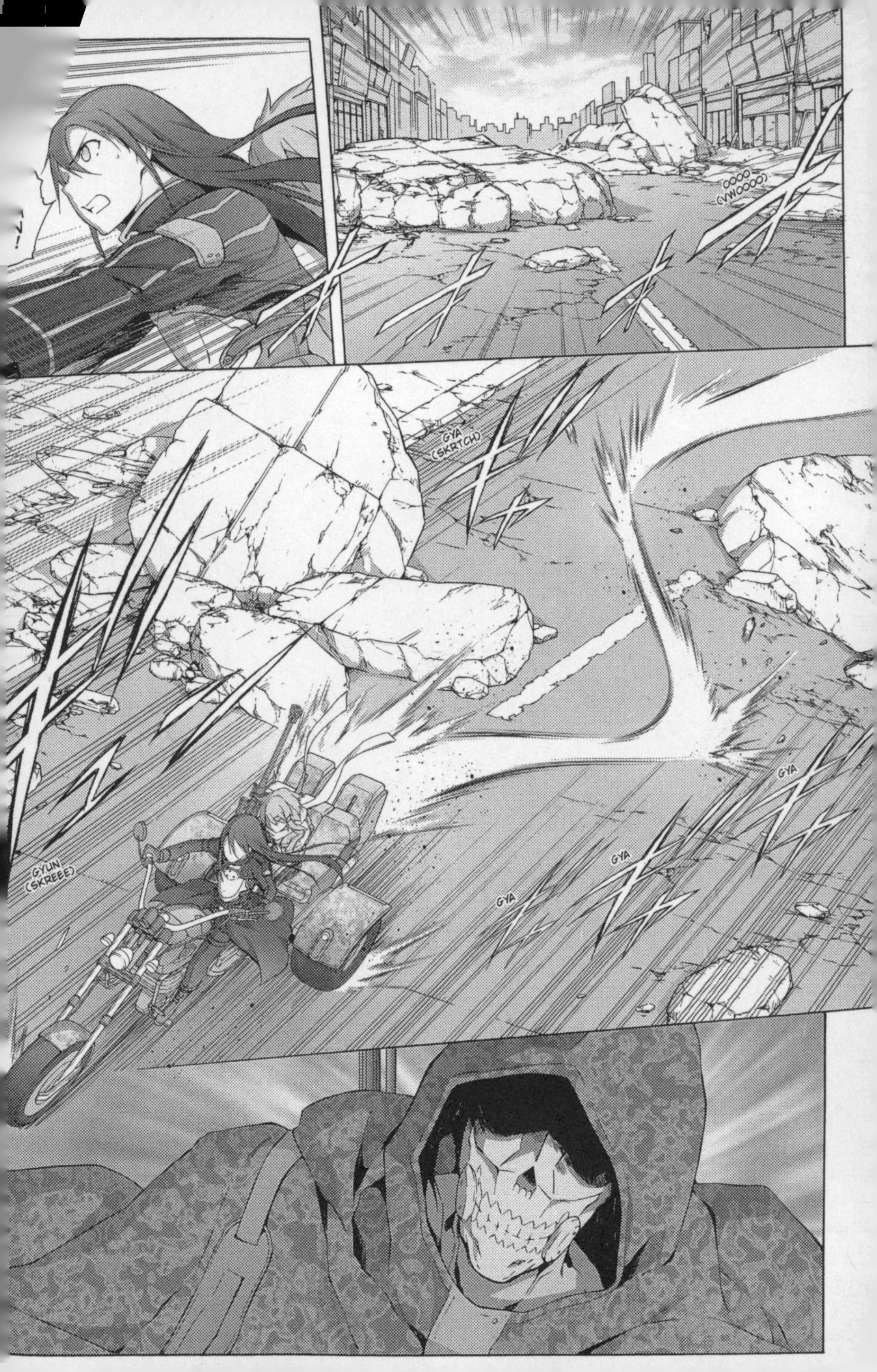
OOOO
(VWOOOO)
GYA
(SKRTCH)
GYA
GYA
GYA
GYUN
(SKREEE)

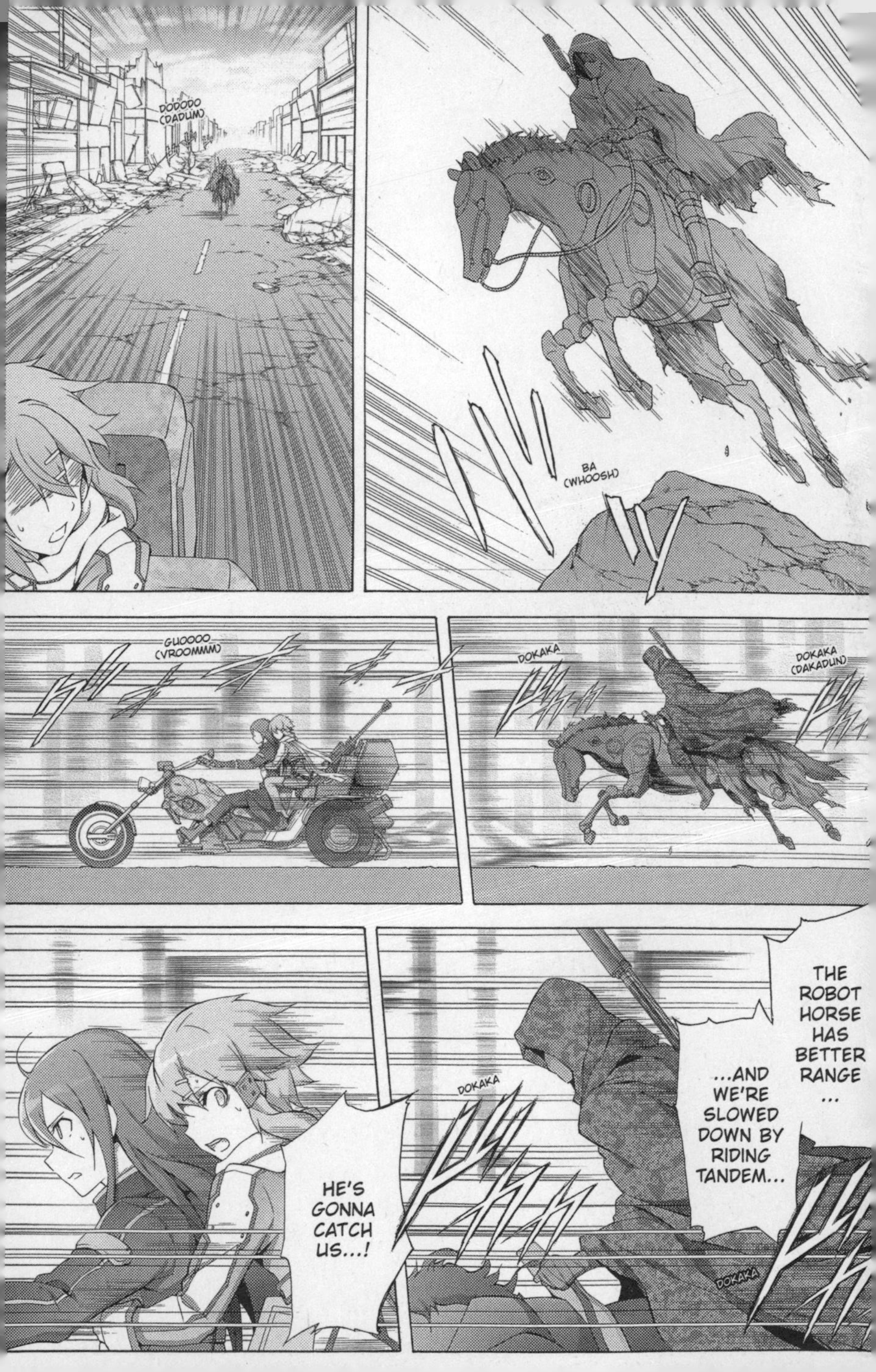
BA (WHOOSH)
DODODO (DADUM)
DOKAKA (DAKADUN)
DOKAKA
GUOOOO (VROOMMM)
THE ROBOT HORSE HAS BETTER RANGE...
...AND WE'RE SLOWED DOWN BY RIDING TANDEM...
DOKAKA
DOKAKA
HE'S GONNA CATCH US...!

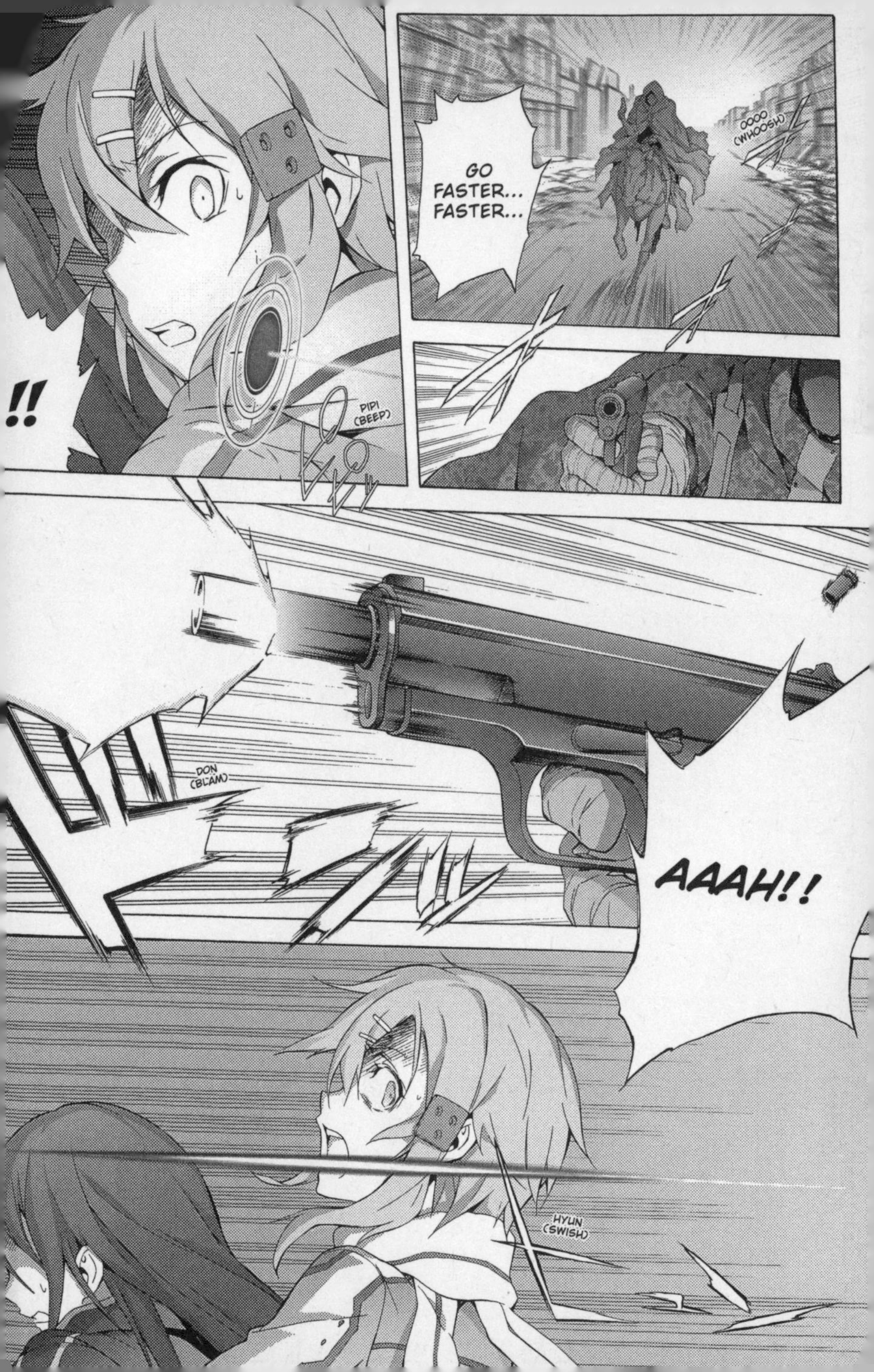
GO FASTER... FASTER...
OOOO (WHOOSH)
PIPI (BEEP)
!!
DON (BLAM)
AAAH!!
HYUN (SWISH)

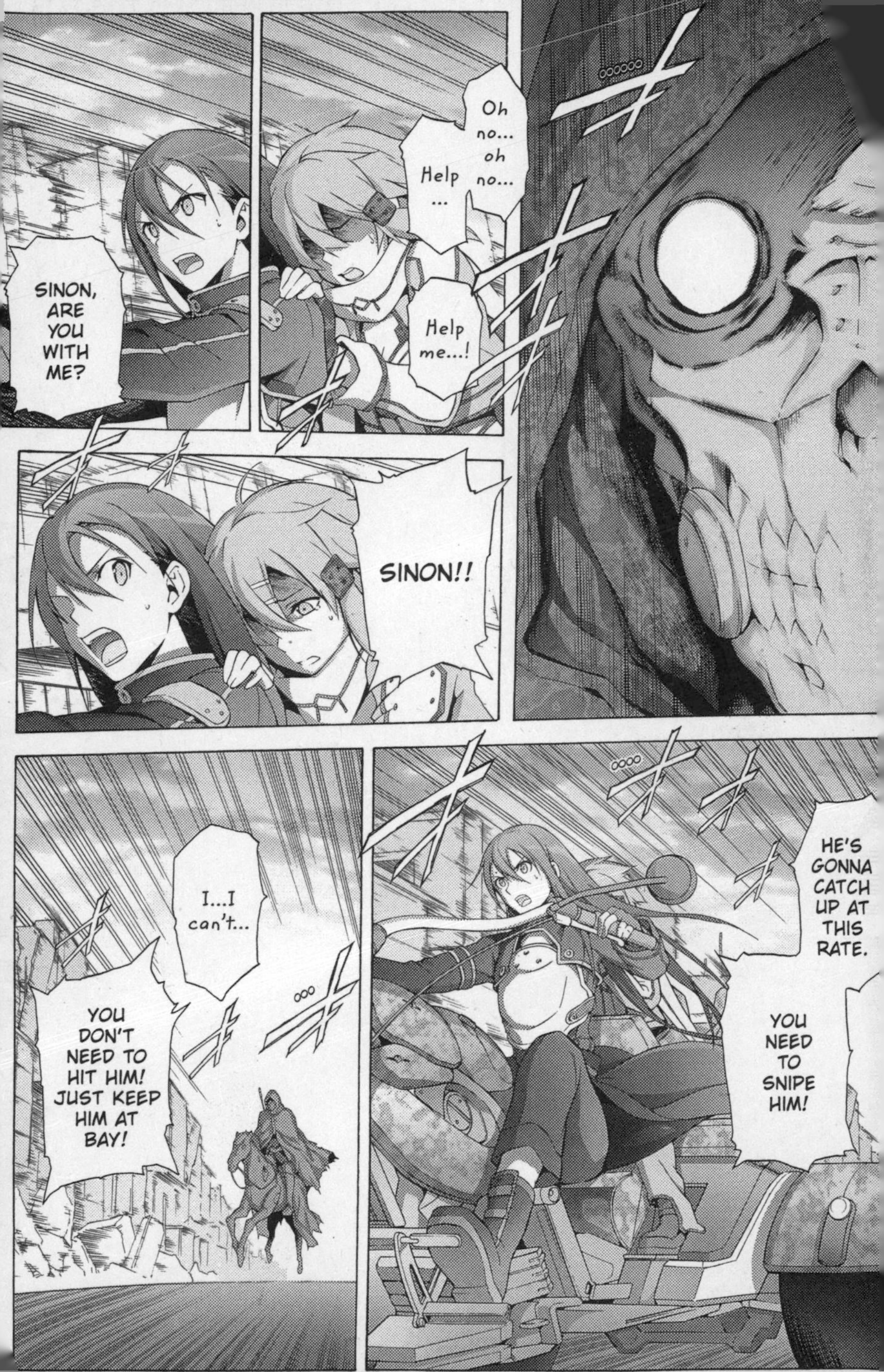
Oh no... oh no...
Help ...
Help me...!
SINON, ARE YOU WITH ME?
SINON!!
HE'S GONNA CATCH UP AT THIS RATE.
YOU NEED TO SNIPE HIM!
I...I can't...
YOU DON'T NEED TO HIT HIM! JUST KEEP HIM AT BAY!

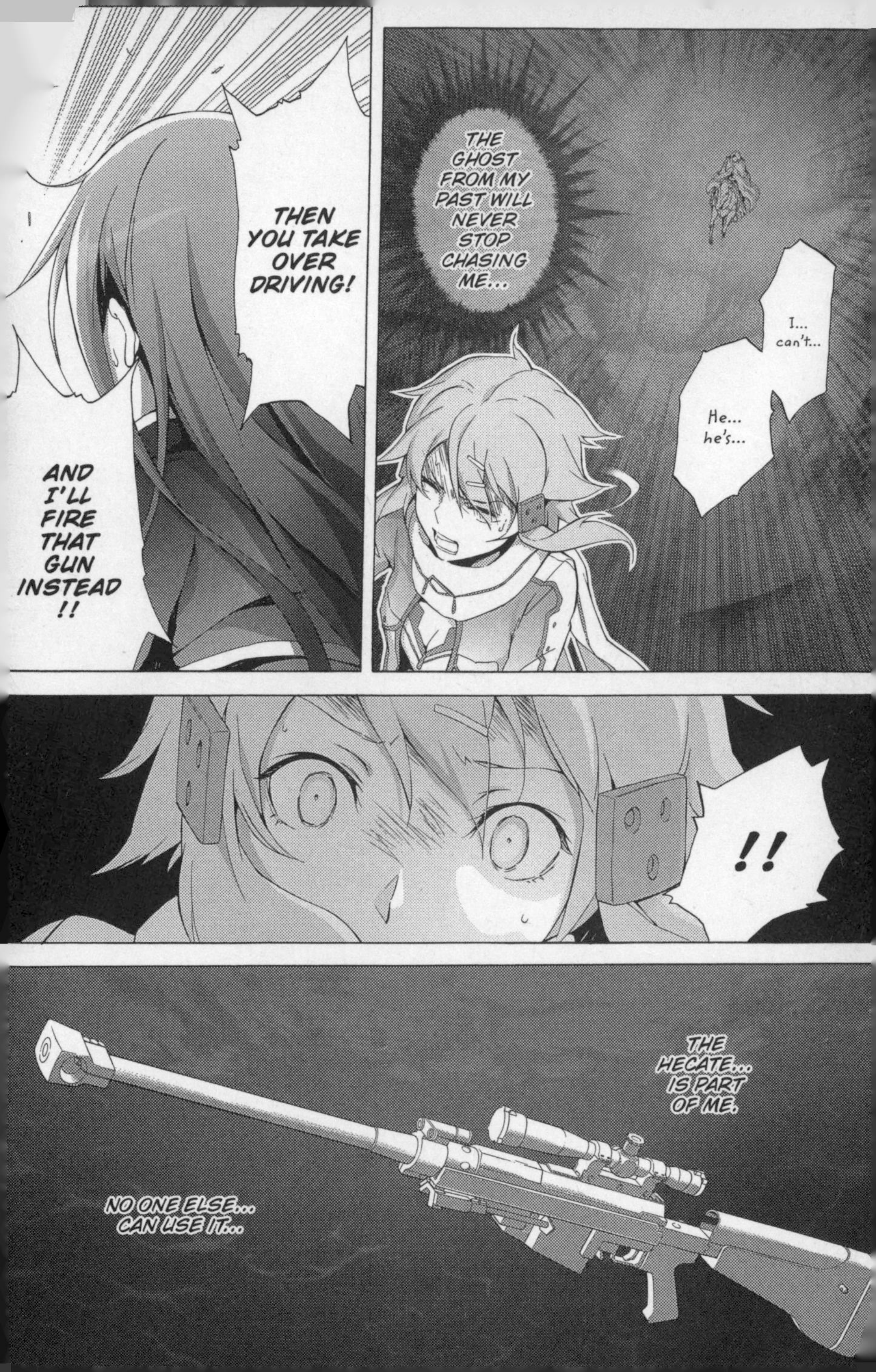
THE GHOST FROM MY PAST WILL NEVER STOP CHASING ME...
I... can't...
He... he's...
THEN YOU TAKE OVER DRIVING!
AND I'LL FIRE THAT GUN INSTEAD!!
!!
THE HECATE... IS PART OF ME.
NO ONE ELSE... CAN USE IT...

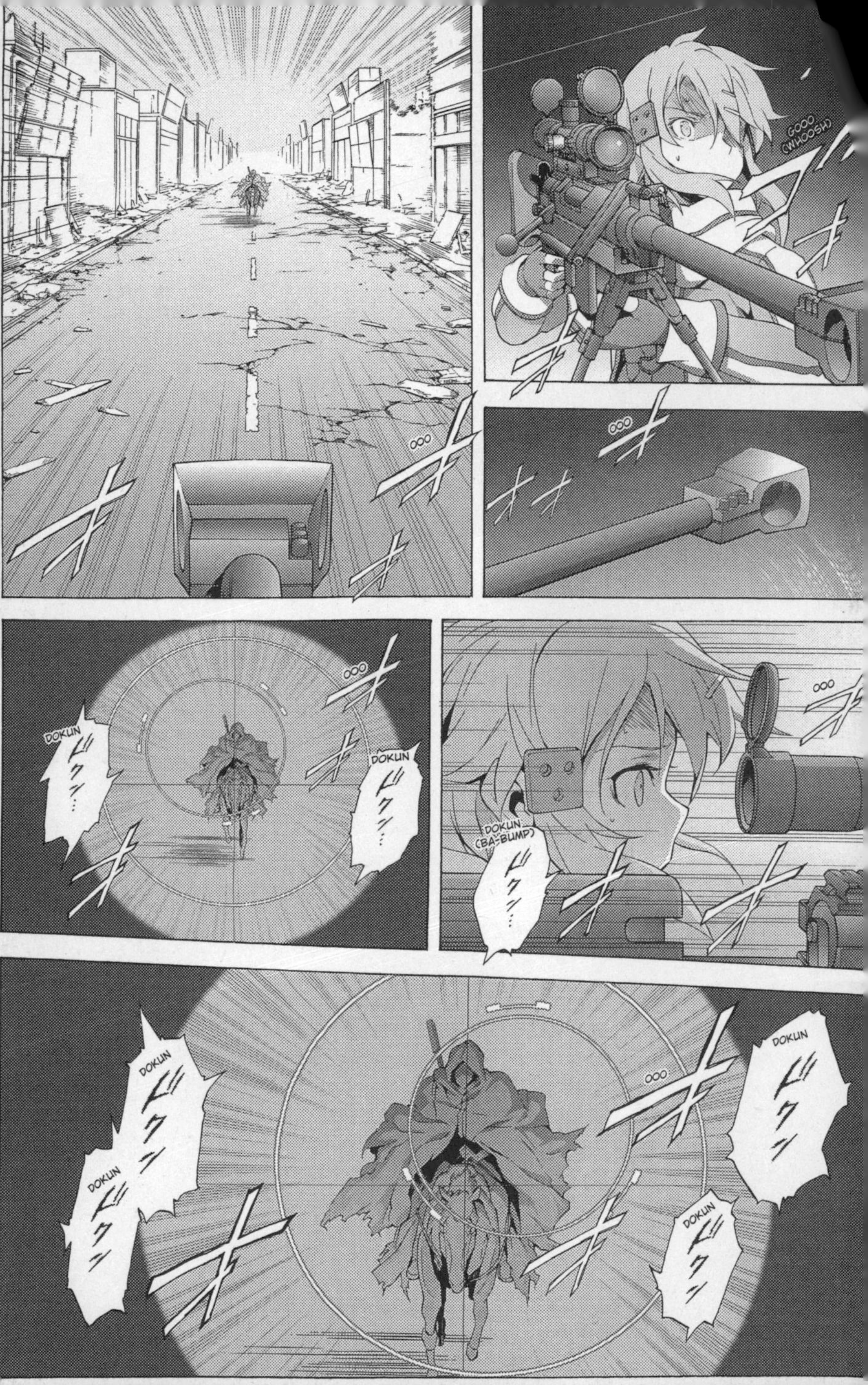
GOOO (WHOOSH)
OOO
OOO
OOO
DOKUN (BA-BUMP)
OOO
DOKUN
DOKUN
DOKUN
OOO
DOKUN
DOKUN
DOKUN

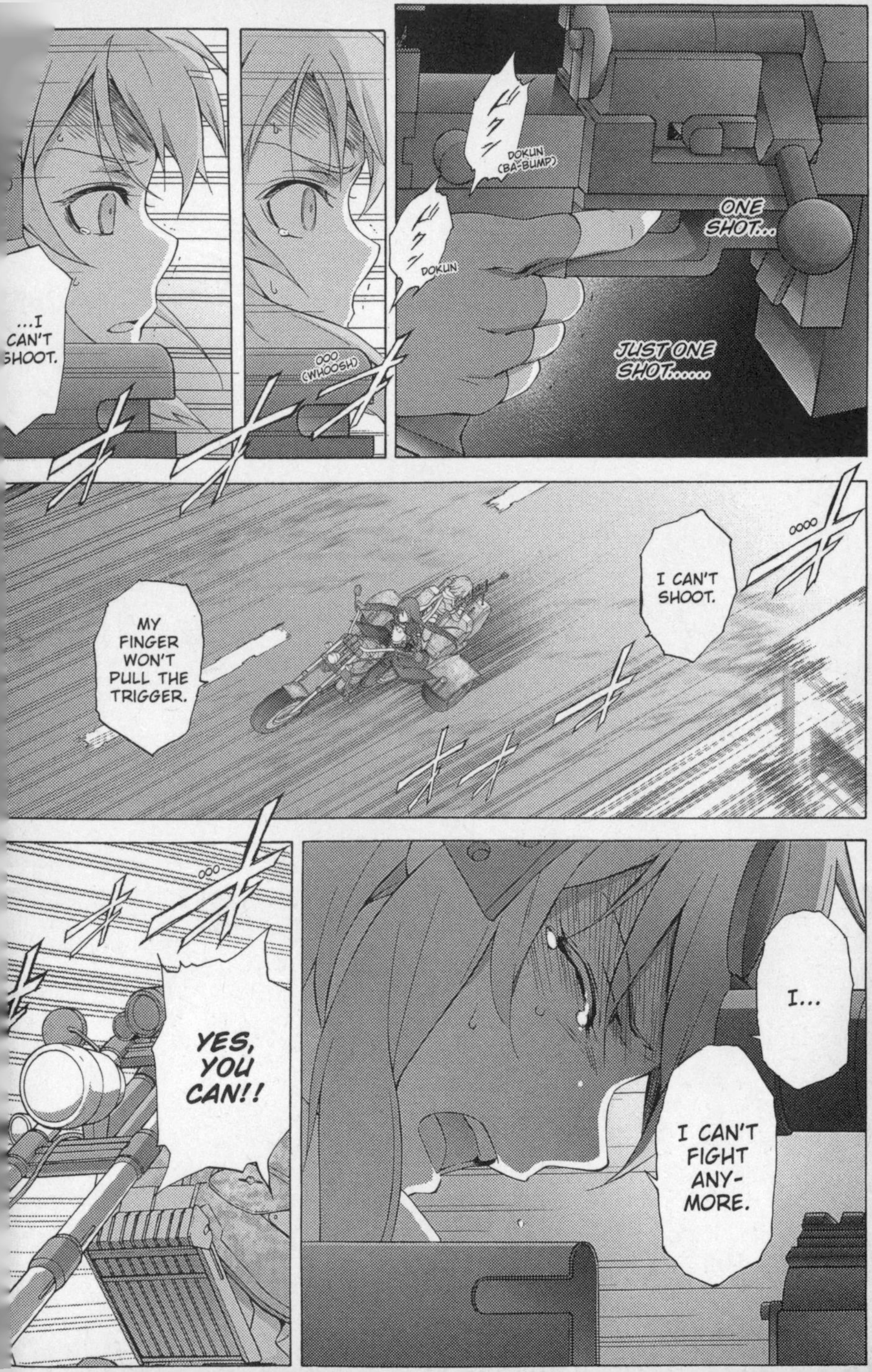
DOKUN (BA-BUMP)
ONE SHOT...
DOKUN
JUST ONE SHOT......
OOO (WHOOSH)
...I CAN'T SHOOT.
OOOO
I CAN'T SHOOT.
MY FINGER WON'T PULL THE TRIGGER.
I...
I CAN'T FIGHT ANY-MORE.
OOO
YES, YOU CAN!!

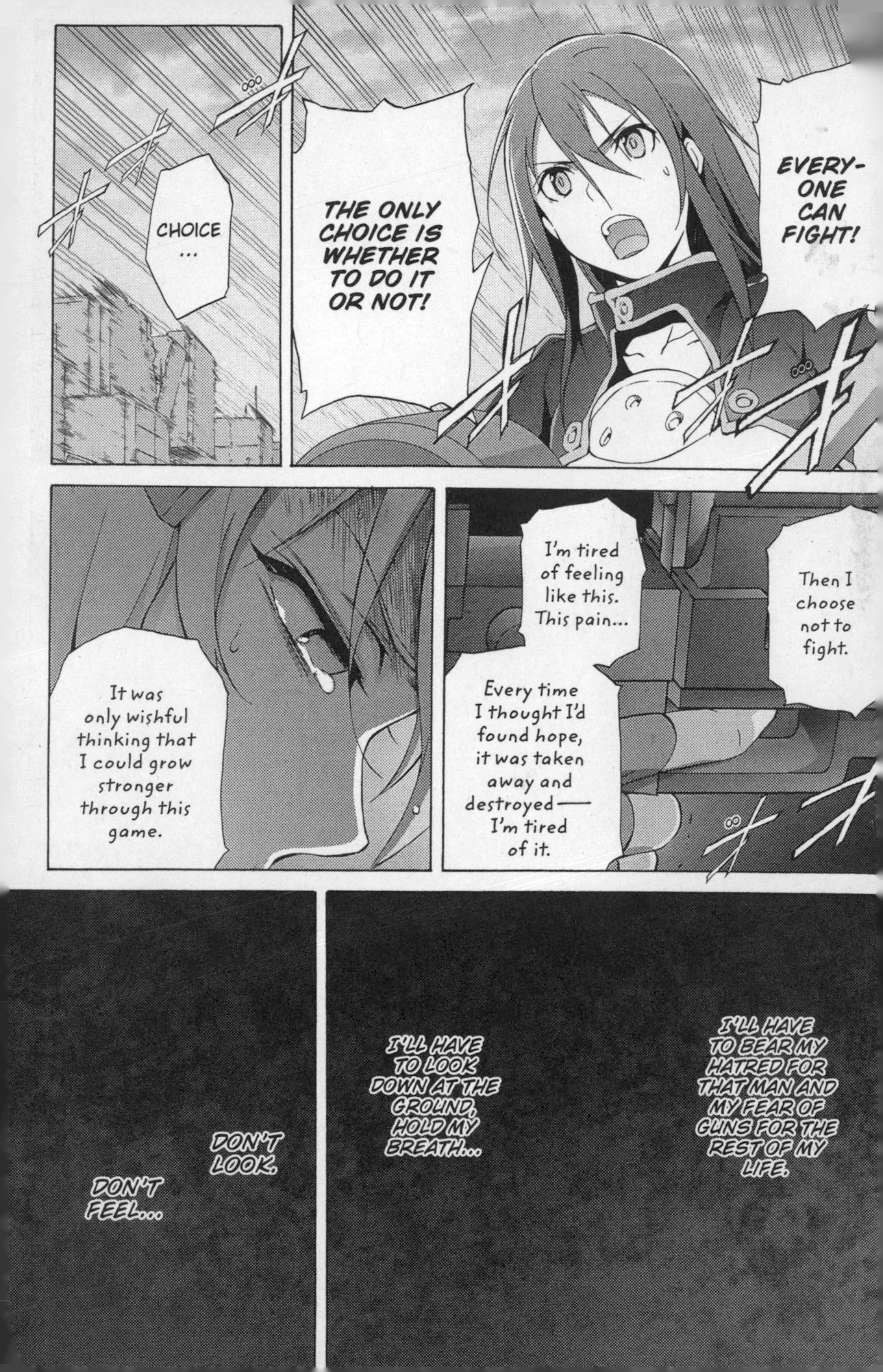
EVERY-ONE CAN FIGHT!
THE ONLY CHOICE IS WHETHER TO DO IT OR NOT!
CHOICE ...
Then I choose not to fight.
I'm tired of feeling like this. This pain...
Every time I thought I'd found hope, it was taken away and destroyed— I'm tired of it.
It was only wishful thinking that I could grow stronger through this game.
I'LL HAVE TO BEAR MY HATRED FOR THAT MAN AND MY FEAR OF GUNS FOR THE REST OF MY LIFE.
I'LL HAVE TO LOOK DOWN AT THE GROUND, HOLD MY BREATH...
DON'T LOOK.
DON'T FEEL...

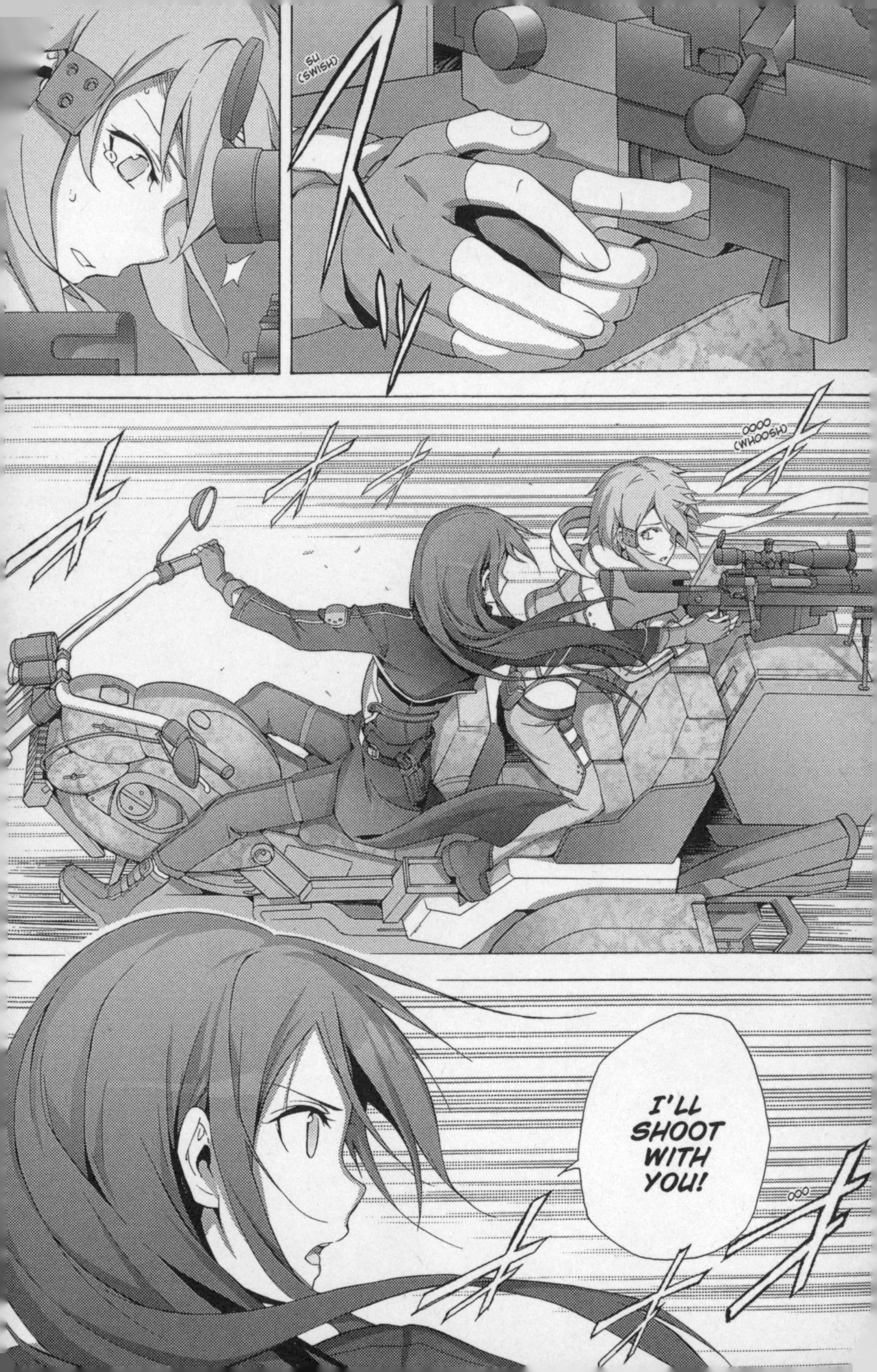
SU (SWISH)
OOOO (WHOOSH)
OOO
I'LL SHOOT WITH YOU!

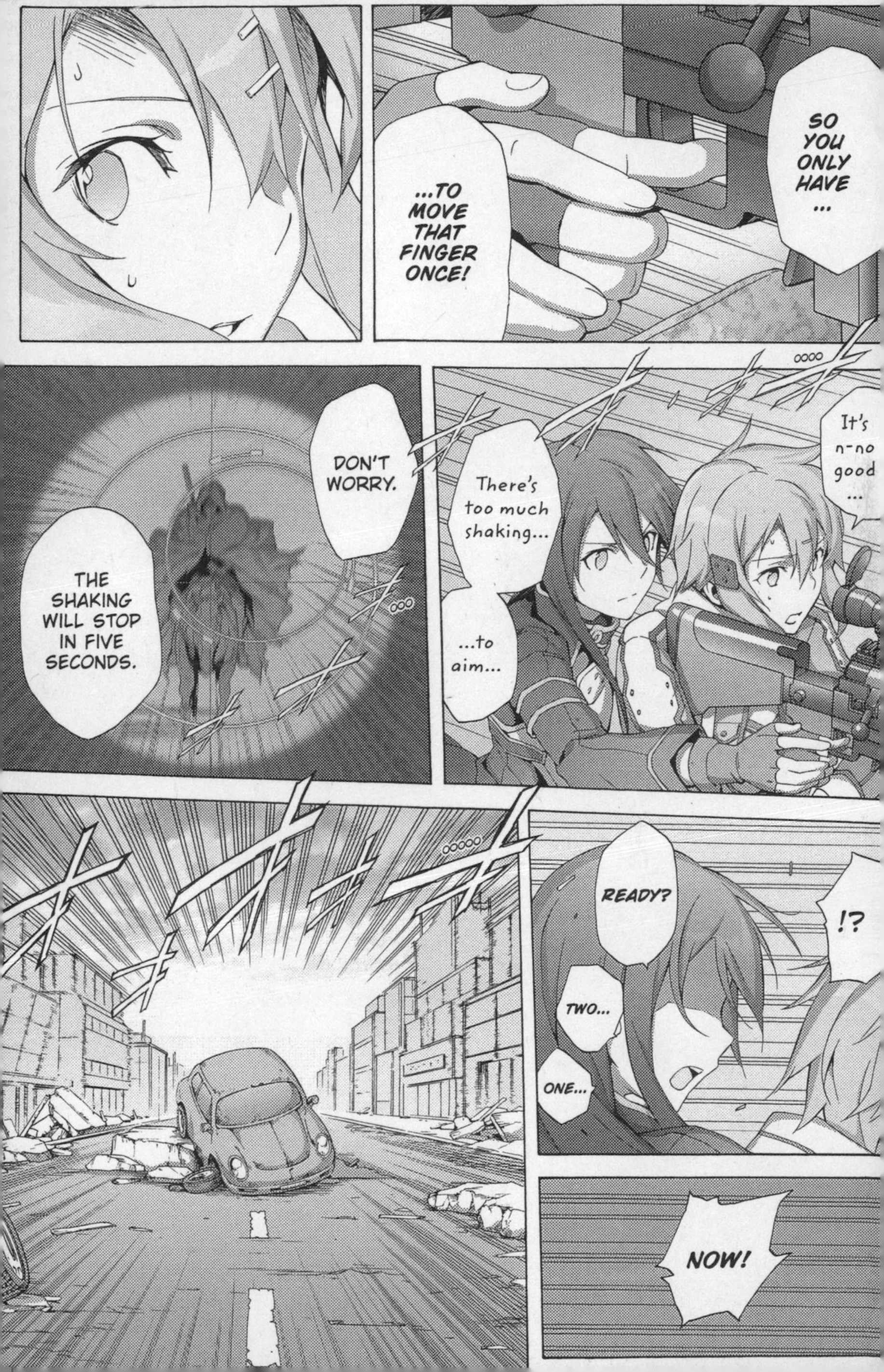
SO YOU ONLY HAVE ...
...TO MOVE THAT FINGER ONCE!
oooo
It's n-no good ...
There's too much shaking...
...to aim...
DON'T WORRY.
THE SHAKING WILL STOP IN FIVE SECONDS.
ooo
!?
READY?
TWO...
ONE...
NOW!
ooooo

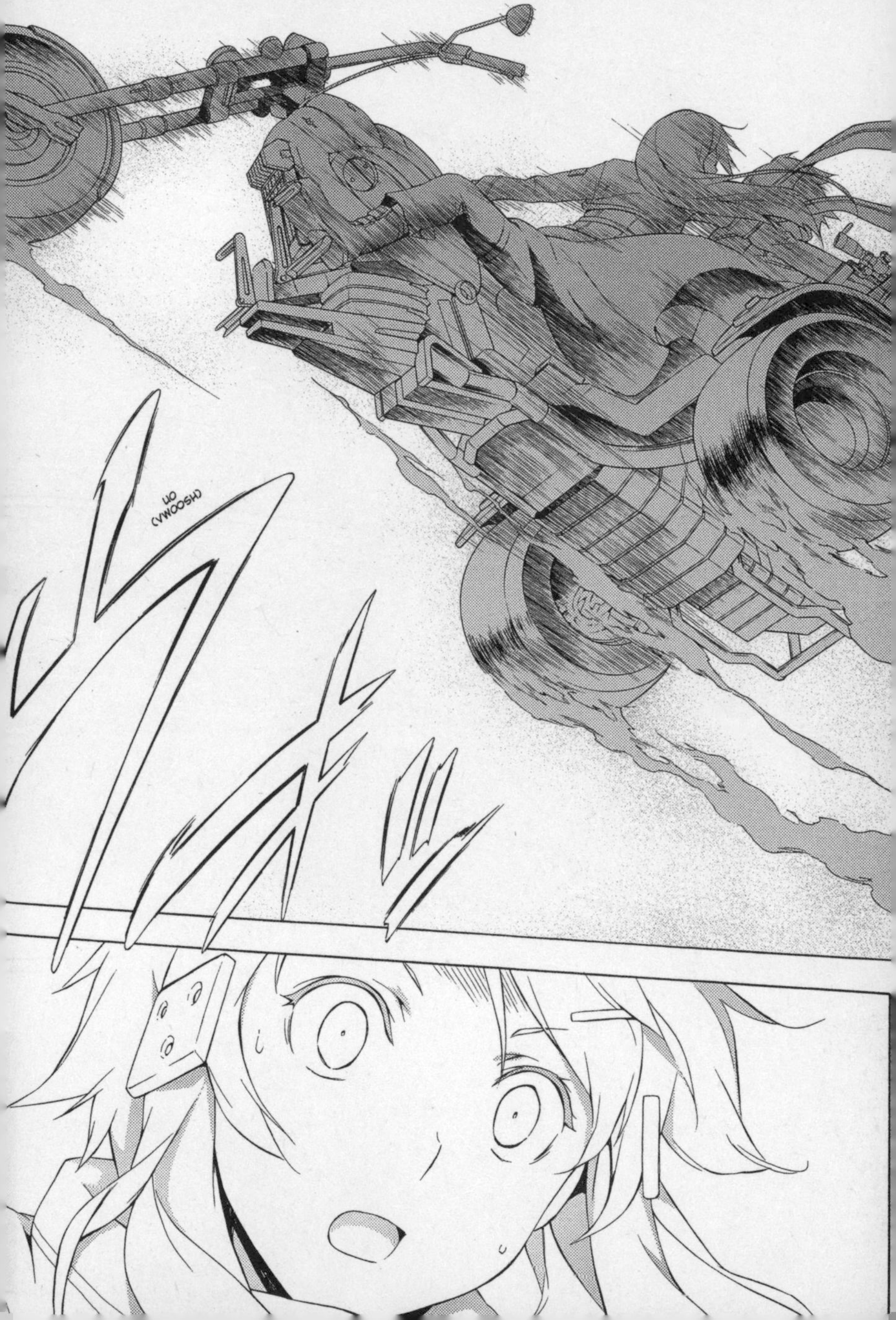
(VWOOSH)
ON

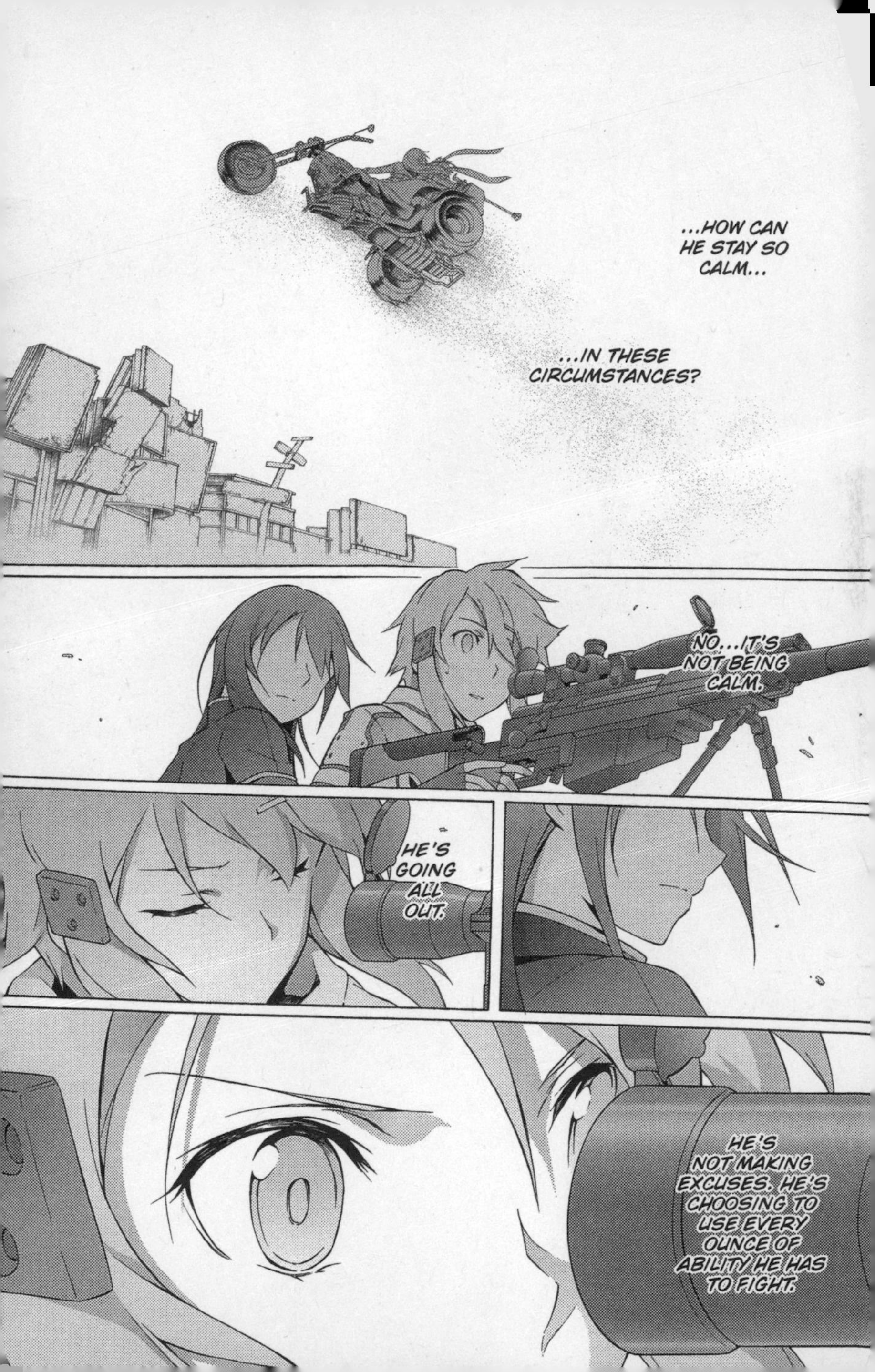
...HOW CAN HE STAY SO CALM...
...IN THESE CIRCUMSTANCES?
NO...IT'S NOT BEING CALM.
HE'S GOING ALL OUT.
HE'S NOT MAKING EXCUSES. HE'S CHOOSING TO USE EVERY OUNCE OF ABILITY HE HAS TO FIGHT.

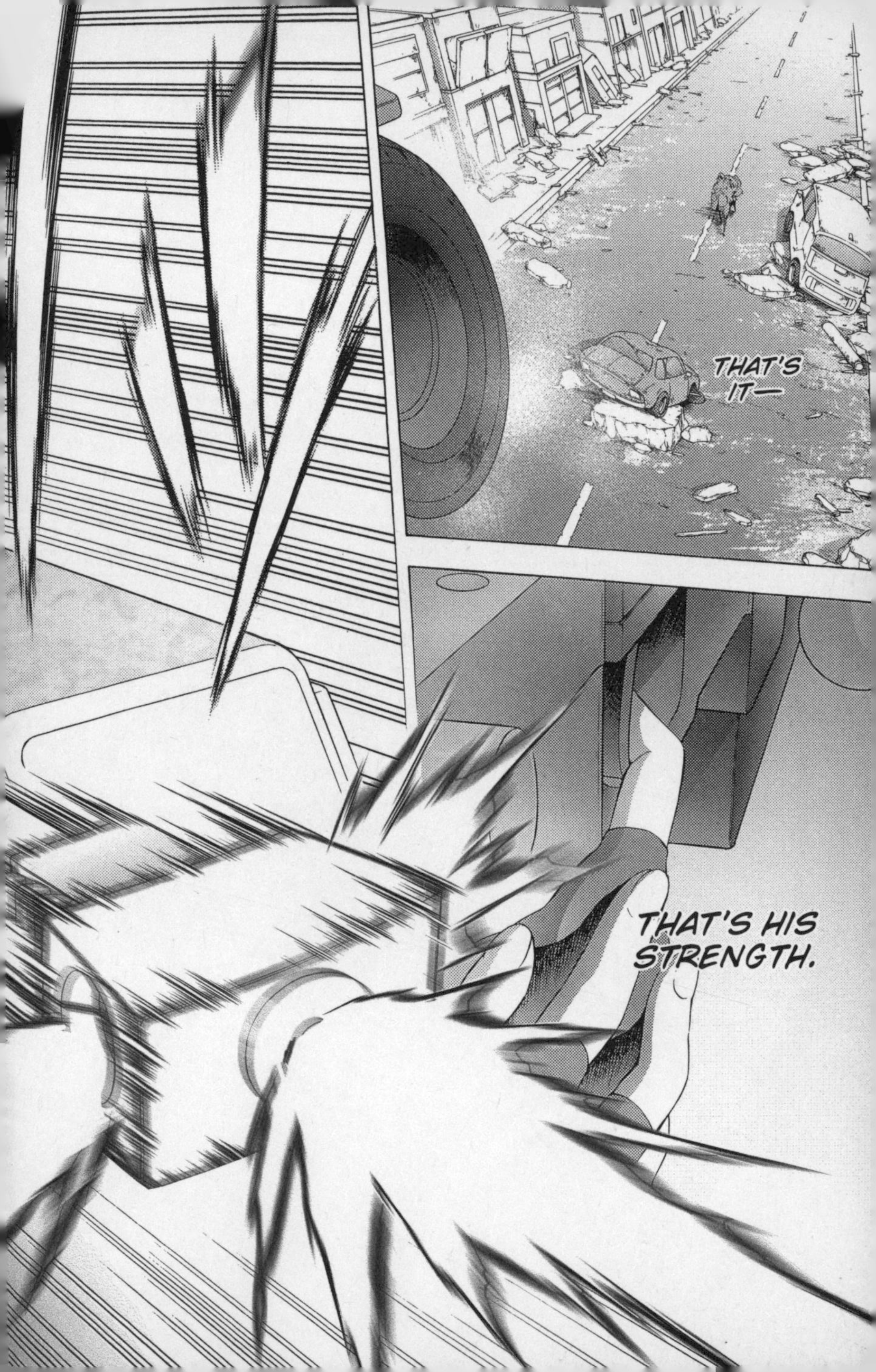
THAT'S IT—
THAT'S HIS STRENGTH.

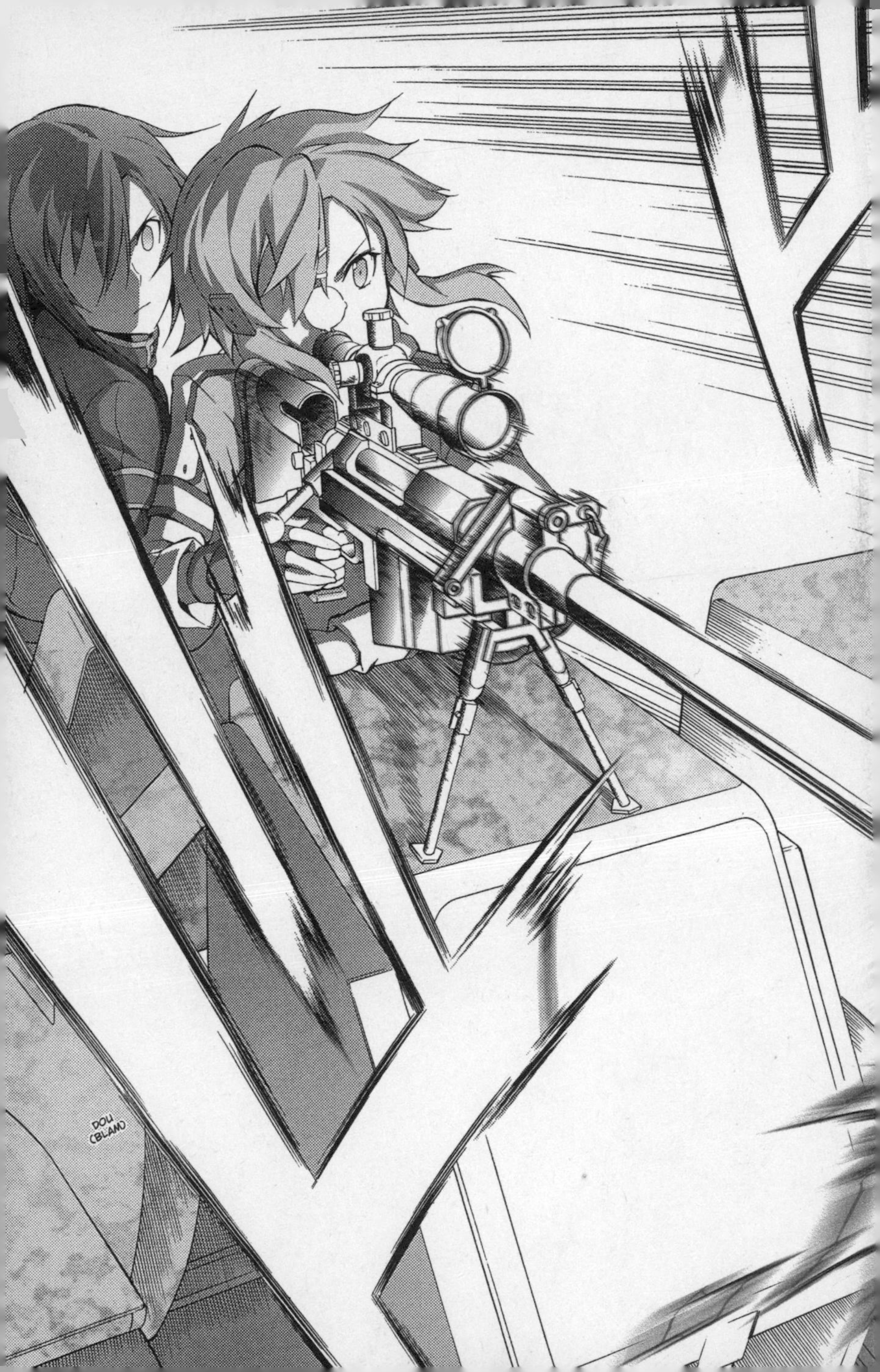
DOU
(BLAM)

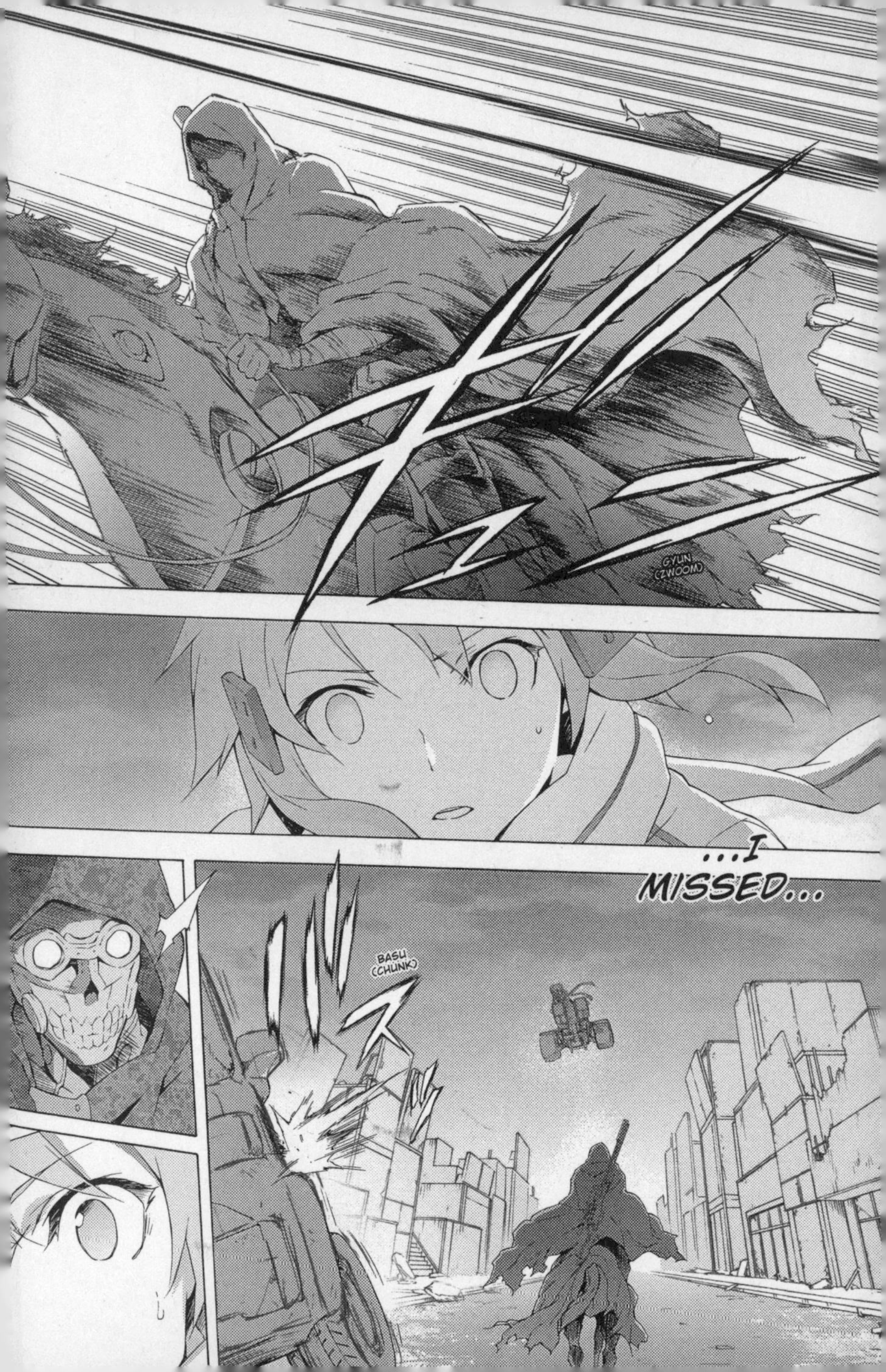
GYUN (ZWOOM)
...I MISSED...
BASU (CHUNK)

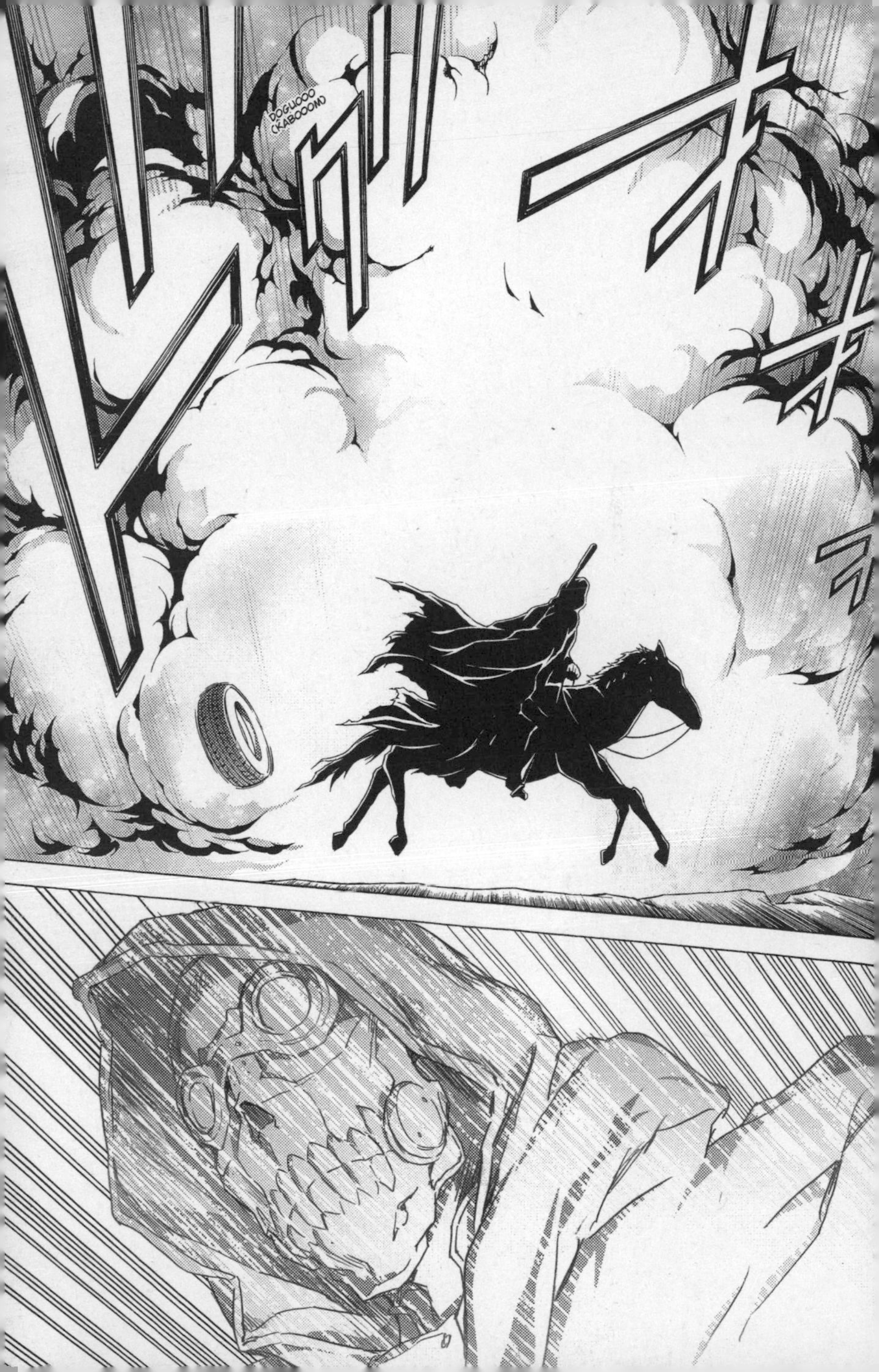
DOGUOOO
(KABOOOM)

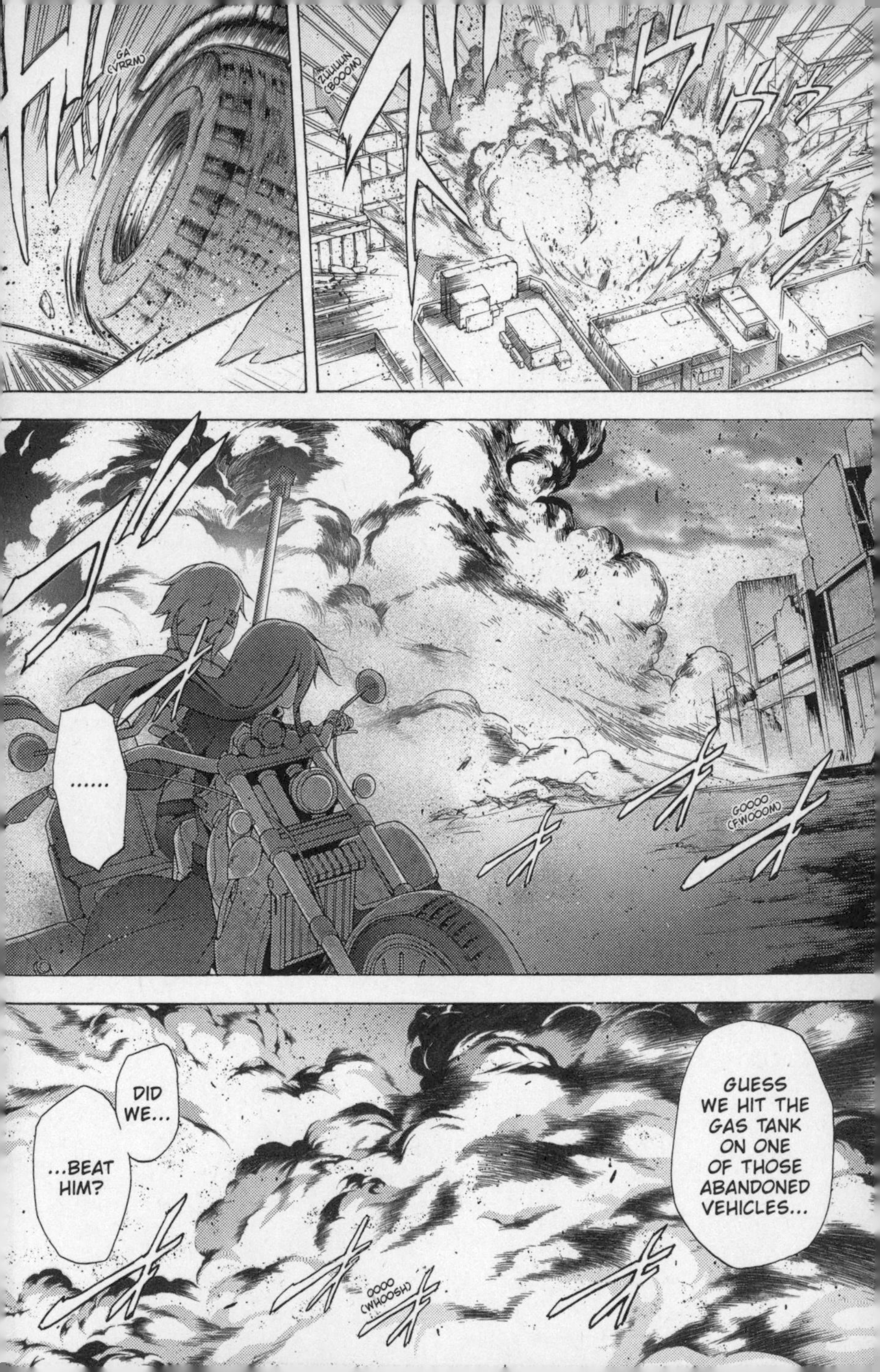
ZUUUUN (BOOOM)
GA (VRRM)
GOOOO (FWOOOM)
......
GUESS WE HIT THE GAS TANK ON ONE OF THOSE ABANDONED VEHICLES...
OOOO (WHOOSH)
DID WE...
...BEAT HIM?

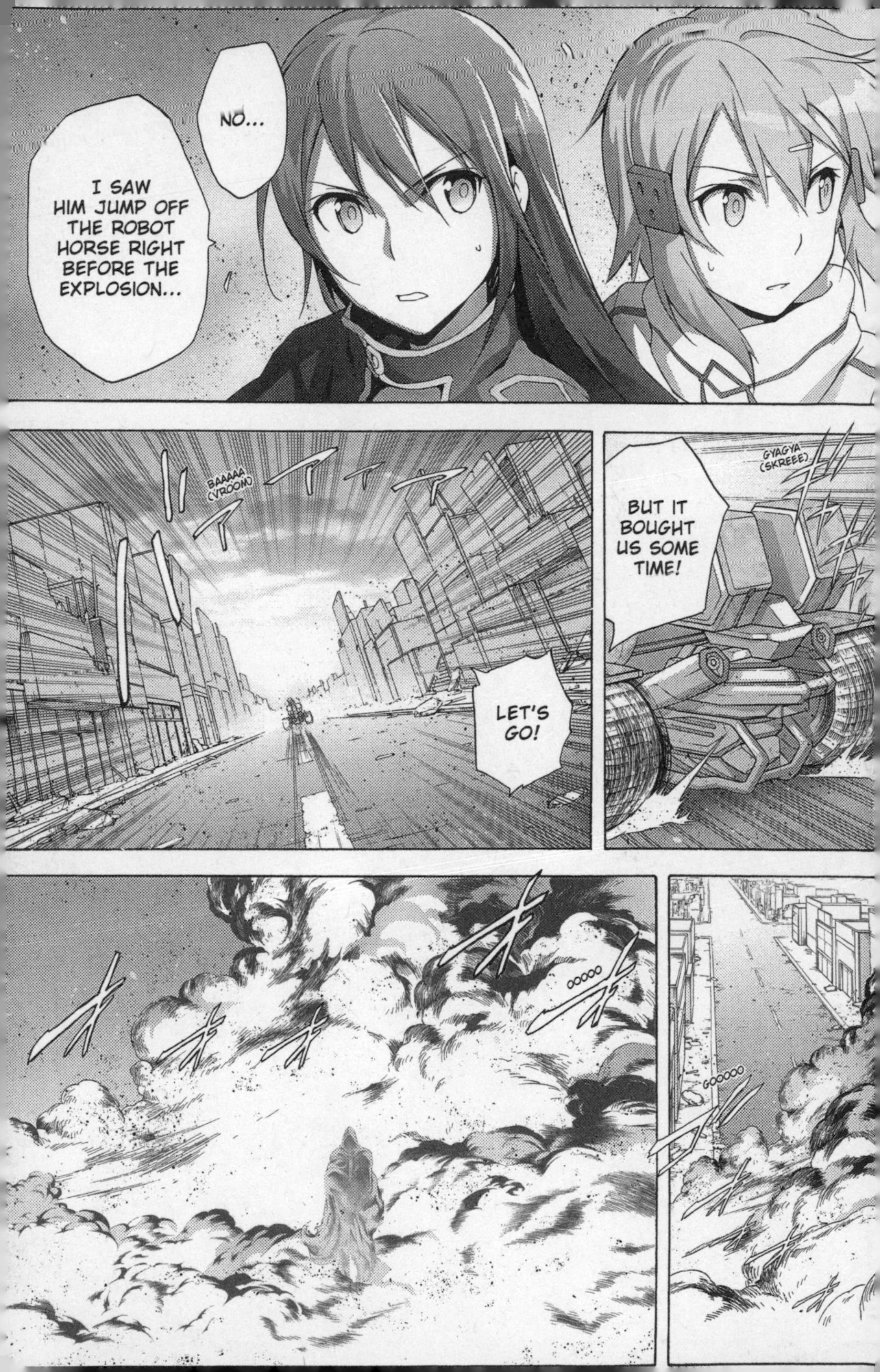
NO...
I SAW HIM JUMP OFF THE ROBOT HORSE RIGHT BEFORE THE EXPLOSION...
GYAGYA (SKREEE)
BUT IT BOUGHT US SOME TIME!
BAAAAA (VROOM)
LET'S GO!
GOOOOO
OOOOO

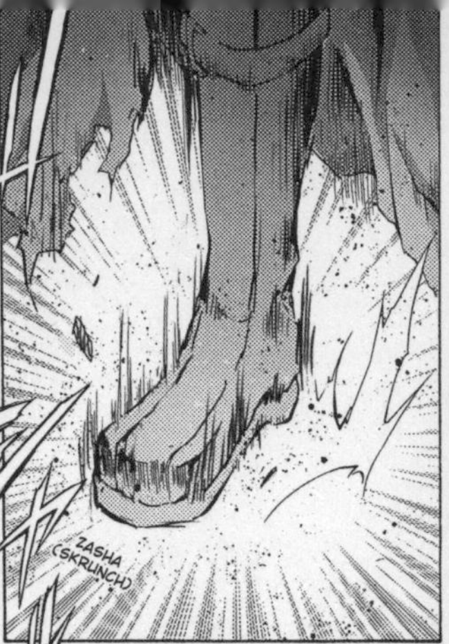
ZASHA (SKRUNCH)

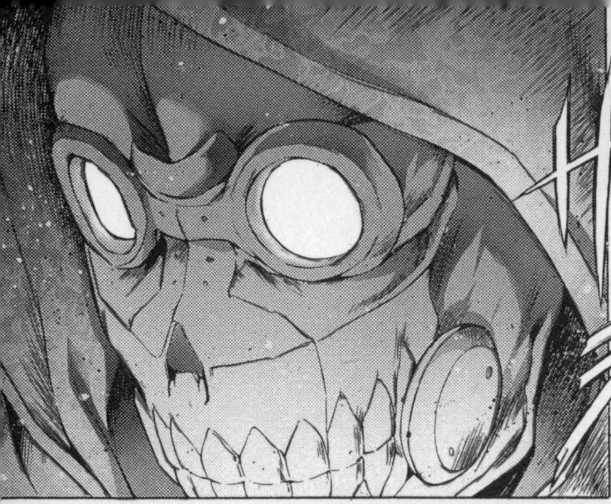

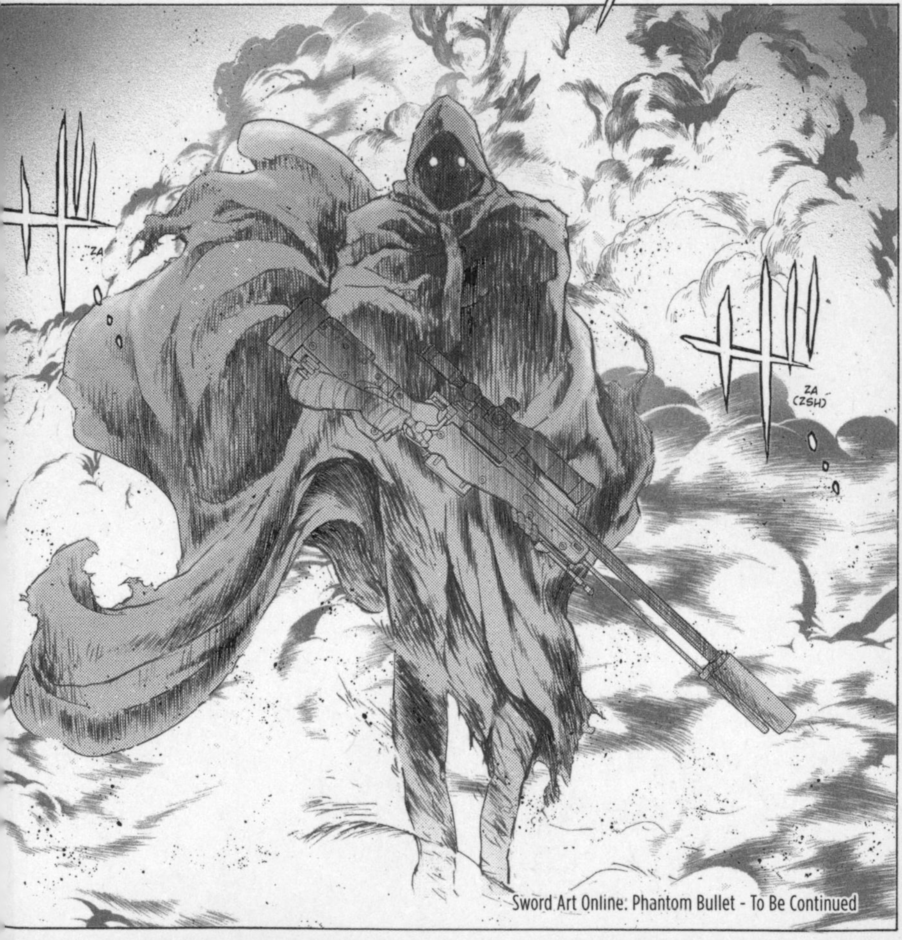
ZA (ZSH)
ZA

Sword Art Online: Phantom Bullet - To Be Continued

SWORD ART ONLINE
phantom bullet

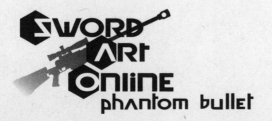

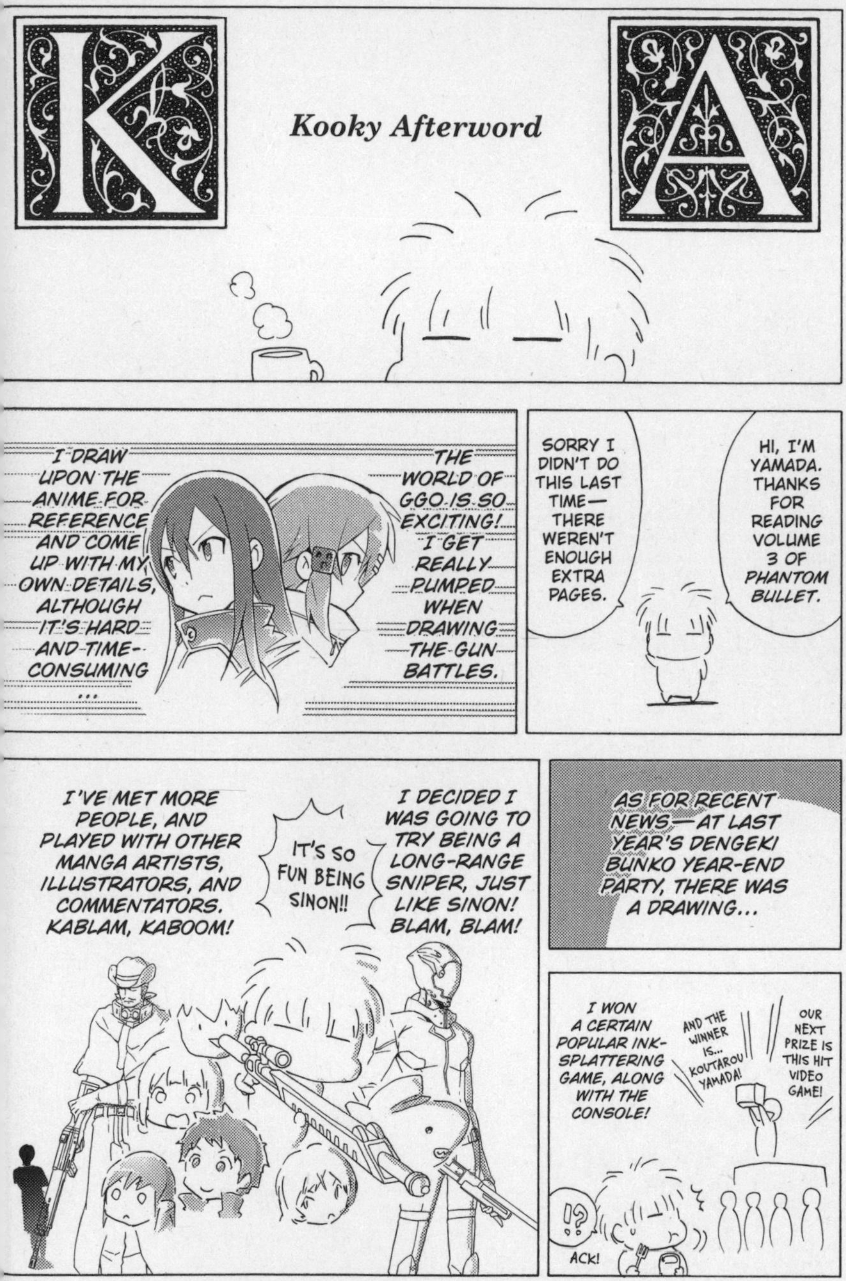
Kooky Afterword
HI, I'M YAMADA. THANKS FOR READING VOLUME 3 OF PHANTOM BULLET.
SORRY I DIDN'T DO THIS LAST TIME— THERE WEREN'T ENOUGH EXTRA PAGES.
THE WORLD OF GGO IS SO EXCITING! I GET REALLY PUMPED WHEN DRAWING THE GUN BATTLES.
I DRAW UPON THE ANIME FOR REFERENCE AND COME UP WITH MY OWN DETAILS, ALTHOUGH IT'S HARD AND TIME-CONSUMING...
AS FOR RECENT NEWS—AT LAST YEAR'S DENGEKI BUNKO YEAR-END PARTY, THERE WAS A DRAWING...
OUR NEXT PRIZE IS THIS HIT VIDEO GAME!
AND THE WINNER IS... KOUTAROU YAMADA!
I WON A CERTAIN POPULAR INK-SPLATTERING GAME, ALONG WITH THE CONSOLE!
!?
ACK!
I DECIDED I WAS GOING TO TRY BEING A LONG-RANGE SNIPER, JUST LIKE SINON! BLAM, BLAM!
IT'S SO FUN BEING SINON!!
I'VE MET MORE PEOPLE, AND PLAYED WITH OTHER MANGA ARTISTS, ILLUSTRATORS, AND COMMENTATORS. KABLAM, KABOOM!

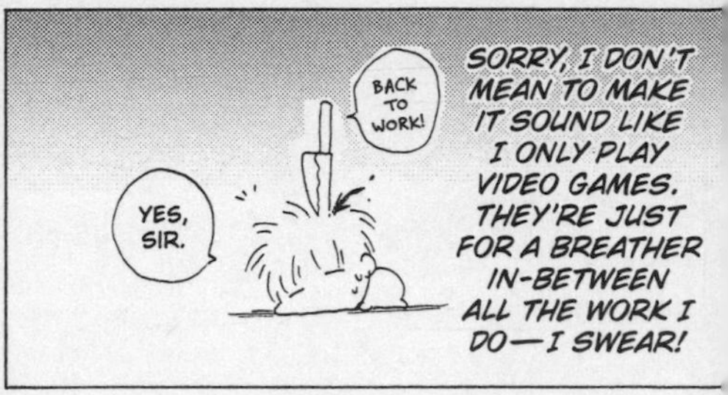
SORRY, I DON'T MEAN TO MAKE IT SOUND LIKE I ONLY PLAY VIDEO GAMES. THEY'RE JUST FOR A BREATHER IN-BETWEEN ALL THE WORK I DO—I SWEAR!
BACK TO WORK!
YES, SIR.

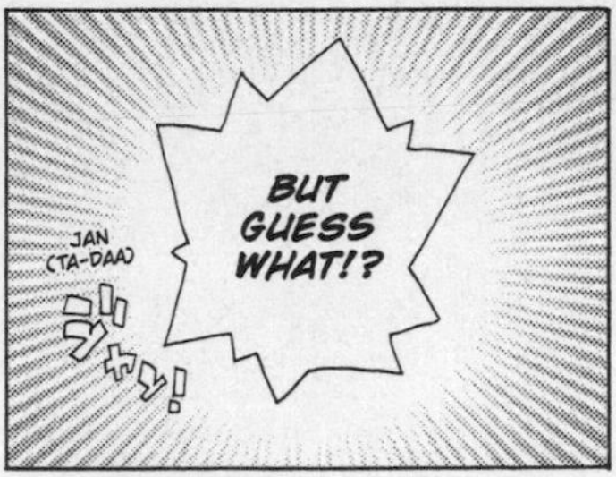
BUT GUESS WHAT!?
JAN (TA-DAA)

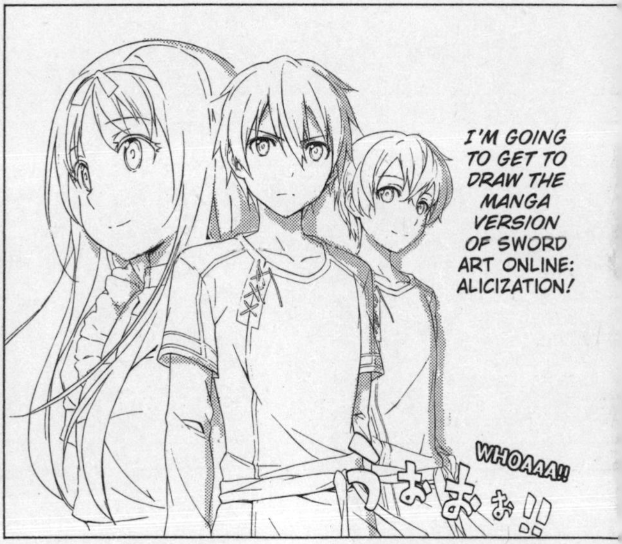
I'M GOING TO GET TO DRAW THE MANGA VERSION OF SWORD ART ONLINE: ALICIZATION!
WHOAAA!!

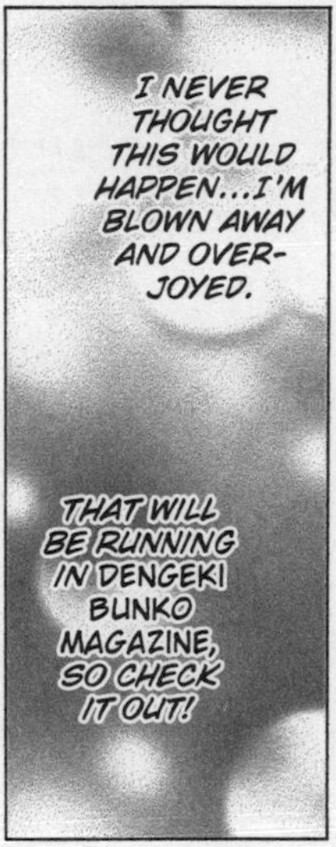
I NEVER THOUGHT THIS WOULD HAPPEN...I'M BLOWN AWAY AND OVER-JOYED.
THAT WILL BE RUNNING IN DENGEKI BUNKO MAGAZINE, SO CHECK IT OUT!

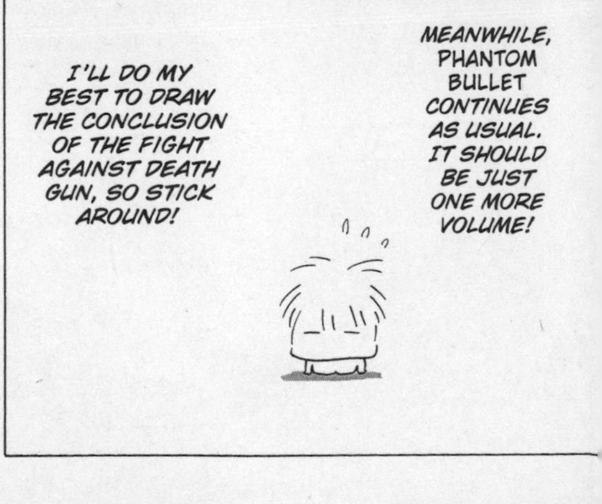
MEANWHILE, PHANTOM BULLET CONTINUES AS USUAL. IT SHOULD BE JUST ONE MORE VOLUME!
I'LL DO MY BEST TO DRAW THE CONCLUSION OF THE FIGHT AGAINST DEATH GUN, SO STICK AROUND!

SPECIAL THANKS:

NAKAMURA-SAN

SAITOU-SAN, TAURA-SAN

OKOMEKEN

BEATNIKS-SAMA

REKI KAWAHARA-SENSEI,
ABEC-SENSEI, THE
ANIME STAFF

KAZUMA MIKI-SAMA
TOMOYUKI TSUCHIYA-SAMA

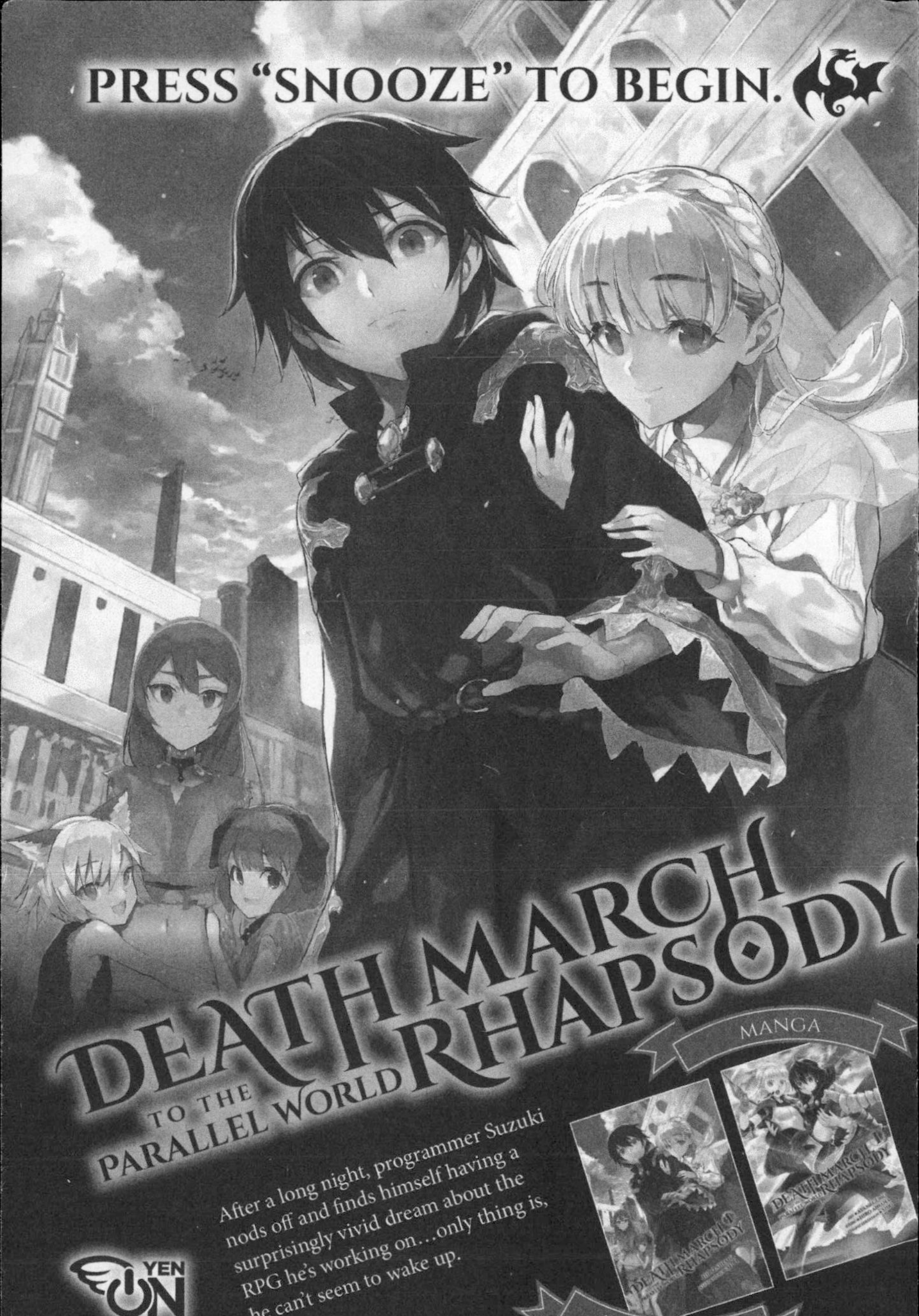
PRESS "SNOOZE" TO BEGIN.
DEATH MARCH TO THE PARALLEL WORLD RHAPSODY
MANGA
After a long night, programmer Suzuki nods off and finds himself having a surprisingly vivid dream about the RPG he's working on…only thing is, he can't seem to wake up.
YEN ON
LIGHT NOVEL

SWORD ART ONLINE: PHANTOM BULLET 3

ART: KOUTAROU YAMADA
ORIGINAL STORY: REKI KAWAHARA
CHARACTER DESIGN: abec

Translation: Stephen Paul
Lettering: Brndn Blakeslee

SWORD ART ONLINE: Phantom Bullet
© REKI KAWAHARA/KOUTAROU YAMADA 2016
All rights reserved.
Edited by ASCII MEDIA WORKS
First published in Japan in 2016 by KADOKAWA CORPORATION, Tokyo.
English translation rights arranged with KADOKAWA CORPORATION, Tokyo, through Tuttle-Mori Agency, Inc., Tokyo.

English translation © 2017 by Yen Press, LLC

Yen Press
1290 Avenue of the Americas
New York, NY 10104

Visit us at yenpress.com
facebook.com/yenpress
twitter.com/yenpress
yenpress.tumblr.com
instagram.com/yenpress

First Yen Press Edition: September 2017

Yen Press is an imprint of Yen Press, LLC.
The Yen Press name and logo are trademarks of Yen Press, LLC.

The publisher is not responsible for websites (or their content) that are not owned by the publisher.

Library of Congress Control Number: 2016296281

ISBNs: 978-0-316-43974-9 (paperback)
       978-0-316-44221-3 (ebook)

10 9 8 7 6 5 4 3 2 1

BVG

Printed in the United States of America